A TEXTBOOK OF
MARXIST PHILOSOPHY

I0406803

A TEXTBOOK OF MARXIST PHILOSOPHY

prepared by

the Leningrad Institute of Philosophy
under the Direction of
M. Shirokov

consisting of Four Parts.

The Last Three Parts –
being an Exposition of
Dialectical Materialism –
have been Translated without Alteration
from the Russian:

But the First Part –
being an Historical Introduction to
Marxist Philosophy
and to the Theory of Knowledge –
has been Condensed
and entirely Rewritten
by the English Editor
who alone takes Responsibility
for this Section.

The Whole Book
has been Translated by
A. C. Moseley,
and the Translation has been Revised and Edited by
John Lewis, B.Sc., Ph.D.

The Publishers are
Victor Gollancz Limited
London

Reprinted in the United States, 2013 by
Red Star Publishers
www.RedStarPublishers.org

CONTENTS

PREFACE

This volume was originally prepared by the Leningrad Institute of Philosophy as a textbook in Dialectical Materialism for institutions of higher education directly connected with the Communist Party and also for use in the Technical Institutes which correspond to Universities in Great Britain.

This particular textbook was specially selected by the Society for Cultural Relations in Moscow (VOKS) as the best example they could find of the philosophical teaching now being given in the Soviet Union not only to students of philosophy but to engineers, doctors, chemists, teachers, in fact to all who pass through the higher technical schools and institutes.

In the original work Part I, which consisted of an historical introduction to Marxist Philosophy and the Theory of Knowledge, was of considerable length and included illustrations which would not be familiar to English students. But as it is really quite impossible to comprehend the philosophy of Marx and Engels without some knowledge of the development of philosophy up to Hegel, this section has been considerably condensed and entirely rewritten by the English editor who takes entire responsibility for this part of the work. The original authors did not cover this familiar ground in the manner of a conventional history of philosophy but from the Marxist point of view, and this whole method of approach has, of course, been faithfully followed in the rewritten section.

The English editor has also contributed an introduction relating the whole work to philosophical thought in the West to-day.

Sections II, III and IV comprise the exposition of Marxist Philosophy by the Russian authors themselves.

In placing this textbook before English-speaking students it is hoped that serious consideration may be drawn to the claims of a philosophy which in its challenge to philosophical orthodoxy raises issues to which recent critical studies in Western science and philosophy are giving increasing attention.

JOHN LEWIS

INTRODUCTION

Some little assistance is needed to those who sit down for the first time to read a book on dialectical materialism, written by Russians for Russian students. The very name of the new philosophy raises questions. What is dialectic? Is the new philosophy really no more than the discredited materialism of the nineteenth century?

The book itself will be the best answer to these questions but it may help towards the understanding of the book if we take these two fundamental difficulties, which probably disconcert a good many would-be students of dialectical materialism, and endeavour to throw some light on them from the standpoint of Western philosophy.

What is Dialectic?

Dialectical thought is the study of things in their relations and in process of development and change. "The opposite of dialectics is the isolated consideration of things, and the consideration of things only in their fixity." It is dialectical to look out for the special characteristics of a thing in a new set of relations and then to adapt one's forms of thought to the new form which reality has taken. Dialectics, therefore, is not an abstract system of logic which men are asked to accept, it is necessary because the nature of the world requires it. There are no fixed properties in the concrete world, therefore there should be no fixed concepts in our science. There are no final scientific laws, therefore our thought must avoid dogmatic finality.

A rationalist may try to make out that nature shows a smooth continuous progression from simple to complex in which the higher, if we knew enough detail, could be predicted from the lower. But this conception of uniformity is one of those static moulds into which man pours his thought and in doing so does violence to reality. For nature is not continuous but discontinuous. It cannot be reduced to mere variations of one fundamental reality. In reality there is novelty and therefore gaps between the old and the new. Now if by reason itself one means precisely continuity and unchangeability then nature is irrational. Dialectics, however, challenges this conception of reason and moulds thought to the changing surface of events. In other words it gives us a conception of reason derived from the living nature of reality, not from a man-made static logic.

Non-dialectical thinking, on the other hand, is always getting itself into difficulties. How, for instance, is the control of the physiological mechanism by mind to be explained? Static thinking finds it difficult to show how mind can possibly affect matter except by a miracle. That is because by matter is meant a physiological mechanism such as is found before mind has anything to do with it. Such matter is mindless. But since mind certainly exists, and since it has nothing to do with mindless organic matter, it must be a thing apart, pure mind. The riddle then is how mind and matter interact. There would be no riddle but for static thinking. Dialectical thought allows the concept of matter to change from one evolutionary level to another. At one level matter is mindless, at the next it is *minded*. Matter itself *thinks* when organized in a brain. Because the properties of matter outside the grey matter of the brain do not include thought, that is not to say that in the unique set of conditions which obtain in the brain quite new properties may not emerge.

Dialectical thinking is particularly important in politics. There it is often called realism. Instead of trying to force social change according to certain abstract ideals, the realist is bound to take the situation as it is at its particular stage of development and frame his policies accordingly.

Quixotic idealists are anti-dialectical. Good tacticians, men of shrewd practical judgment think dialectically, not abstractly.

Every successful scientist, engineer and physician is a dialectician because his thought conforms to the stuff he works in and enables him to handle it. He cannot do his thinking in isolation from reality.

Dialectical thinking is not an esoteric secret, it is simply the way to think in relation to the world one wishes to control, therefore it can be said that *all* effective thinking is dialectical.

Why Materialism?

By materialism we usually mean either the reduction of all phenomena to inert matter and its movements, or the evaluation of life in terms of eating and drinking. Dialectical materialism means neither of these things. Where it differs from every form of Idealism is in its belief that in the evolution of the universe the non-living preceded the living. There was a time when there was no mind. Mind is a characteristic of matter at a high stage of its development. Dialectical materialism fully recognizes the progressive enrichment of evolving matter from level to level, and fully accepts the reality of mind and of spiritual values.

It is only mechanistic materialism thinking statically instead of dialectically that shuts its eyes to such obvious facts. Dialectical thinking is strictly empirical, and this may be regarded as another aspect of its materialism. Whatever facts emerge in experience must be recognized, but transcendental objects it does not recognize. In the Middle Ages there was a fierce controversy between nominalists and realists. The nominalists said that concepts are only products of human thought, and that real existences are always concrete and individual. The realists asserted that ideas and ideals have an actual existence of their own. Plato held that Beauty exists in the ideal world from which it descends to dwell for a moment only in beautiful objects, which all eventually lose their beauty.

In this controversy the dialectical materialist would be wholly on the side of the nominalists and against Plato. Beauty exists, but never apart from beautiful things. Goodness exists but never apart from good people. Thought exists but not apart from brains. The simple truth is that form and matter are inseparable, but at the same time distinct. The form that matter takes may be the form of beauty or of thought, the form is real but it is always a form of matter. That is sound Aristotelianism as well as sound dialectical materialism, and it would trouble no one if we did not so frequently assume that platonic mysticism is the only respectable philosophy.

Dialectical materialism therefore does not believe in the dualism of soul and body. But it does not therefore deny the existence of mind. The modern psychology which does not require "a soul," and therefore rejects both interactionism and parallelism, does not reduce mental processes to physiological, but discovers in the organism at a certain level of brain development a control of behaviour in terms of foresight and purpose. It is as unnecessary to attribute this new function to the indwelling of a soul as to explain sensation in the lower animals in this way. Granted a sufficiently developed brain a new pattern of behaviour becomes possible and actually appears. This shows that the organism when it attains a given complexity has new properties which must neither be reduced to physiological reflexes nor attributed to the intrusion of some alien element.

Emergent Evolution

Dialectical materialism recognizes the emergence of new qualities at different levels.

This evolutionary materialism is sometimes known as "emergent evolution," and has been ably expounded by Lloyd Morgan, Alexander and Roy Wood Sellars. Unfortunately it is sometimes compromised by being combined with philosophical parallelism in order to give to the evolutionary process a teleological character. But it is unnecessary to postulate a directive spiritual force if, as the emergent evolutionists themselves demonstrate, the material factors at any one stage are in themselves sufficient cause for the next. Most evolutionists therefore already hold the dialectical rather than the vitalist or parallelist form of emergent evolution.

The doctrine of emergence is of the greatest importance for the whole question of development and change in nature. Although development implies the emergence of novelty, scientists are extremely sensitive to any tampering with the principle of continuity. But a doctrine of pure continuity rules out the emergence of the really new, since everything is a combination of the original elements. The result is that in defence of continuity evolution itself may be denied, since without real change evolution is meaningless. On the other hand in defence of change continuity may be denied, in which case once again there is no evolution. Two possibilities are open, one can merely assert that as an empirical fact there is both change and continuity. But the mind is unsatisfied with what falls short of a rational explanation. The other possibility is afforded by the new dialectic which repudiates the *disjunctive* method in thinking which is responsible for all these difficulties. The disjunctive method treated existences as mutually exclusive and *owning* their content. The dialectical or conjunctive method treats them as interpenetrating and sharing their content. Thus a special character in some object, is not derived from the character of its components taken severally but from the distinctive relationships of these components, from a special configuration. There is a function jointly exercised. This avoids the error of demanding that if a new quality emerges at a given moment it must have emerged from somewhere. Where was it before it emerged? This puts the whole question wrongly. Emergence is treated like the emergence of a duck from beneath the surface of a pond. If it *appears* it must have been under the water before. But that is not what emergence means at all. When two colourless fluids are mixed and the result is a red fluid the redness was nowhere before it emerged; it is a character belonging to a particular configuration. Dialectical materialism will have nothing to do with hylozoism or panpsychism; it does not believe that life and mind have always existed in imperceptible degrees and had only to grow in quantity until they were big enough to be noticed, thus *emerging.* It believes that they appeared for the first time at a definite period in the history of matter, and that they are the inevitable consequence or concomitant of certain material patterns.

When it comes to defining the agent of change, dialectical materialism has its most suggestive theory to offer. Its conception of movement and contradiction as inherent in all matter and all relationships is, of course, derived by inversion from Hegel. What Hegel and Bradley show to be the inherent instability of any particular relationship *as conceived,* Marx shows to be characteristic of all relationships *as concrete,* as well as conceived. Development through contradiction is not due to some mystical force working within the material content of the world, but is an observed characteristic of all life and matter. Contradictions and their emergence do not have to be projected into facts quite innocent of them, you have only to examine reality to find them. To be convinced of the dialectic of nature, look around you!

The Dialectic of Social Change

It is not only in physical and biological phenomena that dialectical development takes place. It is the driving force behind human evolution and social development.

Man is partly determined by his environment. But his relation to his environment is not a static one. In the first place the environment itself is as much the creation of man as man is the creation of the environment. Interaction is continuous. The changes wrought by man react on man himself and then man proceeds to yet further changes. Man fells forests and practises a crude husbandry, as a consequence soil erosion sets in and man launches vast irrigation projects like the Tennessee Valley experiment, which in turn change the social habits and industrial structure of a whole area, introducing electrification, scientific agriculture, new industries and a new level of social development. But this awakens the fierce antagonism of vested interests outside the Tennessee Valley so that the relation of the district to its environment, politically, brings into existence new internal movements and institutions. It is such mutual influences and corresponding adjustments which lead, not only to gradual change, but, after a cumulative process of parallel modification, to a revolution.

The process of soil erosion is gradual and homogeneous. However far it is prolonged it does not of itself become a series of dams and irrigation canals; but when the social pressure due to erosion and its consequences reaches a certain degree of intensity the social organism produces a mutation and grapples with the environment in a new way. It is human intervention in the manner rendered necessary by the actual conditions that revolutionizes the situation. But it is also worth noting that a failure to interrupt the gradual process of erosion itself leads to abrupt and violent changes, to disastrous floods, to famines, and to social collapse.

To take another example. The pressure of the law of supply and demand on the price of labour power causes the workers to form trade unions, restrict the supply of labour, and get a better price for it, a better wage. The employers' policy thus produces an opposite tendency. But the trade union eventually finds that competitive industry cannot afford to pay a living wage, whereupon it has to fulfil a new role or perish. It must struggle for power, to supersede the employing class, and in so doing pass beyond the two-class economic system in which one section owns the tools and the other sells its labour power. The continuance of the old struggle is rendered impossible by the accumulation of parallel or converging changes resulting from the inter-relatedness of economic factors and social movements. It is not a pendulum movement, or simple action and reaction, but a condition of deadlock, of crisis, to which these converging changes have inevitably led. The impasse shows itself in a choking of the forces of production, a paralysis, leading to fierce competitive struggle for economic existence and, unless something is done, to war and social chaos. But the moment the transition is effected the whole face of things is transformed, the whole structure of things is re-patterned. Certain entities disappear, others come into existence. Eternal laws vanish. Values change. Human nature itself changes. There is no human institution that is the same afterwards. In particular the *weight* of various factors is altered. What had been feeble and unable to grow in the old order is released and stimulated and becomes a dominant force. As an example consider adult education for workers. Under capitalism this remains puny and ineffective nor is it possible to get it beyond a certain point no matter what efforts are made. But in a workers' state, where workers rule and industry is self-governing, an immense impetus to education is received, and a remarkable release of latent forces occurs.

Note the importance and fruitfulness of this conception, how many knots it unties and controversies it clears up. Endless confusion results from persistently refusing to admit the change of properties which a new pattern brings with it, to admit the disappearance of old laws and the emergence of new ones consequent upon such re-patterning.

Our example has been a social one. It might just as well have been biological. It is a similar process wherever you find it. The properties of matter in all its forms are relative. Changes in matter are always arising out of the situation caused by the self-development of a given situation. Such changes always lead to new properties and laws emerging and a new relation between object and environment. Dialectical materialism analyses the laws of evolutionary change and applies them to society as well as to nature.

Dialectics and Metaphysics

Dialectical materialism takes up a somewhat hostile attitude to metaphysics. Why is this? It is because "the persistent problems of philosophy" are not, as is usually supposed, merely problems for thought, but problems inseparably connected with stages in social development which carry with them contradictions insoluble at these particular levels.

For instance the failure of a pre-scientific world to understand nature creates special intellectual problems for the philosophy of that period which only clear up when science advances. Or again, before the discovery of emergent evolution philosophy will be troubled with dualism and vitalism, and there will be no help for it.

These very problems of pre-Marxian philosophy indicate that men are not yet in the position to solve them. Now it is the false formulation of a problem that creates a philosophy. Restate it correctly and the problem disappears – and so does the philosophy! There are no insoluble problems in philosophy but only problems wrongly stated. Hence most contemporary metaphysics is due either to ignorance or to confusion of thought. The list of metaphysical problems which disappear as we proceed to higher organizational levels is a long one and in recent years a school of logical positivists has appeared which threatens to sweep the last of them away. In certain respects the logical-positivists approach the position of dialectical materialism but their view is a purely logical one and takes no cognizance of the changes in thought due to social evolution.

Ayer in his recent book, *Language, Truth and Logic,* says that metaphysics must eventually disappear, because it tries to say something about what is not matter of fact, whereas the only way to avoid senselessness is either to explain the use of the words and special terms we use (called by Ayer and Russell "symbols ") or to say something verifiable about matter of fact. To consider anything at all as existing prior to and independent of the concrete is complete folly unless we are working out mere logical possibilities, clearing up the meaning of language, stating in advance how we propose to think, and what is going to count for us as proof. Apart from this, which is the real job of philosophy, the only other kind of truth is matter of fact, which must be verifiable in principle by some future sense-experience. To affirm what is not empirically verifiable is to talk nonsense. Professor Schlick of Vienna, writes:

> "What about metaphysics? It is evident that our view entirely precludes the possibility of such a thing. Any cognition we can have of 'Being,' of the inmost nature of things, is gained entirely by the special sciences; they are the true ontology, and there can be no other. Each true scientific proposition expresses in some way the real nature of things – if it did not, it would simply not be true. So in regard to metaphysics the justification of our view is that it explains the vanity of all metaphysical efforts, which has shown itself in the hopeless variety of systems all struggling against each other. Most of the so-called metaphysical propositions are no propositions at all, but meaningless combinations of words; and the rest are not ' metaphysical' at all, they are simply concealed scientific statements, the truth or falsehood of which can be ascertained by the ordinary methods of experience and observation. (In the future) Metaphysical tendencies will be entirely abandoned, simply because there is no such thing as metaphysics, the apparent descriptions of it being just nonsensical phrases."

Dialectical Materialism and Contemporary Philosophy

The "logical-analytical method" of Wittgenstein and his followers is by no means the only modern philosophy that approximates in certain points to the new dialectic. Benedetto Croce, for all his errors, is condemning abstractness when he insists that philosophy is identical with history and that both are the self-consciousness of life itself. Troeltsch, many of whose positions are open to the gravest criticism, is right when he insists that the fundamental philosophical question is what is the main trend of historical matter of fact and how does it dominate each special domain, such as law, education, art, politics, and philosophy, and in his insistence that historical activism should supersede historical contemplation. Whitehead's energetic opposition to the whole Kantian bifurcation of nature and mind is a wholesome reaction from dualism.

It would appear, in fact, that not only are scientific discoveries confirming the standpoint of dialectical materialism but that Western philosophers are increasingly discarding metaphysical concepts, though still reluctant to accept an outlook which undermines the buttresses of the existing order.

There is, however, one tendency in recent Western philosophy with which the dialectical materialists are thoroughly familiar, though we are not as thoroughly acquainted as we should be with their treatment of it. This is due to an historical accident. In 1908 a group of leading Russian socialists living in exile in Capri, became profoundly interested in the new positivism of Mach and Avenarius. They proceeded to recast philosophical Marxism along positivist lines. Lenin at once saw that this philosophy was both unsound and also anti-socialist in its implications. He proceeded to write an exhaustive criticism which displayed a surprising knowledge of philosophy and a clear grasp of the question at issue. Lenin's *Materialism and Empirio-Criticism* has never been sufficiently appreciated by philosophers although it was one of the first and most trenchant criticisms of a sceptical system which so far from disappearing has grown widely in recent years. This scientific positivism has been popularized in recent years by Eddington, Bertrand Russell and others in science, and by Dürkheim and Levy Brühl in sociology. As Lenin rightly discerned, it opens wide the door to solipsism and superstition and has been eagerly seized upon by theologians to buttress, irrationalism and supernaturalism. It therefore happens that this criticism as developed in modern dialectical materialism is immediately relevant to much contemporary philosophy and surprisingly up-to-date.

Philosophy and Politics

No exposition of dialectical materialism can proceed for long without an excursion into political controversy. Again and again in this textbook we shall meet with practical applications to contemporary Russian problems. At first this may appear disconcerting and irrelevant, but a great deal would be lost if the theory remained on the abstract plane and never allowed itself to be mingled with practice.

In fact this is quite impossible, for this philosophy first of all *reflects* every kind of material and social change and helps us to understand it, and of such changes none are so important as political changes. Secondly, however, since political change requires above all things just such an *understanding* of events, a philosophy of this sort will itself be an indispensable agent of such change. Hence the political importance of this philosophy. Under these circumstances it is not difficult to understand two peculiarities of communist philosophy, firstly it is taken seriously by everyone in Russia and is studied and debated universally with great insistence on correct conclusions; secondly, no discussion proceeds very far without plunging into political controversy. The first peculiarity will occasion suspicion in those who are influenced by the apparent irrelevance of ordinary philosophy to real problems in life and politics. But is it unimportant to reach correct conclusions in aeronautics? Is it not a matter of life and death? Is it not the responsibility of authority to see that aeronautical engineers are provided with correct and verified formulae? This will explain the earnest and polemical tone of Russian political controversy. On more than one occasion the preservation or destruction of the new civilization has depended on a right understanding of social change and the transvaluations brought about by repatterning. The great collective farm controversy is a case in point. This has become the classical working example by means of which every phase of dialectical materialism is demonstrated.

The second peculiarity arises from the insistence on the material unity of the world. We are here in this real world and all our thinking is about it. Moreover we think about it not as if we were looking at it from the moon, but because it is a going concern and we are on it. Every moment it is doing something and going somewhere, and it does nothing of itself. Its direction and its action are due to our activity and our thought. The job of philosophy is not to explain, to analyse, to sum up as good or bad, as rational or irrational, a finished universe outside itself, but to take the primary responsibility of understanding how the world changes and in directing that change. Philosophy is the self-consciousness of a self-moving, self-directing world in process of progressive development.

Its goodness is not a fixed quantity but may be more to-morrow according to whether we know how to improve it. It is not either rational or irrational. It is as irrational as our ignorance and lack of control.

If philosophy is the analysis of social development we can understand the frequent incursions of dialectical materialism into the realm of social action. The contact is as close as that between the research department of a medical school and the hospital. Western philosophers who feel a little resentful and irritated at this philosophy of action might remember that it was Bradley who said, "There is no more fatal enemy than theories which are not also facts," and that both Plato and Hegel would have warmly approved of this indissoluble connection of politics and philosophy. It is a *fin de siècle* intellectualism that finds itself "above the battlefield."

Determinism and Freedom

This brings us to another characteristic of Russian philosophy. It is often supposed that the materialist conception of history is a form of fatalism. Nothing could be farther from the truth. On the contrary it holds that man is a self-directing organism. But consciousness and physiological processes are not two separate things. The organism man is a physiological mechanism that knows what it is doing. The mistake hitherto has been to make a false antithesis. *If* a physiological mechanism then *not* self-directing. *If* self-directing *then* parallelism or interactionism. Modern psychology, and also dialectical materialism, goes back to Aristotle, man is a "minding" animal. "Consciousness, instead of being a stream outside of the process of physiological change, is simply a characteristic of some facts of organic behaviour."[1] When a particular movement is made which intervenes in the course of events, that particular movement is only explicable on the ground that when it took place the organism knew what the effect on his environment was going to be before it occurred.

This is also true socially. Man is conditioned but not determined by social structure and the stage of economic development. An airman is most strictly conditioned by the laws of flight and his machine, by the changing atmosphere and his supplies of petrol and electricity; but he is free in so far as he accepts, understands, and utilizes those conditions. Freedom is the knowledge of necessity. If you want to loop the loop you *must* do this and that, and there are some things that cannot be done at all. So in politics, you can only find out what to do, what is possible and what impossible, what is profitable and what profitless, by knowing what stage of development society has reached, what contradictions are maintaining the tension of the structure, what forces are weakening and what are strengthening, in what direction society must move to escape impasse or disaster! Moreover such knowledge is not astronomical, as though watching a collision of heavenly bodies which an observer could only predict. It is operative. The measure of knowledge determines the measure and quality of control. There may be stages in which men and whole classes act almost instinctively if they are to carry social development to a farther stage, but this is the age in world evolution at which man for the first time comes to social self-consciousness and takes himself on to the next stage. Hence Lenin fiercely opposed the popular doctrines of "drift," of leaving it to the instinctive upsurge of the masses, the theorists and "leaders" merely coming in at the tail. Lenin even coined the phrase *Khvostism* – "tailism" – to denote this lagging behind. He argued that by "setting up the 'spontaneous' movements of the imperfectly conscious mass into the one law of the labour movement, this theory ruled out the constitution of an organized revolutionary party and had for its inevitable consequence the abandonment of all political action to the bourgeois liberals."[2] Hence the importance of the task of bringing

---

[1] Everett Dean Martin, *Psychology*, ch. v.

[2] Mirsky, *Lenin*, p. 41. See also Lenin, *What is to be done?* Collected Works, vol. iv.

the whole working class to consciousness, since it is their historic mission to emancipate the world. Hence the permeation of the Russian proletariat with genuine political education and philosophical discussion, which is deliberately denied to the masses in fascist countries. It is a genuine attempt at popular enlightenment and self-direction and it has already gone too far for anyone wishing to keep the multitude in tutelage to be able to do so.

The Impossibility of Dogmatism

Should the charge of dogmatism be levelled at this political education one can point to two characteristics of dialectical materialism which are continuously undermining the dogmatic attitude. Firstly its belief in fluid concepts. While avoiding pure relativism, dialectical materialism drills its students, using scores of examples drawn from current politics, in the habit of regarding things as changing with changing circumstances both in their properties and in the laws that govern them, and even as passing over into their opposites. *"Capitalism"* is not a fixed concept. The capitalism of the nineteenth century was progressive. It was releasing the forces of production. Capitalism in the world it has thus created is beset by difficulties for which its very achievements are responsible. It has now become retrogressive. It restricts production and moves in the direction of impoverishment, chaos and destruction. *"Democracy"* is not a fixed concept. At first it sets the bourgeoisie free to develop capitalism, later it may be a facade to delude the politically helpless worker that he is governing himself while really he is being governed by a veiled dictatorship; later an aroused and suffering proletariat trying to use the democratic rights hitherto only nominally theirs may find in the defence of their constitutional rights against Fascism that the preservation of democracy *is* the proletarian revolution. *"Man"* is not a fixed concept. Human nature is not unalterable. His character and habits arise not from fixed instincts but, as psychology shows, from conditioning. He is what his institutions make him, but he made those institutions and can make new ones. "The whole of history is nothing but the progressive transformation of human nature." Now it is impossible for a philosophy of this sort to be dogmatic in the vicious sense and, when we remember its stress on practice, we see here too a characteristic bound up with the doctrine of fluid concepts which also precludes dogmatic rigidity.

For dogmatism always arises out of abstraction. It is when thought is regarded as giving us *in itself,* apart from experience, the pattern of reality that a static system of doctrines is built up and can continue. Dialectical materialism creates systems out of reflection on the facts, verifies them by action on the facts, and corrects and amplifies them by the changes brought about by that very action. Its method precludes vicious abstraction.

If further proof were wanted it can be found in the plain fact that the history of Bolshevism has not been marked by the rigid enforcement of inflexible dogmas. So far is this from being the fact that its enemies have never ceased to reproach it with abandoning its principles. How often have we not been told that Russia has reverted to capitalism, has abandoned Lenin's plans, has betrayed its internationalism and so on. It is the opponents of Stalin and the official philosophy who have stuck rigidly to dogmatic and schematic policies. Of course consistency may be more virtuous than what may be termed vacillation and opportunism, but that is not the point at issue at the moment. If the Russians are guilty of this kind of fault (if it is a fault) they are certainly not guilty of being dogmatists.

Does Philosophy matter?

We are now more in a position to see why such practical people as the Russian communists are deeply concerned about philosophy. It is frequently assumed that a practical man can do very well without a philosophy, that the religious and metaphysical beliefs of a scientist or a politician have no kind of relation to their life's work, and that speculation constitutes a more or less leisure time occupation like music or golf.

But the Russian knows that a man's creed matters, that it may be a positive force behind exploitation and parasitism and that you cannot destroy the social disease if you do not accompany your political and industrial measures with the refutation of capitalist philosophy and the propagation of an alternative. It is for this reason that philosophical discussion plays such an important part in Russia to-day. In every higher technical school, institute, and university philosophy is a compulsory subject in the curriculum. Works chemists, textile engineers, agricultural experts and school teachers are thoroughly trained in philosophy. They know the fallacies of the system they repudiate and they have a system of their own to be "the master light of all their seeing."

This will occasion surprise in those who have always understood that the first principle of Soviet philosophy was the economic determination of ideas. But although no creed comes into existence as a mere development of thought and out of all relation to social needs yet once a creed is born it has an activity and force of its own. If it is believed it will help to perpetuate the social system to which it belongs, if it is overthrown one of the buttresses of that system will be taken away. Therefore the Russian is inclined to believe with Chesterton that the practical and important thing about a man is his view of the universe.

> "We think that for a landlady considering a lodger, it is important to know his income, but still more important to know his philosophy. We think that for a general about to fight an enemy, it is important to know the enemy's numbers, but still more important to know the enemy's philosophy."

There has been no great movement in history that was not also a philosophical movement. The time of big theories was the time of big results. Our modern politicians who call themselves practical and belittle philosophy are mediocrities, and their policies are opportunist and vacillating.

It is not difficult to see why this is so. In the first place the main philosophical tendencies are always closely allied to the conflicting social and political movements of the day. A totalitarian philosophy lends support to State absolutism. Irrationalism fosters political "thinking with your blood." In the last century, when Spencer transformed the biological theory of evolution into a philosophy, its theory of progress through struggle and the survival of the fittest made a popular theoretical instrument for furthering the interests of the economic class that throve on competition. A philosophy may not be consciously advanced with such an aim but it will be seized upon and will spread widely if it reinforces the aims of a large section of the community engaged in struggle with an opposing class.

Secondly, fundamental questions are never of purely speculative interest, but frequently arise out of or are suggested by the urgent social problems of the time. Even the philosopher who isolates himself and devotes his attention to what he imagines to be purely theoretical questions is affected by the spirit of the age and is unconsciously answering its questions. Bradley, a recluse, in his famous essay on "My Station and its Duties," argued that the community was a moral organism which knows itself in its members so that to know what is right we have merely to imbibe the spirit of the community. "It is a false conscience," he says, "that wants you to be better than the world as it is." His essay is largely an apologia for functionalism, and functionalism which accepts the present class stratification as permanent is simply fascism.

Why not do without Philosophy?

Nor is it possible to avoid all contamination with philosophy by becoming the perfect philistine and restricting one's attention solely to the practical sphere – the tendency of British labour leaders. For if the devil of philosophy is thrown out and the empty spaces of the mind swept and garnished, "Then goeth he, and taketh with himself seven other devils more wicked than himself, and they enter in and dwell there; and the last state of that man is worse than the first." The mind that is not made up is peculiarly susceptible both to atmosphere and to passing fashions, it yields all too easily to powerful and specious movements of thought and is "tossed to and fro, and carried about with every wind of doctrine." The human mind is more eager and curious than that of the pragmatic politician, and there will not be lacking vehement and persuasive philosophies of a dubious character likely to infect those not rendered immune by having a considered philosophy of their own.

It is indeed impossible to keep the mind free from philosophy. "We have no choice," says A. E. Taylor, "whether we shall form metaphysical hypotheses or not, only the choice whether we shall do so consciously and in accord with some intelligible principle or unconsciously and at random." The philistine's mind is a mass of prejudices, unexamined assumptions, shallow and insufficiently substantiated generalities and dogmas. The man who says he is no philosopher is merely a bad philosopher.

The Relation of Theory and Practice

This insistence on the importance of "hard facts" is a reaction from speculative theories and pure abstraction, but sound theory is only the eye of practice and practice is blind without it. Just as a doctor must unite a sound knowledge of human physiology and pathology with his practical experience and cannot know too much to be a good physician, so a politician must understand all there is to know of the laws of social change and the structure of society if his leadership is to take the class whose interests he represents anywhere but on to the rocks.

The truth is that if form and content, which in this case are theory and practice, can be divided so as to be merely related they are of little importance. Philosophy and practice that fall below a certain standard can be discussed in this way; above that standard, theory and practice are not opposed, nor merely related; they are one. There is more than a bond – there is union and fusion.

Whitehead contrasts these two aspects of reason; the first seeking an immediate method of action, the second a complete understanding.

> "The Greeks have bequeathed to us two figures, whose real or mythical lives conform to these two notions – Plato and Ulysses. The one shares Reason with the Gods, the other shares it with the foxes. Ulysses has no use for Plato, and the bones of his companions are strewn on many a reef and many an isle!"[1]

Until Philosophers are Kings

If in previous social crises political leaders could do no more than "play by ear" that is not necessary to-day; the knowledge of the social process given by the dialectical approach provides the basis for a conscious transformation of society. The way out is therefore being found by a whole class coming to a consciousness of its destiny and it follows that the leaders of that class must be enlighteners and therefore themselves enlightened. "Till the philosophic race have the government of the city, neither the miseries of the city nor of the citizens shall have an end, nor shall this republic, which we speak of in way of fable, come in fact to perfection."[2]

But if rulers must be philosophers that means that in a State where the workers rule the workers must themselves be philoso-

---

[1] Whitehead, *The Function of Reason.*

[2] Plato, *Republic.*

phers. This accounts for the severe training in dialectical material-ism which is found in all Russian technical and higher education in the Soviet Union. It is felt in Russia that an engineer or a chemist who does not understand the philosophy of Socialism is not likely to be of much use in the new order. That is why thorough training in dialectical materialism is universal. Not only are the kings all phi-losophers in the republic, but the workers are all kings, or kings in the making. They must all be trained for rule and responsibility. "Every kitchen-maid must learn to rule the country."

The result is that every educated Russian has something of that philosophic spirit which Shaw remarked in Marx when he wrote:

"...he never condescends to cast a glance of useless longing at the past, his cry to the present is, always 'Pass by; we are waiting for the future.' Nor is the future at all mysterious, uncertain or dreadful to him. There is not a word of fear, nor appeal to chance, nor to providence, nor vain remonstrance with nature... nor any other familiar sign of the giddiness which seizes men when they climb to heights which command a view of the past, present and fu-ture of human society. *Marx keeps his head like a god.* He has discovered the law of social development, and knows what must come. The thread of history is in his hand."

That the Russians are submitting themselves to a vigorous intel-lectual discipline will be clear from the reading of this book which is not an easy one. It is significant that Hegel's *Logic* has been translated into Russian and has been printed in editions running to tens of thousands. It is doubtful whether fifty copies a year are sold in England. This, coupled with the practical dialectic of unending controversy and argument and with the constant test of practice, has made of the new philosophy a virile and sinewy intellectual instru-ment. Its outlines are rough and its details unfinished. It needs elaboration, expansion, much filling in of detail, a good deal of cor-rection and revision, but in spite of this it is fundamentally an excel-lent illustration of its own thesis, the emergence on a higher level of a new evolutionary type, the fruit of the clash of opposites, the working out of older systems to exhaustion and yet to fulfilment, a reordering of the whole problem of philosophy.

SECTION I

HISTORICAL

CHAPTER I

THE CONFLICT BETWEEN IDEALISM AND MATERIALISM

§ I. THE CHARACTER OF IDEALISTIC THINKING

Man who lives in a world of peril is compelled to seek for safety. The way most familiar to us is the control of nature. We build houses, weave garments, make flame and electricity our friends instead of our enemies and develop the complicated arts of social living. This is the method of changing the world through action.

But there is another method. The method of changing the self in emotion and idea because it is too difficult to change the world. This is the way first of religion and subsequently of philosophy. It begins with propitiation, but passes at length from the attempt to conquer destiny to the resolve to ally oneself with it and so perchance escape destruction. Out of religion philosophy developed as man came to reflect upon this sharp contrast between a feeble, uncertain practice and an imaginative apprehension of a supernatural world of potencies and certainties. In other words out of the conflict of knowledge and practice arises the major problem of philosophy and the conflict between idealism and materialism.

As the mythological elements fell away from the religious attitude philosophy retold the story of the universe in the form of rational discourse instead of emotionalized imagination. The result was the apprehension by Reason of an ideal world of logical constructions constituting, as it was finally declared, "a realm of fixed Being which, when grasped by thought, formed a complete system of immutable and necessary truth."[1] Reason provided the patterns to which ultimately real objects had to conform. But unfortunately science and its world falls far short of the logicality and unity of the world of pure reason. It is, as it were, an inferior world in which things change, which is subject to illusion and in which multi-

---

[1] Dewey, *The Quest for Certainty*, p. 18.

formity is more to be found than uniformity. But this, unfortunately, is the world of action. Activity therefore is always of less importance than contemplation since it deals with the less real. Hence ever since the Greeks philosophy has been ruled by the notion that "the office of Knowledge is to uncover the antecedently real, rather than, as is the case with our practical judgments, to gain the kind of understanding which is necessary to deal with problems as they arise."[1]

Right on through Plato, Descartes, Spinoza, Kant and Hegel the same quest for the rational and the unchangeable was pursued. For Plato the changing and passing forms of this world are but the transitory and partial embodiments of ideal realities laid up in heaven and only to be apprehended by reason. In the same way our virtues are but pale reflections of the perfect virtues which exist in the Absolute. I am kind because a little of the perfect kindness of God dwells in me for a moment. Thus goodness is an almost measurable quality which inheres in men to a greater or less degree.

Descartes, as we shall see, drew the sharpest pattern of a purely logical physical world, so logical in fact as to be mathematical. Spinoza, however, went even farther and embraced mental and physical events in one perfectly rational whole where the order and connection of ideas were proved to be, in reality, the order and connection of facts. Kant was still haunted by the obstinate refusal of the facts to look as orderly and connected as they should, and therefore had to assert that in order to be rational all facts must be considered within the mind and fitting neatly into its logical pigeonholes. Hegel completed the argument by simply declaring that anything which does not fit the pattern is not properly understood and described. If you see it completely you will see it to be rational. If it is not quite rational that is because you do not really see it as it is. You are witnessing something illusory and partial.

The struggle to make things orderly therefore becomes not a struggle with nature, but either with our imperfect theories, which must be scrapped one by one until at last the perfect explanation which comprehends and justifies everything, or with our worldly habit of regarding experience as more valid than the ideal. A really disciplined mind will rise above this appearance of disorder, and

---

[1] Dewey, p. 20.

grasp by spiritual apprehension the goodness and truth that alone is real.

No matter what the detailed conclusions of experience, perfect truth and goodness are ours in ultimate Being, independently of both experience and human action.

Thus philosophers have tended to depreciate action, doing, making, and the reason has not been entirely the impulse of the mind to outrun practical human achievement. Work has been despised ever since a class of labourers was segregated and set to the world's work. From that moment work was done under compulsion and the pressure of necessity, while intellectual activity was associated with leisure. The social dishonour in which the class of serfs was held was extended to the work they did.

Idealism will always be the popular philosophy of a leisured class. This is not a sufficient reason for its existence, but it is a condition which favours its rise. Hence the more complete the separation between mental and physical work, and the greater the degree of exploitation of one class by another, the more is this class relationship reflected in an idealist philosophy.

"The division of labour," says Marx, "does not become an actual division until the division of material and spiritual work appears. From that moment consciousness may actually seem to be something other than a consciousness of the real world and of the activity within that world. As soon as consciousness begins actually to represent something, without that something being a real representation, we find it ready to free itself from world connections and to become a cult of 'pure theory,' theology, philosophy, morals, etc."

It would, however, be a complete mistake to suppose that because idealism is a projection of man's yearning for order in a disorderly world, or because such phantasies flourish among the leisured classes, that it has no justification and no truth. It is justified by the evolution of the world towards the ideal of order. It is true, as Leonardo said, that "Nature is full of infinite reasons *which were never in experience*," and the scientist who does not, in the words of Galileo, make headway with reason against experience is a very poor scientist indeed.

The idealist rightly asserts that it is not the function of mind merely to reflect the universe, it has in some way to participate in it.

The materialist is wholly wrong when he denies the active role of consciousness and asserts that it merely reflects processes that are going on in nature. Consciousness is no lifeless mirror. In the first place it has itself slowly developed along with man and society and is a function of social humanity. In the second place it is *creative*, for it is always developing man and society a stage farther, planning his activities, devising ways and means, creating new institutions. Thus at any given stage consciousness is both limited by the social forms which society takes and yet is striving, not unsuccessfully, to transcend those limits.

This free activity of consciousness can be so isolated from the conditions which determine it as to appear to be the sole creative force of history. In the same way the power to generalize and create concepts and theories can easily be separated from the action with which true thought is always wedded, until this aspect of man's activity becomes dominant, self-sufficient, overshadowing everything else. At last it breaks away from the concrete man and his tasks altogether, especially under such conditions as separate the workers and the thinkers among men, and becomes "pure thought." Scientific concepts, even, become mental fictions or reflections of an "immanent reason" in nature, of the spirituality of the universe. In these ways every break that thinking makes with practice leads to a one-sided idealism. Idealism, in fact, is nothing more or less than the isolation of *one feature of knowledge* from the whole and the turning of it into something absolute, namely the power of ideas to reveal the nature of reality and enable us to control it, the power to abstract from the complexity of life and single out special aspects.

Thus Lenin writes:

> "Philosophical idealism is nonsense only from the standpoint of a crude, simple and metaphysical materialism. On the contrary, from the standpoint of dialectical materialism, philosophical idealism is a one-sided, exaggerated, swollen development (*Dietzgen*) of one of the characteristic aspects or limits of knowledge into a deified absolute, into something dissevered from matter, from nature. Idealism means clericalism. True! But philosophical idealism is (more 'correctly' expressed and 'in addition') a road to clericalism through one of the nuances of the infinitely complicated knowledge (dialectical) of man. The knowl-

edge of man does not follow a straight line but a curved line which infinitely approaches a system of circles, the spiral. Every fragment, every segment, every bit of this curved line can be transformed (transformed one-sidedly) into a self-sufficient whole straight line which, if one does not see the wood for the trees leads us directly into the mire, into clericalism (which is strengthened by the class interests of the ruling class)."

Lenin points out that the result is superstition. What does he mean by that? That it is. by means of such idealism that the legal standards that regulate social relationships are given the sanctity of absolute obligations, and come to be regarded as independent forces which stand above society and determine its structure. In the same way economic laws are regarded as absolute and precluding social change. Utopian socialists come to believe that the way to progress lies in creating an imaginative social structure, and showing that it is compatible with human nature and reason. Idealists believe that social institutions are created by ideas, that human history is the result of the change of ideas. If anything in society changes, it happens because consciousness has changed first. Preachers and educationists therefore seek to alter the world by inculcating improved ideas into people's heads, by moralizing and indoctrinating. Psychologists see the essence of society not in the productive relations of classes but in the instincts, feelings and thoughts of people. Even scientists come to believe that the laws of nature are not objectively determined by nature, but subjectively determined by the consciousness of scientists, that the atom is "only a mental construction," that the theory of evolution is "a useful way of thinking," held because we choose to believe it. Even politicians pursue the will-o'-the-wisp of pure idea. Trotsky believes in his "destiny," in the mysterious "will of the people," apart from strictly defined objective conditions. Like all idealists, "he treats the possible as the actual," he believes in the existence of what he desires should be, thus he sought to skip the stage of a bourgeois-democratic revolution in 1905, and proceed directly to the proletarian revolution. Bukharin lapses into the idealism which substitutes doctrinaire formulae and over-schematized stages of development for a close objective study of the kaleidoscopic changes of the face of society.

Lenin views this whole process of detachment of ideas and ideals, theories and generalizations, from the standpoint of the concrete fusion of theory and practice. This is that idealism, he argues, that is really superstition, that is really myth-making, and the only purpose of such thinking (i.e. what the theory means in practice) is to justify things as they are in the interests of the owning class and to betray reformers into paths of folly and futility.

§ 2. THE CHARACTER OF MATERIALISTIC THINKING

But if wish-fulfilment thinking and the false pursuit of abstractions have led men to idealism, the inexorable demands of the real world have as often pulled them back to realism. Idealism has developed and flourished but so has science. And always with the growth of science we perceive a clearer apprehension of the philosophy of science known as materialism and the sworn foe of idealism. To-day we have learned to trust the scientist and to look to him to get us out of our difficulties. He has had a long struggle with ignorance and class interests, but he has triumphed over all of us.

His attitude is totally different from the idealist. He looks at the concrete world with all its imperfections, not at the ideal world. He looks forward to a richer and fuller life here on earth, not to the spiritual contemplation of absolute values in eternity. He believes it can be realised by man's co-operative effort, utilizing the resources of the earth.

"Trust in science, and the idea that this world is the place of man's destiny, tend to bring about a new attitude toward the question of what we are to believe. For the investigator first set his foot on the road of science when he refused to accept anything as true which could not be confirmed by experimental evidence. The mystic sought the divine vision through fasting and prayer; the philosopher stormed the citadel of reality by logic and reasoning. The scientist turned away from both ways, and was content to make toilsome progress by collecting evidence, sifting and comparing, weighing and measuring, limiting the field of enquiry, remaining in willing ignorance on everything beyond this field. And since he had to fight for his freedom to go beyond the other two methods – since often he had to make his way in conflict with them – on the whole he came to regard his method as necessarily antagonistic to the other two; though in truth I think a sound method has something of all three. His success confirmed him in his method; and thus, to-day, experimental evidence comes to be regarded as the most satisfactory kind of evidence that can be found for statements professing to give information about the nature of things."[1]

Modern science was founded in the seventeenth century by men who were not materialists but who had a materialistic conception of matter, without which, indeed, progress would have been impossible. They held that matter is that which occupies space. It will not move unless something pushes it, and if it is moving it will not stop unless something stops it. It is not alive or conscious.

The obvious effect of this view was to separate matter and mind and make mind a distinct substance, inhabiting the body during life, and withdrawing on the dissolution of the body.

This worked very well as far as matter was concerned, but it raised great difficulties about the relation of mind to matter. The result was that mind came to be regarded as a mere effect of matter and materialism became the popular philosophy.

These revolutionary ideas came not as the result of pure thought, but of the requirements of an economic and social situation. Science was the technical instrument of the rising town civilization of the Renaissance, with its growing commerce and its need for navigation, surveying, and military science. Manufacture was developing, comfort was growing, and men took more interest in civilization and less in the world to come. But the rising burgher class had a stiff fight with the feudal lords, who represented the dominant social force of the preceding period; and on the side of feudalism was the Church.

The new science comes in as the ally of the new class, and its rationalistic and materialistic philosophy as the opponent of the ecclesiastical authority which supported feudalism. If the wall is to fall the buttress must be undermined.

Thus, with many qualifications and exceptions and acknowledging much actual confusion of interests, it may be said that the

---

[1] L. J. Russell, *Introduction to Philosophy.*

struggle for a new philosophy accompanied and assisted the struggle of a new class for economic and political power.

There is no philosophy that is not part of a social system, and in the past that has always meant a social hierarchy. The mediaeval social order, with its privileged classes, was bound up with the cosmogony of a fixed earth around which moved the sun. You cannot weaken the force of the ideas on which the social order depends with impunity. Every society hitherto has regarded man as a volcanic force to be kept in subjection. To dissolve the bonds of society is to invite a volcanic eruption. Hence any views which threaten to destroy an implicit trust in the philosophic framework of society are not only false but highly dangerous. Even the scientist, brought up in the climate of another system of thought, found it almost impossible to believe in a new theory of the universe and probably meant what he said when he defended himself from heresy by saying that his ideas were only speculations.

But the new was coming into existence by its own laws of growth and the older picture of the universe was not so much being argued down as dying out. The old feelings were becoming barren, the old actions unmeaning. New ideas alone seemed relevant and alive, the response to the old ideas flagged perceptibly. When this takes place on a large scale the knell of the older order is sounded. Society has to be made anew.

The new philosophy came first as a demand for freer thinking. Then as an insistence on the need for suspending judgment on a question until sufficient evidence has been collected. Bacon borrows a simile from Dante, "Let this be to thee ever as lead to thy feet, to make thee move slowly, like one that is weary, both to the yes and the no, that thou seest not." Men must call a halt in their speculations and allow themselves to be rigidly limited by brute facts.

But it was Descartes who laid down the philosophical foundations of the new science and the new society. He did this in three ways. Firstly by his new method of thinking, secondly by the mechanistic science which it justified and encouraged, thirdly by the philosophical dualism of mind and matter, of faith and reason which this mechanistic materialism itself rendered necessary.

The new method of thought came as a protest against the uncritical assumptions of medievalism and the huge deductive systems based upon them. This mass of knowledge seemed to the new men pretentious and unsubstantiated. While Bacon and the experimentalists turned from dogmas to experimental facts, Descartes was asking himself whether the instrument of reason if honestly and thoroughly used would not provide a method of separating the chaff of baseless conjecture from the residuum of certain truth. In mathematics pure reason gives satisfactory and indubitable results. What happens if you put the mind to work in a completely rigorous manner firstly on spiritual and philosophical questions and secondly on material questions? Descartes thought that the result was the indubitable proof of the distinction between mind and matter, of the reality of the soul and the certainty of the existence of God. On the other hand he came to the conclusion that shapes and motions were all that existed in the world apart from souls. Motion is the only change we can clearly understand, and therefore all other changes and indeed the whole variety and complexity of the concrete world can and must be reduced to matter in motion. Only when you reduce phenomena to physical and mathematical terms do they become rational. Therefore this is the ultimate scientific truth.

If this mechanistic materialism leaves no place for spirit and religion these are safeguarded because they rest on other but equally indubitable foundations. In the same way he was careful to say that his system of universal doubt was not intended to be applied to religion, where matters were believed on grounds of faith and not reason; nor did he allow himself to criticize society. His aim was to show what was provable and what was unprovable, as far as pure reason was concerned, and to set free the scientific intellect to master the universe.

"As soon as I had acquired some general notions respecting physics, and beginning to make trial of them in various particular difficulties, had observed how far they can carry us, and how much they differ from the principles that have been employed up to the present time, I believed that I could not keep them concealed without sinning grievously against the law by which we are bound to promote, as far as in us lies, the general good of mankind. For by them I perceived it to be possible to arrive at knowledge highly useful in life; and in room of the speculative philosophy usually taught in the schools, to discover a practical, by means of which, knowing the force and action of fire, water, air, the stars, the heavens, and all the other bodies that surround us, as distinctly as we know the various crafts of our artisans, we might also apply them in the same way to all the uses to which they are adapted, and thus render ourselves the lords and possessors of nature. And this is a result to be desired, not only in order to the invention of an infinity of arts, by which we might be enabled to enjoy without any trouble the fruits of the earth, and all its comforts, but also and especially for the preservation of health, which is without doubt, of all the blessings of this life, the first and fundamental one; for the mind is so intimately dependent upon the condition and relation of the organs of the body, that if any means can ever be found to render men wiser and more ingenious than hitherto, I believe that it is in medicine they must be sought for."[1]

In this practical scientific end we see the motive of the new philosophy and what differentiates it from all those idealisms which, as we saw in the last section, make it their aim rather to change the minds of men to conform to what eternally is and must be rather than to change nature in the interests of man.

But although Descartes won for men a new vision of the universe by persuading them to accept only perfectly clear ideas, making a clean sweep of all that had hitherto passed for knowledge, these clear ideas have proved so full of obscurity that philosophers have been arguing about them ever since. It is, perhaps, for this reason that Descartes has been called the father of modern philosophy!

The rigid separation of mind and matter chopped the universe in two with a hatchet and led to what is known as dualism, the existence side by side of two worlds, the physical and the mental, which are incapable of influencing one another. This is an untenable position and two solutions were offered. The first was to hold to the physical and drop the mental altogether. This was the solution of the French materialists. The second was to hold to the mental and drop the physical. This was Berkeley's solution and from it Idealism developed. The only attempt to do justice to both sides is to be found in Spinoza who claimed that mind and matter were two aspects of a higher reality.

---

[1] Descartes, *Discourse on Method*, part vi.

The French materialists represented the purely scientific conclusions of the new philosophy and laid the foundations of the successful scientific work of the following century. Owing to the growing tension between the bourgeoisie and the aristocracy we find the scientific movement taking a strongly anti-religious line and deliberately seeking to undermine the supernaturalist sanctions of privilege. Hence science, rationalism, and the new economic forces worked hand in hand.

During the eighteenth century the capitalistic mode of production in Europe was being strengthened and growing. In France capitalism required the dissolution of feudal relations in the countryside and political guarantees for the commercial-industrial towns. The old feudal order hindered trade, giving the peasantry over to the exploitation of landlords and officials and thus depriving it of its power to buy town manufactures. The contradictions between the new class of bourgeoisie, together with the semi-skilled proletariat dependent upon it, and the peasantry, together with their masters, the ruling feudal classes – aristocrats and clericals – reached a state of considerable tension. The oncoming storm of revolution was felt already in the air. In the course of the decades preceding the Great French Revolution the bourgeoisie produced a number of philosophers and publicists who with unusual talent and force came forward as champions of the bourgeoisie in the realm of theory. In contrast to the leading thinkers of the English bourgeoisie who after a victorious revolution had managed to conclude a union with the feudalists and were therefore inclined even in philosophy to compromises, to agreement with religion; in contrast also to the German bourgeoisie, who were feeble and cowardly and therefore vague and indefinite in their ideology; the philosophers of the French bourgeoisie were daring thinkers and fought against religion and idealistic philosophy fearing neither authority nor God. The most logical of the French philosophers of that time in their struggle with religion arrived at materialistic conclusions and produced remarkable examples of materialistic philosophy. Their severe logic, their fearless thinking, their political acumen in the struggle against feudalism and, in particular, against the Church, the talent and often artistry of their exposition, made these philosophers popular, not only in France, but also even beyond its boundaries.

These French materialists took their stand on the achievements of the science of their day. Science in the eighteenth century had attained remarkable successes. Mechanics, the science of moving bodies, had especially developed. New fields had been opened in the mathematics of that time (analytic geometry, the differential and integral calculus) and these provided an instrument for studying the movements of bodies in space. Great strides had been made too in physics, in which mathematics and mechanics provided the basic instruments necessary for studying the properties of liquids, gases, and light. Medicine, too, had its successes. Many physicians at this period discarded the old medicine, which was full of superstition and prejudices, and tried to explain all the processes in the human organism not by postulating a "soul" to control the bodily functions, but by relying on the sciences of mechanics and mathematics. For some time the telescope (1609) had been known and in use, and also the microscope (1590), which in an extraordinary manner widened the field of natural phenomena and made them immediately accessible to the observer. A number of astronomical discoveries were made which reinforced the heliocentric point of view, which regarded the earth not as the centre of the universe, but only as one of the planets that circle round the sun. The laws of falling bodies were discovered, and the laws of planetary motion; Newton formulated his general law of gravity.

All these discoveries required a unity of method and a unity of world-outlook which might well be in opposition to the world-outlook of religion. The most logical materialistic formulation of such a world-outlook at that time was the work of the French materialists Holbach and Helvetius. The fundamental proposition which united them was this, that nature is material, was created by no one and exists for ever. The view of the Church that matter is fixed, passive and can only move itself and change with the help of spirit was opposed. They asserted that matter was created by no one and is always in motion. No matter without movement and no movement without matter. They rejected any interference of a god with nature, since a god appeared quite superfluous and nature could be explained without him. In nature stern causal law is the ruler, one phenomenon of necessity follows another.

"The universe is the vast unity of everything that is, everywhere it shows us only matter in movement," says Holbach (1723-1789), "This is all that there is and it displays only an infinite and continuous chain of causes and actions; some of these causes we know, since they immediately strike our senses; others we do not know since they act on us only by means of consequences, quite remote from first causes."

This mechanistic world-outlook also determined the attitude of the French philosophers to the question of the origin of consciousness and the role of thought. The Church taught that the consciousness of man is a fragment of the divine spirit, of soul, that thanks to the soul man is able, to think, and by just this is distinguished from the animals. But the materialists denied the self-sufficiency of the soul and held that man is just such a material body as all other animals and inorganic bodies. Man, of course, is distinguished from inorganic bodies, but this distinction, in the opinion of the French materialists, amounts to this, that man is merely a more complex and delicate mechanism than other bodies. Thus La Mettrie (1709-1751) even called his principal work: *Man the Machine.* He wrote:

"All the functions, which I have ascribed to this machine, naturally proceed from the organisation of its several parts no more and no less than the movements of a clock or other automaton proceed from the disposition of its screws and wheels, so that it is quite unnecessary to suppose in this machine, i.e. man, any kind of soul, any special cause of movement and life, other than its blood and the forces within it that are stimulated by warmth."

Diderot, who enters into a deeper examination of the reactions of soul and body, expresses the same thought as La Mettrie.

"We are instruments dowered with feeling and memory. Do you really think that a chaffinch or a nightingale and a human musician are essentially different? Do you see this egg? What sort is this egg? Before it was fertilized it was an insensible, non-living mass. How does this mass change into another organization, with sensation and life? By means of heat. What does this heat produce? Motion. What is the gradual action of this motion? At first there is a moving point, a little thread, which dilates and knits itself together, then flesh is formed, a beak, wings, eyes, claws appear; the yellowish matter separates itself and produces the inward parts of the bird – it is an animal. The animal moves this way and that, cheeps! I hear its cry through the shell. It covers itself with down, it sees. The weight of its swaying head ceaselessly knocks its beak against the wall of its prison, now the wall breaks, the bird crawls out to freedom, walks, flutters, falls down, runs, approaches nearer, has regrets, suffers, loves, yearns, and rejoices; it has all your feelings, all your actions. Between you and the animals the difference is only in organization."

However, although they rejected soul as the source of consciousness and acknowledged that man is only a material body, a machine, yet all the same the French materialists had to explain the origin of our consciousness. This question interested them, and the answer they gave was materialistic, but at the same time, mechanistic. For all the philosophers of the eighteenth century, as also for their predecessors, human consciousness did not develop but was *given* together with man and all that was needed was to define the unalterable mechanism by means of which thoughts arose and were united into chains of reasoning. Materialists and idealists wrangled and fought among themselves over the question whether thought is a product of matter or matter is the offspring of spirit and proceeds from it. But the idea that consciousness is a process, that it develops, that it does not amount to a mechanical union of diverse thoughts and feelings, was known by neither side.

The French materialists saw the origin of knowledge in the action of nature on our senses. Until nature acts on us we have no sensations and no consciousness. We are born, said the French materialists, repeating the pronouncement of the English philosopher Locke, with a mind that is like a clean slate. Consciousness arises in a man in the process of living, as a result of the impressions received by his organs of sense. The more impressions his sense organs receive, the more rich, the more diverse his consciousness becomes.

Sensations are those simplest elements of consciousness out of whose union and combination representations are formed. In the further working out of representations, complex ideas, ideas of relations and finally general ideas are formed. We see, therefore, that in their enquiries into the origin and nature of consciousness the French materialists retained their mechanistic ideas.

The essence of human conduct in the opinion of the French materialists is comprised in this, that it seeks for satisfaction and avoids unsatisfaction. Happiness, therefore, consists of prolonged and durable pleasure. Thus every man is an egoist. The aggregate of egoists constitutes society.

In society, the egoism of one man is limited by the egoism of other people. Consequently, in society, man must strive not only for his own happiness, but also for the happiness of others. To attain general happiness, good social institutions are necessary.

Therefore, in order that people may acquire happiness it is necessary to replace bad institutions by good ones. Here the philosophy of the French materialists outgrows its moral teaching and becomes a political programme, a demand to change the feudal structure of society. This demand was that element in their philosophy which particularly attracted the attention of the bourgeoisie and inspired all the progressive people of that epoch. In their social views the French materialists appeared as bold fighters against feudal relations both in town and country. They showed special hatred to the Church as the bulwark of feudalism. Their teaching became a theory of revolution. The French bourgeois sought to realize their ideas in revolution.

Yet personally the French materialists were not revolutionaries. They did not teach a revolutionary, violent overthrow of authority. They made no call to insurrection. To the question how to change social institutions they answered: It is necessary to change the morals and habits of people, to assist the enlightenment of the masses, since the political structure depends on this. But to the question how to change the environment, they had no helpful answer, which reveals the inadequacy and shallowness of their thinking and its speculative character. They rested their hopes of changing feudalism not on the masses but on enlightened, absolute monarchs from whom they expected reforms. The helplessness of metaphysical materialism to resolve problems of social development was in this fashion made absolutely plain. It was this which led to the belief that an enlightened law-giver was necessary in order to change the social structure. As if a king in relation to social institutions acts like a mechanic in relation to a machine the separate parts of which one can rearrange by external action.

The immense encouragement which this philosophy gave both to the growth of science and the growth of religious rationalism must not blind us to its grave defects. It failed signally to explain how any real change can come about. If all the variety of life is to be reduced to the mathematical arrangements and rearrangements of atoms, all actual differences are really denied. This is what Plekhanov called "the transformation of a phenomenon into a fossilized thing by abstracting it from all the inner processes of life."

The only way to explain phenomena is to study things in their development, in their arising and dying away, letting the object freely and spontaneously expound its own characteristics.

But French materialism was incapable of this dialectical treatment of nature.

§3. SUBJECTIVE IDEALISM

Rationalistic materialism reduces the universe to mathematics, but does so by assuming that certain ideas are fundamental and self-evident. The English philosopher Locke thought that the rationalists assumed too much and endeavoured to show that we have no innate ideas in virtue of which we possess knowledge apart from experience. He held that the only way in which to cut entirely free from error and dogmatism is to confine ourselves rigidly to experience. He found that most discussions ended in futility because people would insist on raising problems beyond the limits of possible human knowledge. It then occurred to him

> "that before we set ourselves upon enquiries of that nature, it was necessary to examine our own abilities, and see what objects our understandings were or were not fitted to deal with. For by extending their enquiries beyond their capacities people raise questions and multiply disputes, which only increase their doubts."

Locke then proceeded to argue that there was nothing in the mind that was not first in the senses; that out of sense material the mind puts together more general ideas. Sensations are copies of the fundamental characteristics of the external world, extension, shape, solidity, number, motion. What we call sensations of colour, smell, sound, and taste are really subjective effects produced in us by the more fundamental qualities of the real world.

Locke is thus a materialist because he believes that the entire content of consciousness is derived by impression from the material world. But he is also a dualist because these experiences are mental, whereas the world from which they are derived is material.

This dualism led straight to Idealism, that is to say to the acceptance of the spiritual half of Descartes' divided world. This was the second alternative to which dualism must ultimately come, just as materialism was the first.

Berkeley simply showed that if colour does not reside in the coloured object but is the effect in the mind of the physical properties of an object, if warmth is not a property of the fire but is the end effect of the nerves which are agitated by the molecular disturbance known as heat, if tickling is not a property of the feather that tickles but of the mind of the person tickled, then it is possible to push the whole argument back one stage farther and show that even sensations of extension and solidity are only sensations and that we can never get beyond contemplating our own mental states. If we want to base all knowledge on experience, experience is at bottom purely mental, and when we believe that it tells us of an external world of which sensations are a copy that is merely an inference. Things cannot exist apart from our consciousness of them, and to ask whether they continue to exist if we no longer have sensations is absurd. Things are sensations.

Hume carried this scepticism one stage farther. We think that at any rate we have a self that is formed of a chain of successive experiences presumably grounded in the identity and unity of the personal soul. Hume declared that just as Berkeley had shown that there was no material substance in which qualities resided, but only pure qualities, which are pure sensations, so he could show that there was no spiritual substance which had experiences, but only pure experiences one after the other.

Berkeley of course did not for a moment mean to say that the objective world did not exist and that we were shut up to our own sensations. He was simply arguing that you cannot prove that such sensations are the sensations of a material world. Nevertheless they are perfectly objective, we cannot help them and we cannot vary them at will, they constitute a rigid, objective world of sensed objects existing independent of our will. Sensed objects but not *material* objects.

Berkeley had his own theological answer to the problem which this raises. The objectivity and permanence of the cause of our sensations must, he argues, be due to the continuous activity of an eternal creative Mind, God. It is God's power which causes our sensations to be arranged in the particular order which they follow one another. The external world, therefore, continues to exist even when we cease to perceive it, because God's perception sustains it.

We see then where the argument from experience leads. And the sensationalism from which it springs is itself derived from Descartes' dualism of mind and matter, which treated matter as in itself merely mechanical.

But if matter had been conceived as developing, as active, and mind as the coming to consciousness of matter, we should find ourselves with neither a dead materialism nor a groundless subjectivism but a living unity of mind and matter.

Spinoza was the first to work out such a system. Rejecting dualism he held that the universe was one system, which was neither pure spirit nor pure matter. Mind and matter are the two ultimate attributes of substance, that is to say substance itself is not dead matter or pure spirit but *has* body and *has* mind. But actual bodies or objects are particular forms of matter, just as actual minds are particular forms of thought. In a human being we have a double manifestation (body and mind) of the two ultimate attributes which make up fundamental Reality.

Spinoza also held that all things constitute a perfect system. Every finite object or event is dependent on innumerable others which ramify in all directions and are each of them similarly dependent on innumerable others. Everything is necessary in its appointed place within the whole. Nothing is possible save the actual, and nothing is actual save the necessary. "From the infinite nature of God all things follow by the same necessity, and in the same way, as it follows from the nature of a triangle from eternity to eternity that its three angles are equal to two right angles."

The mechanism which Descartes saw in matter alone, Spinoza sees in God and mind as well. But the entire Universe is a live, and not a dead mechanism, for the order of things is the order of perfect goodness and wisdom and is continuously sustained by the intense consciousness of God. Yet, once again, God is not above the Universe or within the Universe, but his mind "is all the mentality that is scattered over space and time, the diffused consciousness that animates the world."

This is pure mysticism in its sublime confidence in already existing perfection. But in the conception of the Universe as *one* system, which is wholly material from end to end, and in which whatever mind we find is not extraneous to matter but an attribute of substance, parallel with and interpenetrating matter, we have the conception that inspired Hegel and after him Marx. But for Spinoza it is an unchanging, undeveloping whole.

§4. KANT AND HEGEL

Kant's great contribution to philosophy lay in the combination he effected between reason and experimental fact.

Hume had not only dissolved the soul into a succession of experiences; using the same argument he overthrew the whole conception of law on which both Descartes and Spinoza had built up their rational universes. Hume argued that we can never *prove* cause and effect, we merely infer it from the frequent occurrence of two successive phenomena. It is merely mental habit that makes us think that if the first phenomenon occurs the second is bound to follow. A law is simply a convenient formula summing up what usually happens. We have no guarantee that the sequences hitherto observed will reappear in future experience.

Now materialism had attacked religion in the name of science and philosophy. Then Berkeley had refuted materialism with its own arguments about matter and sense impressions, but now Berkeley's doctrine of experience in the hands of Hume has overthrown the doctrine of the soul, the necessity for God, the rationality of the universe and the very existence of science itself.

Someone was badly needed to rescue religion more effectively than Berkeley and also to rescue science. This Kant did by pointing out that Locke was wrong in imagining that a series of impressions falling on the brain could build themselves up into a systematic picture of the universe. They could not do this but for the inherited structure of the mind. All knowledge needs two factors, sense data and pre-existing mental forms in which to fit them. These mental forms make up the empty framework of a perfectly rational universe. We cannot apprehend anything at all without using this already functioning notion of a rational world in which cause and effect links all phenomena. Hence all the facts we absorb simply fill out this picture and cannot be to us other than orderly facts. In practice therefore we never get the scheme of a scientific world without multitudes of facts to prove it, but all those facts have only entered the mind through the gateways of the logical forms so that they could never be to us other than logical.

This ingenious justification of science leads straight to those modern scientific conceptions which explain scientific theories as symbols, convenient fictions or arbitrary forms. It is really the profoundest scepticism. Things as they really are can never be known. Our subjectivism is double, not only are our experiences subjective but the forms which order them and build them up into our experience of an objective world are subjective too.

Now the mental machine which produces for us a scientific world cannot by its very nature give us anything else. It is therefore useless to ask it to prove the existence of God or speak to us of goodness and beauty. But the mental machine is only a part of the mind. It has other faculties equally valid and important. We are not always thinking scientifically. The practical[1] reason, as opposed to the scientific reason, gives us our power to apprehend God and duty.

In our day Bergson has given us his own version of Kant. Reason is a tool for doing things *with* the world. Intuition is a direct apprehension of the entirely irrational world as it is in itself. The scientist investigates *part* of the world and investigates it for a *special purpose.* He assumes that part of the world to be a machine. He therefore further assumes that the whole universe is an aggregation of machine-like bits and makes up one big machine. But the scientific abstraction kills what it dissects out, freezes what it immobilizes, and is wholly false to life as a living, moving whole. Life itself is apprehended not by reason or science but by intuition. Thus Bergson grows out of Kant and at the same time helps to explain his great forerunner.

Lenin described the philosophy of Kant as

"a reconciliation of materialism with idealism, a compromise between the two, a combination in one system of heterogeneous, opposed philosophical tendencies. When Kant allows that to our representations there corresponds something outside us, something in itself, he is a material-

---

[1] By "practical reason" Kant does not mean scientific reasoning but the very opposite, reasoning which takes life in all its concrete richness, including moral and religious considerations.

ist. When he declares this 'thing in itself' to be unknowable, transcendental, of another world, he is an idealist."

What is valuable in Kant's theory is his demonstration that there is no nature for us that is not made over by social man. That man does not stand over against nature contemplating it as an unpeopled universe, but is himself an active part of the nature he is observing. Mind is active and science is not a photograph of the physical universe but the product of man's activity upon nature and nature's corresponding reaction upon man. There is no "nature in itself" but only "nature for man."

But why should that mean that human science is a fiction or other than a genuine reflection of an objective world? The most that it can mean is that it is partial and incomplete, which may be readily admitted. But it is true as far as it goes and it is always going farther. From this point of view there is not the slightest need to make a mystery of man's apprehension of the non-physical side of nature as though this required another type of reason. It is the same reason but concerned with other and sometimes wider aspects. In fact apart from these wider social ideas and plans the narrower tasks of science would never be attempted, for it is civilization as a whole that gives the scientist and the specialist their jobs.

Out of Kant's idealism grew the systems of Fichte, Schelling and Hegel, all of which criticized him while building upon him. By far the most important was Hegel's. Hegel, like Spinoza, believed that the world was one rational system and that everything was interconnected. In order to understand anything it must be seen in all its relations. Now this is the basis of Hegel's distinction between appearance and reality. Kant's distinction was between scientific appearance, the world as known to reason, and the reality of things in themselves, the world not known to anybody. Hegel's distinction is between appearances which are partial and incomplete, like Bergson's view of science, and reality which is all-embracing and complete, like Bergson's *whole* world as apprehended by intuition.

Now most of experience is obviously partial. It will therefore show manifest signs of incompleteness if carefully examined. It will be seen to imply other things on its fringe or on which it depends just as one small portion of a picture really implies the whole composition. Now if reason gets to work on any portion of experience and seeks to find out all that is implied in that experience, including

the contrary truths which the very existence of so many truths imply, reason will be driven onward to include more and more in its
embrace, ever seeking to clear up seeming contradictions until at
last it includes all the facts and the whole truth and there are no
more contradictions and partialities. This final truth will be the
whole truth about everything.

Now this mental process of passing from the part to the whole,
from the self-contradictory to the self-consistent is the dialectic. Is
it, we now have to ask, a purely mental activity, which a sufficiently
powerful mind could engage in with nothing to start with but a *chip*
of concrete reality and at last come to know everything? Or is it a
real historical unfolding of all the implications of a universe in embryo, like a chick growing from an egg?

The first alternative suggests a palaeontologist reconstructing a
prehistoric monster from a single bone, or a detective reconstructing
a crime from a single clue. The second suggests the evolutionary
process as the working out of the potentialities of the universe.

Hegel himself seems to have meant both. But by the expanding,
unfolding universe he meant, among other things, the development
of Absolute Spirit itself. It was here that Hegel was a pure idealist.
But in so far as he never splits the world in two, never thinks for a
moment of mere mind, as Berkeley did, never considers spirit as
opposed to matter, as Descartes did, but, like Spinoza, holds firmly
to substance as containing within it both mind and matter and constituting one Universe, Hegel is always thinking of the concrete
working out of the pageant of history, of biological evolution, of
political and legal institutions. He is a realist all the time. But because he is an idealist too he sees all these solid, concrete things as
manifestations of the unfolding of objective spirit, whose moments
are not only individual consciousnesses but also all the creations of
human thought, all forms of society, all aspects of the State, in a
word, all that exists.

Heraclitus had spoken of the continuous transition of phenomena from non-existence to existence and vice versa. There is a per-
petual flux from one form to another, from the unity of opposites
into their division and from the division back to unity. This inspired
guess Hegel turned into the basic principle of a new logic worked
out by himself, and on this base he constructed a whole system of
philosophy to show how "absolute spirit," objective consciousness,
is developed from "nothing," a pure abstraction, into an absolute

idea which grasps all and contains all in itself. There is no doubt that the absolute spirit of Hegel is that same God, that same divine reason which as it were realizes itself in human history in the productions of philosophy, art, law and in social institutions. Hegel, however, made God descend from his immutable perfection and proceed along the path of development, contending with himself and enriching himself with new content. But how, according to Hegel, does absolute spirit make its dialectical way, how does this dialectical process of development take place? Hegel sees the essence of development in the unity and strife of opposites, in the fact that every phenomenon contains an internal contradiction that drives it forward and brings it ultimately to destruction and the transition to something else. However, the destruction of one phenomenon is at the same time the emergence of a new one which denies the last phenomenon but also contains it in itself. Hegel demonstrates this idea by citing the history of philosophy, of art, and the material of human history. One philosophic system changes itself to another. Every philosopher down to Hegel held his system to be absolute truth and all previous systems to be delusions, but Hegel showed that such a view is naive, that every philosophic system is a step in the development of absolute spirit. Absolute spirit in every historical epoch knows itself in the form of a definite philosophy that corresponds to the historical content of the given stage of its development. In another epoch this form appears as antiquated and yields place to its successor, which denies it and at the same time contains in itself the positive content of the superseded philosophy. "The philosophy, latest in time, is the result of all preceding philosophies and therefore must include them all in itself." The same holds true of religion, law, art, and social institutions. All these fields of absolute spirit were studied by Hegel as connected with one another, and were found to be in close mutual relations. Hegel taught that "only in the presence of a given form of religion can a given form of State structure exist, only in the presence of a given State structure can a given philosophy and a given art exist."

But Hegel was seeking the fundamental cause of the historic process, the principle which determines the dialectic of development of nature and society, seeking it in the development of contradictions within absolute spirit, which finds in nature and society its own form of disclosure and development, whereas Marx saw this basic cause in the very real contradictions of the material processes both in nature and society.

When Napoleon tried by means of the bayonets of his army to introduce bourgeois relationships into Germany, Hegel, who at that time was creating his dialectical method, was in sympathy with the French Revolution and greeted the entry of the Napoleonic troops into Jena as the historical incarnation of a new form of absolute spirit. They say he then called Napoleon "the "absolute spirit on a white charger." But twenty years later, when the feudal monarchy of Frederick William III was being consolidated in Germany, Hegel had lost his revolutionary ideas and had become the State philosopher of the Prussian monarchy.

The dialectical method had made it possible for Hegel in his youth to generalize in idealistic form all the scientific experience of his time, all the course of the historic process, and from idealistic, perverted positions to criticize the one-sided, mechanistic methods which the science of his day was using. Hegel harshly criticized the completely formal logic that ruled up to his time, disclosed its internal contradiction and showed the impossibility of understanding dialectical processes on its basis. Hegel first formulated in idealistic form universal laws for the development, the transition of certain phenomena into other phenomena. These phenomena proceed, according to Hegel, by means of "a negation of a negation." Marx in *The Poverty of Philosophy* expounds this theory of Hegel as follows:

"But once it has placed itself in thesis, this thought, opposed to itself, doubles itself into two contradictory thoughts, the positive and the negative, the 'yes' and the 'no.' The struggle of these two antagonistic elements, comprised in the antithesis, constitutes the dialectic movement. The yes becoming no, the no becoming yes, the yes becoming at once yes and no, the no becoming at once no and yes, the contraries balance themselves, neutralize themselves, paralyse themselves. The fusion of these two contradictory thoughts constitutes a new thought which is the synthesis of the two. This new thought unfolds itself again in two contradictory thoughts which are confounded in their turn in a new synthesis. From this travail is born a group of thoughts. This group of thoughts follows the same dialectic movement as a simple category, and has for antithesis a contradictory group. From these two groups is born a new group of thoughts which is the synthesis of them. As from the dialectic movement of simple categories is born the group, so from the dialectic movement of the groups is born the series, and from the dialectic movement of the series is born the whole system."[1]

Thanks to such a development of absolute spirit by means of its internal contradictions, no one stage of it is fortuitous, but each flows out of all the preceding history that it contains in itself. "Everything that is real," said Hegel, "is rational, and everything that is rational is real." By this Hegel meant to say that all existing social institutions and forms of ideology are determined by the development of absolute spirit, are steps in the movement of reason. Here Hegel is formulating his idealistic principle of dialectic; the development of reason is also the development of reality. This proposition has served as the ground for charging Hegel with reactionary tendencies, with justifying every infamy, every social tyranny, since for him everything that exists is rational. Hegel in the last years of his life was indeed inclined thus to interpret this dialectical proposition of his, it was also used thus by an official philosophy mainly concerned with self-preservation. Hegel's philosophy at one time became the official philosophy of the Prussian monarchy. We know that this idea in Russia too was the cause of much agony of thought in such people as Belinsky, who could not persuade themselves that the regime of Nicholas was rational merely because it existed! But Hegel's dialectical method offered foundations for quite different social conclusions. Because, granted that that which is rational is real, then if the real should prove to be irrational and cease to correspond with its idea, it means, according to Hegel, that it has become antiquated, doomed and subject to destruction. The monarchy was irrational, therefore it was unreal. The monarchy exists, but the moment it becomes irrational it has already ceased to have its roots in life, in reality, it no longer corresponds to the new stage in the development of society and therefore must perish. Thus the Left-Hegelians were able to interpret this proposition of Hegel so as to aid them in the struggle with the monarchical order and religion. They were able to show that Christianity and religion are irrational

---

[1] Marx, *The Poverty of Philosophy*, p. 117.

and therefore must perish, and so it is necessary to contend with them. Thus the Russian Hegelians argued also, fighting against Tsarism. They proved the irrationality, backwardness, and savagery of the Tsarist regime and hence the necessity for its overthrow, and they sounded the call to fight against it.

The main contradiction of Hegel's philosophy is reflected in the fact that the proposition we have quoted can be interpreted in two opposite ways at once.

In Hegel's philosophy we find an expression of the ambiguity of the ideology of the bourgeoisie of that time – the progressive and the reactionary sides of it. On one side it is characterized by a desire to destroy everything that is antiquated, irrational and doomed to pass away, and to replace it with the new that has grown within the womb of the old; on the other side it is characterized by a dread of the new, a dread that was strengthened by what they saw of the French Revolution, and by the conviction that the *status quo* in Germany must remain, that it was not subject to change. But Hegelianism cannot logically defend the *status quo.* Dialectic is revolutionary, it sees in everything processes of change, phenomena in constant flux; every assertion of absolute rest, eternity and immutability contradicts it.

In the further development of the class struggle within capitalist society, both the Hegelian idealism and the Hegelian dialectic were used as theoretic weapons. The radical bourgeoisie of Germany tried to use Hegel's philosophy as a theory of bourgeois revolution. However, experience soon showed that the philosophy of Hegel, as such, either grows quickly into a reactionary ideology of the conservative elements of the bourgeoisie and takes on the character of a rationalistic religion, or it is used by the revolutionary groups of society.

As long as Hegel was alive these opposing camps developed the two contradictory sides of his philosophy and yet carried on their struggle within the Hegelian system as a whole. But, as we know, in the years 1830-31, a wave of revolutions rolled over Europe, affecting a number of countries from Spain to Poland. In Germany philosophical disputes under the influence of this revolution took on an openly political character. The matter reached the point at which groups of "right" Hegelians, of the "centre" and of the "left" were formed within the Hegelian school, the last mentioned eventually breaking off as an independent group. The revolutionary wave, however, very soon subsided, and the revolutionary strivings of the liberal bourgeoisie in Germany did not lead to any real political achievements. They found their outlet only in philosophic disputations. But for this very reason the philosophical struggle grew in importance and intensity, especially in the sphere of theology where the new philosophy engaged in radical criticisms of the dogmas of the Church.

Marx and Engels took a direct part in this movement of the young Hegelians. Marx, however, soon ceased to be satisfied merely with the philosophic criticism of religion, and began to play an active part in the political struggle as editor of the *Rhenish Gazette*. In 1842 he even broke with the "free men," as the young Hegelians in Berlin called themselves. Marx wanted a serious struggle and not empty declamation, although this bore a revolutionary character.

"I required," wrote Marx, "that there should be less noisy phrases and self-flagellation and more definiteness, more knowledge of the matter and penetration into its concrete essence. Further, I expressed the wish that when they criticized religion they should push forward as the first thing to be done to a criticism of political conditions, and not merely criticize the political conditions in their religious setting, because the former approach is more in accordance with the spirit of the paper and the level of its readers: religion, in itself lacking content, dwells, not in the sky, but on earth and itself collapses along with the dissolution of the distorted actuality, whose theory it presents."

Feuerbach, who studied under Hegel, was the most significant of his liberal disciples. This "left" wing began by criticizing orthodox religion from an Hegelian point of view, contending that the new philosophy far from buttressing orthodoxy reduced dogmas to myths and led to a naturalistic pantheism. Feuerbach went even farther, and showed that religion was nothing more than the imaginative projection of human needs and hopes. Man, in so far as he is rational, is to himself his own object of thought. Whenever man is thinking of God, or infinity, or law, or love, he is not really thinking of the Eternal at all, but of outward projections of his own nature. Feuerbach recalled philosophy from unsubstantial metaphysics to the solid facts of human nature and natural science. "Speculative philosophy," says Feuerbach, "is drunken philosophy; philosophy must again become sober. Do not strive to be a philosopher as distinct from a man; just be a thinking man." What is Feuerbach getting at? He is criticizing Hegel for falsely solving the contradiction between being and thought by transferring it into the interior of one of the primary elements, namely thought. According to Hegel thought is also being, nature is postulated by the idea, material being is created by spiritual being, by God. Kant was only saying the same thing when he affirmed that the outer world receives its laws from reason, instead of reason receiving its laws from the outer world. In what is this really different from the conception that the divine reason dictates to the world the laws which regulate it?

But this means that Idealism is not really establishing the unity of being and thought at all. It is rupturing that unity for it is leaving real being entirely out of the question. The truth is that thought is conditioned by being, not being by thought. It is matter that thinks, it is the body that becomes the subject, the real material being is the subject, and thought is its function, its predicate.

This is the real solution of the problem of thought and existence, of mind and body, the only solution which does not suppress one of the elements of the contradiction.

This is very like the philosophy of Spinoza. It asserts that the purely subjective spiritual act of thought is objectively the material action of a physical body. What is this but Spinozism without its theological lumber? The unity of thought and extension in one substance minus the unnecessary equation of that substance with the concept God?

Feuerbach's weakness was pointed out by Marx. His materialism only contemplates the material world. The mind is only acted upon by the world it thus comes to know. Knowing is the mind's real activity – yes, but that is only half the truth. We know the world only by acting upon it, and when we act upon it and change it, we change our own nature too and our knowing mind with it.

§ 5. RECENT IDEALISM

I. Fictionalism in Modern Science

Of recent years we have witnessed a strange revival of subjectivism in certain novel theories of the true nature of science. Avenarius in 1888 and Mach about the same time came forward with a methodological positivism which, while rejecting much in Kant, nevertheless admitted a subjective or voluntary factor in knowledge. Mach *identified* the physical object with its sensible appearances. Science, therefore, deals only with the last events in a chain of supposed material causes and effects which events are merely experiences. Man groups these "experiences" in scientific systems mainly as a matter of expediency. A *thing* is a construct of a selection of impressions, the mind or ego perceiving the thing is also a construct of the same impressions plus others of a different order. These primary experiences we describe in their modes of occurrence by a system of reference designed solely for purposes of economy. We may speak of "space," "force," "mass," "cause," but these are only short expressions for regularities of behaviour among successive or simultaneous impressions. Science, therefore, is not really explaining anything, still less is it describing an objective scientific world. It merely describes observed relationships among impressions.

Le Roy and Poincare gave even greater emphasis to the subjective element in scientific thought. We apply to an unorganized and amorphous nature a purely conventional system which works with some measure of success. Nature is more easily ordered by one such system than by another, but that is as much as we dare say, the system cannot for a moment be held to be a true *description* of nature.

Le Roy argued that one of the reasons why the facts seem to fit the theory is simply that we only collect such facts as are relevant to that theory, they are therefore bound to fit. The theory is true to the extent that there are enough facts to make it credible, but another theory might be equally true, and be able to amass its own verifactory data too.

In more recent times Eddington has argued that the system of pointer readings, which really constitute science, is not a picture of reality but only a symbol. The pointer reading is no more truly representative of reality than a telephone number is like the subscriber who is so designated. Science in abstracting only the measurements of things, has really let the things themselves, in their richness and complexity, go. Hence to apprehend reality in its fullness some other logic than that of science is required, call it the sense of values, religious intuition, what you will.

These subjectivist attacks on the validity of science were severely criticized by Lenin in his *Materialism and Empirio-*

Criticism, where he pointed out that the whole system of error is due to the old, discredited subjective idealism of Berkeley and the confusion between experiencing an objective world, and merely having experiences. This new scientific theory about scientific theories is only idealism once again, only Kant in a fresh guise, only a re-hash of subjectivism. If matter cannot think, then thought must indeed have an existence in a world of its own in spite of all difficulties. But the only result of such a dualism will be the endless confusions of philosophy. But if matter can think, in the brains of men, then there is no need to go skating on the thin and dangerous ice of subjectivism. Science becomes the imperfect but largely satisfactory picture of man's universe which is validated by his successful practice in controlling nature, and which he has discovered in the process of handling nature and thinking about it.

Thus nature is not a final order of the world of experience which must be accepted as given. It is still an unfinished business. It is neither the terrifying thing the primitive mind envisaged or the lifelessly rigorous affair that rationalists have depicted. Nature is never permanent. Man himself takes a hand in the creative process, and suffuses purely physical and biological events with the aims and desires implied in mind.

"Nature is involved in life, and life is, of course, involved in nature. Life seems to be an expression not of some fixed mood of nature, but of its evolving processes, and not of processes that are fixed for ever in a single groove, but of processes that interminably weave and interweave, yielding moments for the interference of intelligence; so that, if we learn how, we may help, age after age, to select processes artistically intelligent enough to produce an ever finer human living, and a nature as well that will accept and foster that finer human living."[1]

2. State Absolutism

Hegelian Idealism takes a characteristically modern form in the philosophy of the hierarchical totalitarian state which is really only

---

[1] Hart, *Inside Experience,* p. 115.

the absolutism of Bosanquet and Bradley worked out to its logical conclusion.

According to this theory the State is the living organism in which alone the individual finds his true self-hood and true freedom. It is the actualization of freedom, because in its institutions, its law and its actual creation of functional individuals, like bees in a hive, it provides firstly the concrete opportunity and secondly the men to take advantage of it. The State as such stands for an entity over and above the sum of individual wills, and a lawful will to which every individual must submit. In sharing in the common life the individual, therefore, not only fulfils himself but transcends himself.

> "Representing as it does that aspect of the individual's will which harmonizes with the will of others, his will, that is to say, for the good of all, including self, as opposed to his will for the good of self at the expense of all, it is of necessity always rational and always right."[1]

This is that confusion of the actual with the possible so characteristic of idealism. Here it means that absolute idealism sanctifies all existing institutions including the class relationships of modern capitalism. Hegelian idealism in the hands of the English idealists has been turned into an ideological weapon.

The truth of the matter is that the organized community exists only to serve the interests of the individuals who comprise it. The individual does not exist merely to serve the interests of the community. Where the latter theory is held it merely disguises the exploitation of the many in the interests of the few. The "State" or "Community" that is served being nothing more or less than the minority that wields the State machine, the owning class.

The idealist method of attributing a higher will to the individual which is nothing to do with what he desires, but which enables him to transcend his merely individual self is simply a device for giving an appearance of justice and democracy to what must otherwise appear the purely arbitrary and tyrannical acts of a class state.

---

[1] Joad, *Modern Political Theory*.

CHAPTER II

DIALECTIC AS A THEORY OF KNOWLEDGE

§ I. PRACTICE AS THE BASIS OF KNOWLEDGE

Dialectically evolving matter is the initial point in the Marx-Leninist philosophy. In the dialectic of the development of material actuality the very emergence of social history, the very emergence of thinking individuals find their explanation.

Thought is a property of highly-organized matter which has reached the highest stage of its development. In the eternal development of matter there arise, decline and anew create themselves, infinitely varied forms of material movement and among them there arises, in some maybe unimportant part of the world-structure, a peculiar form of material movement, namely organic life, and after it social history.

The capacity for knowledge proper to men in the social historic epoch is the highest product of the development of matter, and is the property of a high form of existence of material actuality.

"Matter," says Engels, "moves in an eternal cycle, completing its trajectory in a period so vast that in comparison with it our earthly year is as nothing; in a cycle in which the period of highest development, namely the period of organic life with its crowning achievement – self-consciousness, is a space just as comparatively minute in the history of life and of self-consciousness; in a cycle in which every particular form of the existence of matter – be it the sun or a nebula, a particular animal or animal-species, a chemical combination or decomposition – is equally in transition; in a cycle in which nothing is eternal, except eternally changing, eternally moving matter and the laws of its movement and change. But however often and pitilessly this cycle may be accomplished in time and space, however many countless suns and earths may arise and fall, however long it may be necessary to wait until in some solar system, on some planet appear conditions suitable for organic life, however many countless beings may fall and rise before, out of their midst, develop animals with a thinking brain that find an environment that permits them to live, be it even only for a short period, we are, nevertheless, assured that matter in all its changes remains eternally one and the same, that not one of its attributes may perish, and that that same iron necessity which compels the destruction of the highest earthly bloom of matter – the thinking spirit – also necessitates its re-birth at some other place, at some other time."[1]

At what moment does this process of knowledge arise? At what degree of development of material actuality are the conditions created which are necessary for the emergence of knowing beings?

The process of knowledge, which is a process of reflecting the ever deeper connections of the material world, can arise only when the conditions are ripe for the development of real social *history;* when socially controlled production becomes possible, when organic life is no longer subject to the merely unconscious operations of cause and effect, but comes under conscious and deliberate social control.

Social knowledge can only come into existence on the basis of a development of material production in the process of which every new generation receives from its predecessor, together with the accumulated heritage of productive forces, a heritage of experience embodied in a known sum of knowledge.

Materialism before Marx was only a contemplative materialism, since it considered the question of knowledge apart from its connection with social-historic practice. The problem for Marx is to explain man's sensuous experience, his hate and love, his joys and sufferings, by the historically existing form of social practice and the class struggle. Only by such a method can we understand the significance of human experience and the actions arising therefrom, which are not the same for people of different epochs and different classes.

In material production the subjective experiences of people are not separated from the material objects of the external world. The material objects of nature are in practice found in unity with the social action of people and, through such action, are also found in unity with the process of knowledge of these people. When we con-

---

[1] Engels, *Dialectic of Nature* (1930), p. 125.

sider the objects of material production, for example the appliances of material production – machine-tools, turbines, tractors, we find in them the subjective action of people, the social practice of many generations of men, which has passed into the definite forms of these objects.

The article which appears to exist in objective reality, without dependence on people or their knowledge, is seen in social practice to be in union with the action and knowledge of people. In the process of material production, and on the basis of human productive activity, a knowledge of material nature becomes a necessary factor in the production of articles. In any tool of production a definite historic stage of social practice and knowledge is embodied. Modern machines assume not only a modern level of development of people's productive activity, but also in conjunction with it more than twenty centuries of scientific development.

The transition of the action of social beings into an article is actualized in the process of production. Marx shows in *Capital* that during the process of labour that labour is continually changing from the form of action into the form of being. In the process of labour subjective action enters into the article, enters into unity with the article by working on it. In social practice the forms of a material article are changed. From an external object of nature, independent of society, the article is turned into a social article indissolubly linked up with the whole complex of social practice. Thus in the process of material production, in social practice, a material object becomes a social object, and the social subjective action of people becomes objective. Thus in practice is realized the unity of subject and object. So we see it is only possible to resolve the question of the mutual action of subject and object, of thought and being, in social practice.

§2. PRACTICE AS THE CRITERION OF KNOWLEDGE

Social practice is not a form of activity that is independent of the time-factor; it emerges in a quite definite form at each given historical stage of social development. In such a concrete historic form Marx regards the question when he speaks of the criterion of practice. Every social class has its determinate criterion of practice. In every historic epoch this criterion is changed; it is changed along with the development of the class in the course of its historical role. The material content of practice, the historically determined processes of material production were, and are, for the classes concerned, the criterion of truth and the criterion of the understanding of objective material reality.

The patriarchal tribal society with its primitive ways of production was unacquainted with the productive possibilities of coal. The possibility of using coal was only discovered at the period of the merchant capitalist relationships which arose in the feudal period in the twelfth century (near Liege in Belgium).

The extraction of iron, copper and silver has now proceeded for nearly 6,000 years. But neither the Assyrian treatment of copper, nor the working of iron in very ancient China, nor the mining industry in ancient Rome could serve as a practical basis for wide geological generalizations. For wide theoretical generalizations there was needed a long process of mining production, a wide extension of mining, the knowledge of how to remove subterranean water, and the utilization of a great many other technical devices. The development of the commercial-capitalist type of industry in the sixteenth century allows the whole practice of mining to be transformed into a science. The experience of mining production became so wide, and the diversity of mine workings so great, that the science of geology may be said to begin from this time.

Experience is the sum, the result of social practice. Only in that experience which is the aggregate of the practical attainments of society do we disclose the objectively existing material reality. "In experience," according to Lenin, "emerge objects of understanding, independent of understanding."

Periodic winds and sea currents existed long before the appearance of organic life, existed millions of years before the appearance of the social practice and knowledge of men. But a long period of development of practical navigation was necessary before it was possible to understand these winds and currents. Navigation, although considerably developed by the Phoenicians, by the Greeks, and by the Alexandrians of the first and second centuries, had not yet accumulated sufficient experience for these scientific discoveries. Only the changes resulting from the rising capitalist organization of production created the practical foundation for such knowledge.

The basis of knowledge in the example we give was merchant-capitalist practice, yet in its experience of sea-travelling this class summed up not only its own practice but also the practice of those stages of social evolution that had preceded it. Shipbuilding, the building of wharfs for boats, and many different ways of rigging a ship, were already known in periods of more primitive methods of production.

All the earlier developments of historic practice are summed up in the experience of every epoch. That is just why Marx-Leninism seeks to resolve the question of knowledge and experience on the basis of all social practice. This implies a radical change in the manner in which these problems are to be approached.

By including the criterion of practice in the theory of knowledge, Marxism leaves no place for the Kantian "thing in itself." For Kant the "thing in itself" was a secret, unknowable essence, inaccessible to our senses and to our knowledge alike. The material object ceases to be a secret, "thing in itself," as soon as it emerges in the process of production, as soon as it is reproduced in industry.

The development of the productive process actually changes the objects of material nature; where at first they were virtually unknown and unknowable, they eventually take shape and become known. "What we can *do,*" as Engels rightly declared, "that, of course, we cannot call unknowable."

"For the chemistry of the first half of the nineteenth century," wrote Engels, "organic compounds were such unknown things. But to-day we are succeeding in making them one after the other by means of the synthesis of chemical elements and with no recourse to organic processes." The objective material world is revealed by practice. Processes that seemed to be inaccessible to knowledge and to exist independently of knowledge emerge as part of the practice of a particular stage in social development. Thus a whole range of entirely new laws in thermodynamics, chemistry and electricity have been discovered in the process of modern social practice.

This explains what we mean when we say that practice is the real key to our knowledge of the external world. "The question whether objective truth can be attributed to human thinking is not a question of theory but is a practical question. The dispute over the reality or non-reality of thinking which is isolated from practice is a purely scholastic question," says Marx in his second thesis on Feuerbach. The best refutation of Kantian and Humist agnosticism as of other philosophical fancies is practice, or as Engels rightly says: "The success of our actions proves the agreement of our perceptions with the apprehensible objective truth of things."

However conditional and imperfect our knowledge at any stage may be, it reflects objective material reality, approximating to absolute truth. The fact that we can and do know the truth and are really in touch with objective material nature is proved to us by our practice, which turns our knowledge into actual existing objects of production and remakes and changes material actuality.

But it would be a crude distortion and vulgarization of Marxism to see in the Marx-Leninist doctrine of practice as the criterion of truth a negation of the vast importance of theoretical analysis and theoretical verification of different logical conclusions. Dialectical Materialism has nothing in common with the cheap rule-of-thumb thinking that has no use for abstract thought and general ideas. "Practice is higher than theoretical knowledge," says Lenin, "because it has not only the virtue of generality, but also of immediate actuality." A logical development of ideas is possible because the mind engages in the task of interpreting and working over the historical process which it reflects. But all such thinking, even when it uses the generalizations of preceding practice, must instantly be tested by scientific experiment and social practice.

Pre-Marxian philosophy tries to find the criterion of truth in knowledge itself. Descartes sees the criterion of truth in clearness and precision of ideas. Kant saw the criterion of truth in the universal and necessary character of knowledge itself. Contemporary mathematical logic, in the person of Russell, Cantor and others, perceives the criterion of truth in the logical formal succession of mathematical conclusions. None of these forms of rationalistic idealism makes any attempt to find the criterion of truth in the external world. But knowledge considered as an abstract system of ideas, however self-consistent, clear and precise that system may be, can never be a criterion of objectivity.

When Marx speaks of finding a criterion of truth by subjective practice he does not mean by subjective what Berkeley or Mach would mean, he means that the subject only reaches truth in so far as and in the manner in which he engages in activity in relation to the external world, in the course of which activity he changes that world. The practical point of view is the subjective point of view in the sense that it proceeds from the concrete activity of social man. True subjectivity is the breaking down of the separation of idea and object, and it is obviously one and the same thing as practice. The objective world (objective truth) is through practice reflected in knowledge and ceases to be a strange world separate from human knowledge.

§3. BOURGEOIS PRACTICE AND KNOWLEDGE

In class society there cannot be extra-class practice and extra-class knowledge. The criterion of truth in class society is the practice of the given class.

In the sixteenth, seventeenth, and eighteenth centuries, when the bourgeoisie was struggling with feudalism for mastery; and in the first half of the nineteenth century, when capitalism had not yet arrived at the period of its decay, capitalist practice was the criterion of progressive knowledge.

The philosophic systems, natural-scientific theories, social-political views of that epoch remain among the greatest achievements of the history of progressive social knowledge.

But however progressive the views of Bacon were in comparison with the scholastic philosophy of the Middle Ages, whatever shattering arguments from the idealistic point of view Hegel brought against the Kantian "thing in itself," the philosophic views of these giants of theoretical thought retain their bourgeois limitations.

The dialectic of Hegel remained a mystical idealistic dialectic. "The whole Darwinian teaching about the struggle for existence," writes Engels, "is simply a transference of the bourgeois economic teaching on competition (and also the Malthusian theory) from the sphere of society to the sphere of nature."

The capitalistic means of production could make possible the emergence of a number of theories – scientific, technical, philosophic – among which, some have reflected, though in a distorted form, others have only guessed at, different sides of objective actuality. The capitalist practice of a given time could be the basis of progressive knowledge. But at no stage of the development of capitalism, even in the epoch of the revolutionary uprising of the bourgeoisie, could its historically limited practice create a theory of knowledge correctly reflecting the contradictions of objective actuality.

At the heart of capitalism lies that principle of exploitation which called into being a development of the productive forces unheard of until that time, with which development a remarkable expansion of the mathematical and natural sciences was closely connected; but at the same time it was this very principle of exploitation that was responsible for the distorted representation of the main forces of capitalist production, especially of the essential principle of capitalism itself, which appears in a curiously mystified form.

The basic contradictions of bourgeois thought are rooted in the contradictions of the capitalistic mode of production itself. And so such works as *Capital* by Marx, *Imperialism as the Latest Stage of Capitalism* by Lenin, which uncover the contradictions of capitalism, acquire great importance for the theory of knowledge.

Marx discloses the character of capitalistic relationships, beginning with the simple categories of capitalist economy, from that period when capitalistic relationships were not yet dominant, and ending with the period of their revolutionary overthrow.

In trade and finance, in capital and profit, in wages, in the form of surplus value, in the reproduction of capital, etc., Marx discloses the mystification, the distorted conception of actual relationships, that is proper to bourgeois practice itself.

In bourgeois society mutual relationships between people "in the social-productive process lead," says Marx, "above all to this, that their own productive relationships which stand outside their control and outside their conscious individual action, take on a 'thingified' character, in consequence of which, all the products of their work take on the form of commodities."

Relations between people become possible only through the means of things, through the "thing"-form of commodities and money, by means of capital, and interest, and so much per cent. And so the social relationships between people are distorted, are mystified.

Even a long time before capitalism became supreme, wherever trade and money circulation appeared, there appeared at the same time distortions of actual human relationships. "All forms of society," says Marx, "to the extent that they reach the stage of commodity production and money circulation, are to a more or less degree characterized by such a distortion of actual relationships."

On the basis of the dominance of the bourgeoisie, thanks to the lordship of capital in production, the social forces of labour present themselves to the bourgeoisie in a distorted aspect, as if they generate themselves in the womb of capital itself. Thanks to an objectively existing exchange a distorted conception of profit is created, as if it arose out of circulation and not by the appropriation by a capitalist of the unpaid labour of a worker.

Marx establishes that *capitalist practice in the whole complex of its social relations gives to itself such a form as does not correspond with its real nature.*

The capitalistic sources of income and forms of income "express," says Marx, "the relations of capitalist production in a fetishistic form. Their nature, as it appears on the surface, is cut off from its hidden connection and real origins. Thus ground becomes the source of ground-rent, capital is the source of profit and labour the source of wages."

Marx is not concerned with passing a moral judgment on capitalism, or expressing indignation at its injustices in the manner of Rousseau who declared feudalism to be "contrary to nature." Marx discloses the actual distortion that exists in the capitalist order of production which is reflected in the distortions and mystifications that exist in bourgeois ideology.

The capitalist means of production, in the light of this distorted bourgeois consciousness, is accepted as an eternal immutable phenomenon, as the relationship of natural man to nature (as was thought in the epoch of enlightenment in the eighteenth century) as the sole form of relationship of man to man (vulgar political economy), hired labour being supposed to comprise all possible forms of labour.

Bourgeois thought always considers the capitalist means of production as historically unchangeable, permanent and existing everywhere that men exist.

It moves in a constricted fashion within the limits set by capitalist social relationships. The system of exploitation, the movement of capitalist forces, fix the very forms of thought just as they determine economic practice.

It is for this reason that bourgeois economics suffers from such severe limitations. Even its most useful ideas remain in some degree under the sway of the distortions of actual relationships that capitalism cannot but produce and reproduce. True their own criticisms have already destroyed many of the dogmas of orthodox capitalist economics, but since they are not free to break completely away into socialist economics this only deepens the confusion and illogicality of their latest theories. Hence their half-way policies and hopeless contradictions, while the actual laws of capitalist production remain for them an unguessed secret. Bourgeois thought cannot pass beyond the stage of discrediting the semblance without revealing the essential truth which it has obscured, just as Kant shows that phenomena are only the *appearance* of reality but is entirely unable to tell us anything about the unknown "thing in itself."

In every sphere of thought bourgeois thinkers will be found creating individualistic theories, interpreting the universe in terms of the sanctity of private property, and separating man from his necessary place in the community. Philosophers as different in their outlook as Spengler, Max Stirner, Fichte and Hume, will all be found exalting the individual and his sensations and the individual and his private property as the criterion of reality and the key to the understanding of the universe.

But the reactionary elements in individualistic bourgeois thought emerge most clearly in our own epoch, in which the contradictions of capitalism have been sharpened to the limit – the epoch of imperialism and proletarian revolutions.

The concealed laws and connections of the capitalist system can be actually disclosed and known only from an anti-capitalist proletarian point of view.

When human society is really understood and capitalism is revealed as one of its necessary forms of development, the class struggle is seen to be the basis of its movement, of its progress into a new and higher form. From this point of view, which was that of Marx, the laws of the rise and fall of capitalism, of the movement of the proletariat and of the proletarian revolution are revealed. From the standpoint of Marx the revolutionary destruction of capitalism has become historically necessary and also the building up under conditions of proletarian dictatorship of a socialist society, of a collectivized society.

In distinction from other oppressed classes, the proletariat goes through the grim school of large-scale capitalist production. This form of exploitation and the struggle against it train the proletariat in habits of joint social work and create the possibility of party political solidarity and organization.

The proletariat is the only class that is able, logically and finally, to struggle against capitalist exploitation and private property in the means of production, against the actually existing irrationality and mystification of the practice of capitalism.

> "Only that class among the oppressed classes which
> has been taught, united, disciplined, tempered by decades

of industrial conflict, which has assimilated all the culture of urban, industrial large-scale capitalism and which has the ability and determination to defend, to preserve and further develop these achievements, to make them accessible to all the people, to all workers, only that class which knows how to endure all the burdens, torments, misfortunes, great sacrifices that are inevitably laid by history on whosoever breaks away from the past and courageously opens up for himself a road to a new future – only that class which has passed through the hardening school of toil and knows how to inspire with respect for his labour every working man, every honourable man – only such a class can destroy the classes which it supersedes by its own dictatorship" (Lenin).

Lenin, as we see, in his approach to the question of the independent class-movement of the proletariat, attributes great importance to the character of the work of the proletariat under capitalism. The working class in the conditions of capitalist production is the greatest productive force. The proletariat is the immediate producer in bourgeois society. It is their activity and not that of the capitalist that transfers itself to and comes into unity with the material object.

The conditions of large-scale capitalist industry foster in the revolutionary class such habits of approach to the object as are not possible to the capitalist, whose basic motive of action is "exchange value and its increase." Therefore only the ideologies of the working class can work out a logical materialistic attitude towards the object, towards those actual processes in which the proletariat itself takes part as a producing force.

The dialectical point of view towards material actuality, as we shall trace in detail further on, has as its most highly developed form the logical revolutionary political struggle of the proletariat which is directed to the destruction of capitalism.

While it is true as we have seen that the very character of the activity of the proletariat has already created all the necessary conditions for working out a logical materialistic philosophy of nature and society, we must yet remember that in capitalist society there exists between the worker and the means of labour a severance which is conditioned by the whole economic structure of capitalism.

The means and instruments of labour are the private property of the capitalists. The progress of capitalist technique and of industrial organization emerges as a hostile force in relation to the worker, as a force that increases unemployment and exploitation.

The social character of labour is itself under capitalism "a kind of force foreign to the worker" (Marx). For the condition that makes real the social character of labour, of co-operation of workers in the process of material production, is such that the worker only feels it as an external force.

Capital makes use of every available means to distort the consciousness of the worker. The bourgeois school, the Church, the Press make it their task to suppress in the worker his power to oppose capitalism, to foster in him the ideology of the slave who is content in his slavery.

In the epoch of imperialism sections of the workers, because of privileged material conditions, identify their interests with the success of their capitalist masters, and help to spread the ideology of capitalism among the workers. This particularly applies to the trade union and political bureaucracy, which with the spread of democratic institutions is increasingly drawn into the State machinery for the preservation of the existing system, and is therefore led into opposition to the forces making for social change.

The bourgeois political education of the workers is being assiduously promoted by every one of the political parties of the bourgeoisie, whose first and radical task is a pitiless struggle against the party of the proletariat, the communist party. But the more the contradictions of capitalism deepen and the fiercer becomes the class struggle, so much the more conscious and revolutionary become the working masses and with still less success can the bourgeoisie apply its methods of deforming and distorting the consciousness of the worker.

§4. PRAGMATISM

Bourgeois individualism when it becomes the ideology of monopoly capital, an ideology which is organically at one with the aggressive politics of imperialism, emerges stripped of all disguise. One of the clearest examples of the decay of bourgeois thought is to be found in the pragmatic theory of knowledge, which reduces the whole question to one of practical advantage and the wishes of the individual. For me, says William James, the founder of pragmatism, only that which is practically useful is truth. Truth is not actuality reflected in our thinking, but that which happens to suit the needs and feelings of an individual personality. Such a view is far removed from the conception of knowledge as a reflection of material reality.

The British representative of the pragmatist philosophy, Schiller, develops a number of possible definitions of truth. Truth as necessity, as correspondence with an object, as that which is self-evident, as authenticity. All these definitions are from Schiller's point of view only expressions of the different psychical states of the subject. Truth is not arrived at in the process of reflecting material reality by the thought of social man – truths are created by man. Of the numerous definitions of truth, man selects those which are most suitable to him at a given moment, those which best express his will, his desires and personal interests. Truth is a working hypothesis which has no relationship to the actual development of the material world and always remains merely an hypothesis. The only things with which truth can agree are the personal acts and aspirations of man.

Pragmatism means that instead of allowing truth to reflect objective reality whether we like what we see or not, we construct a version that suits our desires and see whether we can maintain it in the face of the facts. For so long as we can do so this version is truth.

Thus a financial swindler wishes to persuade his victims, the public, his fellow financiers and the law that his schemes are perfectly honest. He therefore constructs a complete case and puts it about with all the conviction he can muster. It is very much to his interests that it shall be believed. Now according to pragmatism as long as he can get it believed it is "true." Conformity to fact, according to pragmatism, is no test at all. For after all what *is* fact? There are only the facts as they appear to you and me, and very often they appear quite different to you and me, as visitors to the U.S.S.R. discover! Actually there are no bare facts, there are only human judgments about facts, and judgments are really points of view not photographs of reality.

The only useful evidence is the evidence produced by the financier and in his hands, as we know, the facts come to look quite different, much more innocent than they did in the hands of a suspicious lawyer.

Thus Pirandello, in his play *"You're right if you think you are,"* gives us two versions of the inaccessible "thing as it is," which are quite contradictory and yet each of which can be made to appear as true as the other.

> "You want documentary proofs in order to affirm or deny! I have no use for them, for, in my opinion, reality does not lie in these, but in the mind of these two persons into which I cannot enter unless by that evidence which they themselves give me."

Pragmatism was advocated by Papini the Italian fascist philosopher and exerted a powerful influence over Mussolini. Under fascist rule pragmatism means that whatever view of events you can persuade the world to accept is "truth." Have supreme confidence in your own version of affairs, trust your own optimistic presentation, insist on it, get it accepted. It is as true as any other. It is the only truth *if you can get it believed* in preference to any other version of the facts.

Whether you are convincing the outside world or your own people the principle is the same. As long as propaganda keeps the system going because it goes on being believed, your world view, your "Third Reich," your renewed nation, your fiction, is successful, maintains itself, and is therefore true.

There is not a country in the capitalist world today in which a great myth has not to be believed in the interests of the *status quo.* The United States has its great myth, Great Britain and the Empire, the toiling millions of Japan and India. Every myth misrepresents the facts. But every myth holds the masses hypnotized in subjection. Therefore it is true. Hence the immense popularity of pragmatism in a decaying world in which it is not convenient for the masses to know the truth. Truth, pragmatism claims, is what is valuable to the knower. But what is most valuable to a capitalist knower is a successful lie, so that lie is the truth as long as he can get it believed.

But it is in opposition to such "value" determinations of truth that the whole of science has made headway. Enlightenment and criticism mean little more than conscious discrimination against fictions which are merely useful and not true. The scientist has to learn to forgo the pleasing and the hopeful hypothesis. Knowledge is a means of adaptation to experience not in proportion to its pleasantness and hopefulness, but in proportion as it dispels illusions, be they ever so grateful and inspiring.

But suppose the class conscious workers come forward with their own theory and after a revolution impose their ideas on the masses and on the bourgeoisie. Once again we have a theory, this time the Marxian theory, that works. Is it not regarded as true on just the same grounds as the fascist theory? Does it not maintain itself by just the same vicious propaganda? Not in the least. The fascist theory is held to be true only because it works in the sense that by propaganda the system keeps going. The Marxian theory works because it is true and if it did not work it would not be true. The fallacy is a logical one. Because every true theory works that is not to say that every theory that works is true. Many false theories work for quite a long time yet they are not true even while they are working satisfactorily.

Marxism is true not because it works in this sense but because it is always being tested by the facts and because it arises out of the facts. Therefore for the great mass of the people it is believed not because it is put across by successful propaganda but because it corresponds with the facts known to the workers, because as a working hypothesis it is repeatedly verified by social experiment and achievement.

Verifying an hypothesis by the test of facts is a very different process from choosing an hypothesis because we like it. An hypothesis is verified by finding out what facts would follow from it, and then looking to the facts to see whether they are as the hypothesis demands. The unfavourable answer is taken as well as the favourable and the hypothesis modified accordingly.

Marxism is always being verified by experiment. Fascism presents conceptions that are only believed because the desire to do so outweighs all the factual evidence against them.

Pragmatism is the decadent philosophic ideology of imperialism. For the bourgeois of the epoch of imperialism the objective processes of development, the laws of social history, are something foreign to his personal will, his actions and his interests. At every step of his action he encounters movements of working-class revolutionary action that are strange to him – crises, the contraction or disappearance of markets. This is where pragmatic philosophy comes to his aid, for it "easily proves" that crises are not conditioned by active law, that one ought to seek the truth, not in them, but in the practical interests of the agents of the capitalist means of production. Truth is given not in the process of reflecting the object, but in the subject and its personal actions. Only by personal actions based on individual interests is it possible, from the pragmatic point of view, to establish or refute a given truth.

"About pragmatism," wrote Lenin, "the philosophic journals say just about everything. Pragmatism ridicules metaphysics and materialism and idealism, exalts experience and only experience, acknowledges practice as the sole criterion, completely accepts the positivist flux in general, holds that science is not an 'absolute copy of reality,' and happily deduces from all this a God who exists only to serve man's practical aims, only for practice, without any metaphysics, without any reality, beyond the bounds of experience."[1]

Pragmatism is one of the extreme forms of bourgeois subjectivism. Only that which "helps us and works on us" is true for us, says Dewey. Truth is an instrument and not a reflection of the material process, and the theory of truth is the theory of the instrument. Wherefore John Dewey calls pragmatism instrumentalism.

Monopoly capitalism has brought to extremity the contradictions of bourgeois society. Attempts to reconcile the demands of individuality with the objective process of actuality on the basis of an adequate reflection of the latter are being made less and less frequently. To most bourgeois philosophers of the imperialist epoch the view that knowledge can be the reflection of the objective process of development appears as something monstrous.

Pragmatism has most accurately formulated the turning of bourgeois knowledge away from the attempt to disclose the essence of the contradictions of the objective process of material actuality. We cannot know the actuality of the material world and its internal contradictions, as realities independent of us, say all pragmatists without exception. Knowledge is a working hypothesis (James), an instrument which depends on our interests and advantages (Dewey), on our "internal sensation" (James). The only thing accessible to us is our practice, everything that goes beyond is unknowable.

---

[1] Lenin, vol. xiii, p. 279.

CHAPTER III

MOMENTS OF KNOWLEDGE OF ACTUALITY

Only by proceeding from material social practice as the basis of the theory of knowledge were Marx, Engels and Lenin able to resolve the problem of the connection of subject and object, to uncover the historical, evolutionary character of that connection. Human knowledge of reality passes in the course of its development through different moments or gradations that mark the comprehension by man of the ever more deep and many-sided connections of the material world. Lenin expounds as follows the movement by which knowledge attains greater and greater depth.

"At first – impressions, as in a flash, then – something is distinguished, then – ideas of quality are developed (leading to a definition of a thing or phenomenon) and subsequently, ideas of quantity. Then study and reflection direct the thought to questions of identity and difference – basis – essence. All these moments or steps of knowledge are directed from the subject to the object, verify themselves by practice and proceed through this verification to truth."

From the direct perception of reality, of sense data, of separate impressions, received by the aid of our senses, man proceeds to the stage of defining a thing and reaching an "idea" of it, to the disclosure of its connections, the law of its development, and all this he verifies in practice.

Among all these different moments of knowledge the problem of the relation and connection between sense data and idea, between immediate and developed knowledge, the problem of the importance and role of each of these at each stage of knowledge, has occupied a central place in philosophy through the whole course of its history. Even in ancient Greece the question was being raised in a general way. What is truth, sense perceptions or "logos" (reason)? If sense perceptions then how are we able to make any kind of unity out of their diversity? The question is really this, if by truth we mean that our understanding reflects reality, how can we be sure that it is possible to pass from a number of separate sensations to these general ideas through which we understand? The failure to solve this question led to scepticism and relativism (the admission by the Sophists of the absolute relativity of all that exists – including our knowledge), to the denial of the reality of movement (the Eleatics), to the construction of idealistic systems (Plato, for whom the sensed, material world is virtually non-existent).

In the working out of dialectic as a theory of knowledge Lenin insistently stressed this problem of the transition of one moment of knowledge to another and the helplessness of pre-Marxian philosophy to solve it. He sees in this failure one of the stumbling-blocks of the Greek and also the modern philosophers.

Lenin shows that a successful approach to this problem must unite the different streams in the history of philosophy, for example the Sophists with Kant and Mach; Hegel and Plato with Epicurus and Locke.

The ancient Greek rationalist Zeno regarded movement as "sensed truth." But he did not limit himself to the mere admission of this as a fact. He was one of the first in the history of philosophy to show the contradictory aspects of movement – the contradictions of discreteness and continuity, of rest and motion. He was one of the first to set before himself the problem of understanding the connection of these aspects and in this is his great historical service. But being a metaphysician he could not comprehend this contradiction in terms of fixed concepts, and therefore as a rationalist came to a denial of the reality of movement, and opposed to it, as to a deception of the senses involving hopeless contradiction, rest and identity (grasped in metaphysical conceptions) as the real essence of things.

Lenin formulated Zeno's problem thus – the question is not whether there is such a thing as movement, this is acknowledged as a fact of experience, but how to express it in the logic of fixed concepts.

In the history of recent philosophy the different attempts to solve the question whether scientific knowledge is based on sense experience or reason, give rise to different philosophical movements, sensationalism, empiricism (from the Latin word "sensus," the faculty of feeling, and the Greek "εμπειρία," experience) and rationalism (from the Latin "ratio," reason).

Sensationalism was at the basis of the theories of knowledge of the various materialistic schools which emerged in the struggle with mediaeval scholasticism and with the thoroughgoing rationalism of classic German idealism; these schools were represented by the English philosophers Bacon and Locke, the French materialists of the eighteenth century and Feuerbach. Nevertheless from this same sensationalist point of view, philosophers have also been able to draw subjective idealist conclusions.

The classic representatives of such sensationalist idealism were Berkeley and Hume. How was it that such a remarkable combination of two sharply opposed philosophies should be found in this common derivation from sensationalism? Special attention must be paid to this problem because it demonstrates clearly that the "freezing" of any one "moment" of knowledge and the tearing of it out of its connection with knowledge as a whole in an abstract, metaphysical fashion, serves as a loophole for the idealist, and, in a favourable class setting (which always helps one or the other party in philosophy and fortifies its conclusions), may be converted into a whole idealistic system.

Over what did Berkeley and Hume and in our day Mach stumble when they found themselves compelled to deny in one form or another the objectivity of the external world, although they had set out by admitting sensation as the sole source and material of knowledge?

The course of their reasoning is as follows:

To man are given directly his perceptions, his sensation. They are the only material of knowledge. In the perceptions themselves there is no internal necessary connection. Connection is nothing else than particular combinations of perceptions in the stream of the psychical experiences of the subject. Wherefore any statements about the objectivity of the logical categories – causality, interaction, substance, etc. – are pure metaphysics reflecting nothing real in the sensed material of knowledge. The logical categories are only schemes which we use for organizing sense data, and for this or the other evaluation of them. But these schemes and this evaluation are entirely subjective. They are subjective first of all in relation to the external world, for which there is no more evidence, from the sensationalist point of view, than there is for, say, the devil (since experience offers evidence for nothing but itself); secondly, these logical schemes are subjective in relation to the very sense data of knowledge themselves, since they are determined by the peculiar constitution of the subject, i.e. in the last analysis, by the aggregate of the subject's former psychical experiences as well as by that group of sensations on which its attention is now directed.

The assertion of materialists, namely that the necessary objective connection between sensed phenomena is confirmed by experience and practice, is an elementary logical mistake, because experience itself, and therefore practice, is nothing other than a mass of psychical experiences, so that its unity and connection are derived not from the external world, but from the mental states themselves. The world of man is limited by its "human experience" and beyond its bounds, for a "positive" scientific knowledge, there exists nothing.

And so the root error of sensationalism, which has been developed by subjective idealists into a whole philosophic system, consists in this – that it has concerned itself solely with the question of the source and content of knowledge and has left out of account the question of the forms of knowledge and their foundation, in which are expressed the connections arid transitions given in sensed experience itself. Subjective idealists have turned their sense data, in which sensationalism rightly saw the final means of knowledge, into the sole object of knowledge.

Proceeding from the ground that every object of knowledge in the last resort appears before us in its sensed form, they have exalted to an absolute, the discreteness, the specific character that belongs to it as a moment, and have in this way deprived the object of every internal necessary connection. For example, to a bored man time seems "an eternity," to a cheerful man "an instant," to the soldier, who goes on the march with fresh powers it is nothing to cover forty versts, but to the tired man even *two* versts appear to be a big distance. In this way the subjective idealists have returned to the position of the ancient Greek sceptic Protagoras, who said that "man is the measure of all things" and took away from science its only basis – the objective, law-governed connection of phenomena.

Actually, by remaining on the ground of mere sensations, it is impossible to show, for example, that it is not the sun that goes round the earth, but the earth that goes round the sun, that thunder and lightning appear simultaneously and not one after the other. In this way, by contending for the rights of the senses in knowledge, as the sole source of "real givenness," by contending against "metaphysics," against the lessening of the rights of the senses by "wilful reason," subjective idealists inevitably arrive at a self-destructive conclusion, at complete disbelief in sense experience, since in effect they have deprived it of its objective content and of those laws which made it rational. Lenin has many times drawn attention to this: "Phenomenalists like Mach and Co." – he says – "when they attempt to deal with the question of law and necessity unavoidably become idealists."

The weakness of resting in the moment of simple perception and the kind of idealistic error this involves, is clearly seen in Plekhanov's theory of knowledge. We have in view in the first place, his so-called "hieroglyphic" theory. Plekhanov borrowed the theory of hieroglyphics principally from the natural scientists, Sechenov and Helmholtz.

Helmholtz in particular expresses with remarkable clarity that distrust of all sense experience which springs from the isolation of the perceptual moment of knowledge. He tries to prove that visual perception is completely relative. For example, people perceive the colours of flowers differently. There are even those who suffer from so-called Daltonism, to whom violet appears green, yellow – pink, and so on. Indeed, even to the eye of a healthy man an object may appear differently. For instance, if the image of an object falls on the so-called "blind spot" of the eye, then the man cannot see the object at all; he will see it again only by shifting the retina. From the relativity of our visual perception, Helmholtz concludes that the image of the object in our consciousness is quite unlike the object itself, that it is only a hieroglyph, a symbol (conventional sign) of some object that exists outside our consciousness. We know that this object exists, because we feel its *action* on us (and only the results of this action can we know, in the opinion of the agnostic), but we never know the object itself, and can never define it. We can only say that to the relations between sensations there are corresponding relations between real objects, and to the changes of sensation there correspond changes in the object. But we shall never be able to know what these objects are and what is the real nature of the changes that go on within them.

Engels in his time showed Helmholtz's fundamental mistake to lie in his separation of sensational and logical knowledge. "Helmholtz forgets," said Engels, "that thought also is united with our eye."

This same agnostic "theory of correspondence" was borrowed by Plekhanov too from those scientists who fell into Kantianism and was adopted by him in place of the Marxist theory of reflection.

Later on Plekhanov sought to explain away his mistake by ascribing it to unsuccessful terminology, to the abuse of the term "hieroglyph," but continued to hold the "theory of correspondence" without realizing its Kantian significance. The core of this agnostic error of Plekhanov was shown by Lenin in *Materialism and Em-*

pirio-Criticism. In defence of the hieroglyphic theory against Lenin's criticism, Axelrod came forward declaring that contemporary science also took the same attitude towards the "symbolic" character of knowledge. But if sensationalism is incapable of showing the validity of the system of scientific laws which underlies the connections and changes of things, can we not turn to the rationalist philosophers who regard the logical working of the mind as the real ground of rational knowledge? Descartes, Spinoza, Leibnitz – the chief representatives of the rationalistic tendency of the philosophy of the seventeenth century – regarded sense knowledge as something dim and untrustworthy. The task of the true method, in their opinion, is precisely this, to purify knowledge from fluidity, unsubstantiality, and its overload of ephemeral fortuitous appearances which sometimes seem, as it were, to add additional and unreal data to sense knowledge. And so the conclusion to which the rationalists arrive runs as follows: The freer that logical thought is from sensation, the more truly will it reflect the essence of the object. Thus, in absolute knowledge (about which all the rationalists speak as about something attainable by every thinker who possesses the right method) thought finds itself "in its own sphere," being perfectly free from all the elements of sensation. Quality of "intellect" consists, above all, in its complete insulation from sense experience.

It stands to reason that by remaining in the sphere of thought itself rationalists could not explain the development of thought, its ever deepening comprehension of actuality. Truth, in the teaching of the rationalists, presents a picture of death-like immobility, a grey frozen waste unstirred by a breath of movement.

The marks of truly scientific knowledge are, from the rationalist point of view, the generality and necessity of its propositions. By generality is meant applicability to all experienced facts without exception, and by necessity that the minds of all men must compel them to acknowledge such a truth. These are obviously the marks of purely logical knowledge, not the knowledge derived from sense experience. But whence does the rationalist derive his unified system of relationships which according to him underlies the deceptive appearances of things?

Why should it be supposed that because these ideas are clear and self-evident, because they form a logically consistent system, they necessarily constitute a true picture of the external world? The classic rationalism of the seventeenth and beginning of the eighteenth century does not state these problems in a fundamental manner and does not solve them. It proceeds from an *assurance* that "the order and connection of ideas are the same as the order and connections of things" (Spinoza), but does not establish this coincidence in fact. Moreover attempts to establish it led rationalists to the idea of a "pre-determined harmony between world and spirit" (Leibnitz), to an "occasionalism" that saw in every act of knowledge a miracle, which one could explain only by the constant "assistance of divinity." To bridge the gulf between consciousness and matter, between the "thinking" mode and the extended, was beyond the power of Spinoza who by his teaching of the unity of extension and "thought" in the one substance approached incomparably nearer than the others to the materialistic solution of the question.

Basing themselves on the conviction of a primordial coincidence of the laws of thought and the laws of being, the rationalists saw the task of knowledge thus: To construct by thinking an object in accordance with the laws of thought itself, proceeding each time from clear and evident premises. But the rationalist could base these premises only on other ideas, and ultimately on those ideas which were, in his opinion, the most universal, the most clear, and belonged to every human consciousness. Thus the rationalists proceed to the theory of "innate ideas" (Descartes), of *a priori* categories and laws of thought, as the final sources and means of scientific knowledge.

But rationalism, in spite of its efforts, could not get away from sense experience. It could neither relegate to sense experience the mere function of setting a task to logical reason, nor dissolve the whole extent of such experiences into logical constructions built up with the aid of *a priori* ideas. And so Leibnitz was compelled to recognize along with "truths of reason" also "truths of fact," i.e. truths of observation and experience.

An attempt to overcome the one-sidedness of sensationalism and rationalism was made by Kant. But the ambiguity, the compromising character of Kant's philosophy, declared themselves in his solution of the problem of sensation and reason. The sensational and the logical moment of knowledge do not have, according to Kant's teaching, a common basis, there is no transition between the two. The sensed, in Kant's opinion, arises in consequence of the external action on us of some "thing-in-itself," the logical has its basis in our thought, which is sundered from the material world. Ideas, according to Kant, do not grow up out of the sensed world, but are already given before it by the *a priori* categories of reasoning. These grasp, with dead tentacles, the living, multiform, ever-changing material of sensations, but themselves remain fixed. Similarly the question of the variety and at the same time the unity of scientific knowledge was resolved by Kant not by disclosing the process by which knowledge grew out of experience, or describing the slow transition from the one to the other, not by showing how these two mutually enrich one another, but by setting up the multiplicity of sensation over against the unity of rational knowledge in a thoroughly mechanical way.

The defect of the Kantian solution of the problem of the connection between sense data and logical form was demonstrated from the position of dialectical idealism by Hegel. Hegel's fundamental reproach of Kant is this, that "the latter wished to learn to swim, before getting into the water," that is, he solves the problem of scientific knowledge outside the process of knowledge itself.

The new element introduced by Hegel into the solution of the problem is this – he proceeds from the dialectical movement of thought from a lower grade to a higher and on this ground resolves the question of the connection of the sensational and the logical, criticizing the one-sidedness both of empiricism and rationalism. In his *Phenomenology of Spirit,* Hegel shows the path along which, in his opinion, consciousness travels, raising itself from the level of sensation to the "realm of pure thought." It is necessary to remember that this consciousness is conceived by him in a doubly abstract form, separate both from the material carrier of consciousness, and also from social man.

But however brilliant was the new approach to this problem made by Hegel, his idealism frustrated his attempt to solve it. Idealistic contempt for the material basis of sensation had as its result this fact, that instead of the logical construction of knowledge actually developing on the basis of working upon the ever richer material given by sensation, the process of the ascent of consciousness to ever higher levels was represented by Hegel as the course of a gradual emancipation or "purifying" from the sensed.

The point at which we may first be said to have reached truth is where we have escaped from "sensed concreteness."

The connection of the sensed and logical thus appeared in a significant manner to be unreal, since sensation according to Hegel is a necessary accompaniment of only the lowest grades of knowledge. The attempt to restore the importance of the sensed moment of knowledge, which had been pushed into the background ever since the days of French materialism, belongs to Feuerbach. In a vigorous criticism of the abstract Hegelian rationalism he tried to overthrow the position that only by the help of thought arc we able to grasp the connection of the various aspects of the object and make generalizations.

"Is it possible I see only leaves and not trees also?" he writes as against Leibnitz. "Is it possible there is no *sensation* of identity, of uniqueness, of difference? Is it possible the law of identity is not at the same time a law of sensation, is it possible that in the last count this law of thought does not depend on the veracity of sensed contemplation?"

And in his statement of the question Feuerbach is right. This is how the matter stands: Sensations are not merely raw material, that in an external fashion is in opposition to thought (as the German idealists supposed). On the contrary they are the starting point of the logical *understanding* of reality. The connections of the objective world, that are finally reflected in logical ideas (identity, opposition, causality, necessity, etc.), have already been reached in rudimentary form in sensed representations. Thus, we observe a known likeness, a difference, we detect sequence of one phenomenon after another. We see how day is replaced by night, we hear that a blow is accompanied by a sound, etc. All this serves as a basis for a mental conclusion about law, causality, the mutual dependence of the different sides of actuality.

But Feuerbach, as Marx showed, regards sensation as sensed contemplation in which consciousness is merely made aware of the existence of external objects and is not apprehending them through human activity. But the sensation of the subject is not simply an aggregate of definite physiological acts of perception determined by its bodily organization, but is always only *relatively* a direct knowledge of the world, since it is the apprehension of an individual in a particular historical situation.

The *direct* perception of actuality at a *given* stage of social development, by a member of a *given* class, is affected by the whole of the past experience of society and of that class, in other words it is not merely perception but apperception.

The sensed and the logical, direct perception and apperception, are not different, independent aspects of social knowledge, not distinct stages of it. The difference between them is relative. Direct perception becomes knowledge permeated by past experience, that is to say apperception; sensed knowledge becomes logical knowledge.

In its solution of the problem of the sensed and the rational in knowledge, dialectical materialism is equally removed from mechanistic materialism and from idealism. And on this question it wages an irreconcilable struggle on two fronts.

Mechanists attribute the rational to sensation, in effect they see in the rational nothing else than a general representation, within whose vague contours the specific features of the separate sense-representations are mutually overlaid. It is the property of truly rational ideas, that grow up out of practice and are confirmed by it, that they represent a working-over of the sensed in such a way that in it are reflected all the essential connections of the object. Such a property can never be understood by the mechanists.

When the mechanist is confronted by the problem of the development of class consciousness, his attribution of the rational to sensation forces him to deny a qualitative difference between class psychology and class ideology, he will assert an elemental development of class theoretical consciousness as a passive product, he will, it follows, degrade the role of revolutionary theory and the whole theoretical front of class struggle.

Nay, more, mechanists like Feuerbach treat human sensation as a physiological function of the organism, as mere reflexes so to speak, and therefore wipe out any distinction between the sensed reflection of actuality in a human consciousness and the sensations of an animal. But that is just why they cannot see even in the rational side of human consciousness, in human theoretical thinking, any qualitatively new stage as compared with the germs of instinctive "analysis" and "synthesis" that animals possess.

That which other mechanists do not openly confess is frankly stated by Zeitlin.

He is assured that "the statement that animals too have *ideas* about matter can be shown to be strictly scientific." He seriously analyses the character of animal philosophy and comes to the conclusion that "the Berkeleyan and empirio-critical understanding of matter as an objectivised stable connection of sensations is very near to the animal understanding of matter."

However, dialectical materialism regards even the physical basis of human sensation not as something given in a ready-made form with the biological nature of *homo sapiens*, but as a quite special product, arising in distinction from merely animal sensations upon the basis of historic social practice.

Quite mistaken also is the assertion of rationalistic idealism, which is upheld even by our Menshevist idealists, that the development of social knowledge is only a development of rational knowledge and has nothing to do with sense experience. The development of social knowledge is the development and enrichment of both the sensed or direct form of knowledge and the rational, apperceptive form of knowledge, at the basis of which lies the development of social practice. The new theoretical approach to problems, brought forth by new practice, carries with it a new direct perception of actuality, which grows up out of the same practice. The sensations as well as the ideas of a savage are so low as not to be compared with those of a modern civilized man. His thought and sensation alike are determined by the extremely restricted range and low level of his material practice.[1]

The position of the Marx-Leninist theory of knowledge in resolving the problem of the sensational and rational moment in knowledge has been shown with extraordinary clearness in the analysis by Marx and Lenin of the formation of the class consciousness of the proletariat.

In the elemental period of the worker's movement we do not yet have on the part of the workers a scientific understanding of actuality. The worker is directly in conflict with the individual capitalist. In his daily disputes with his employer his experience includes actual details of cruel exploitation, the indignation of separate groups of workers, their mutual assistance, acts of treachery, etc. All these facts are accepted and interpreted by him, not as by a "naked physiological Individuum," but in large measure from the standpoint of the petty-bourgeoisie, whose entrance into the ranks of the workers was the historic source of the education of the prole-

---

[1] Anthropology has even established on a basis of actual measurement that savages possess no special acuity of vision or smell.

tariat. At this stage his "direct" knowledge appears mainly as nought else than the prejudices of a petty-bourgeois. Many of the facts of capitalist exploitation that the worker has observed he is inclined to ascribe to the personal qualities of his own employer. The employer, in the consciousness of the worker at this period, emerges as distinct from the class of capitalists as a whole, just as the worker does not realize himself as also part of a whole – the proletariat. The different aspects of capitalist reality do not yet emerge in the consciousness of the worker as manifestations of a class antagonism running through the whole of society, but as chance things with no interconnection.

To this very stage of the development of proletarian consciousness, in which the world of actuality emerges still in its "primitive, formless indefiniteness," there correspond in the development of theory different forms of pre-scientific socialism, including also Utopian socialism the immediate predecessor of scientific socialism.

> "Such phantastic pictures of future society, painted at a time when the proletariat is still in a very undeveloped state and has but a phantastic conception of its own position, correspond with the first instinctive yearnings of that class for a general reconstruction of society" (Marx).

However, even at that stage in the consciousness of the proletariat there is already something which makes possible the transition to a scientific understanding, to a complete, connected synthesis of the facts. This is found in the ideas derived from and actually reflecting the worker's experience of collisions with his employer. It is such ideas that make it possible to escape from the limitations of disconnected experiences, for they reflect the objective relations of concrete reality, even though they may do so in a distorted fashion.

To develop these ideas so that they scientifically explain their objective content, the concrete experience of the worker must be permeated by the knowledge derived from the world-historic practice of mankind by all the cultural thought and knowledge of his century. Knowledge of the complex capitalist actuality, which includes in itself the sum of the development of all the foregoing history of mankind, requires generalizations so wide as to be beyond the range of separate groups of the proletariat (taking into consideration their situation in capitalist society) and far beyond the bounds of their immediate circle of vision. Such a theoretical expression of the whole experience of the workers' movement on the basis of an inspired generalization of the movements and tendencies of world-historical development, on the basis of all the positive attainments of all human culture, was given by the creators of scientific communism. It was they who raised the consciousness of the workers to the level of the class scientific theory. Just in so far as the workers accept the Marx-Leninist theory, so is the "conflict" between the objective content of their experience and the form in which that content is understood entirely removed. Different disconnected experiences, which grasp only the surface appearance of things, fortuitous external connections between concretely existing facts (which make the "given" material stage of consciousness "rudimentary" in relation to more rational forms) receive a "necessary," stable character. Every different fact of class struggle appears now as part of a whole system of social relationships.

The wholeness, the survey of all the facts in their universal mutual-dependence, the simultaneous grasping of the many sides, is just that which characterizes the scientific knowledge[1] that reflects reality and distinguishes it from the direct perception of the object. This characteristic of the understanding of an object has been many times stressed by the exponents of dialectical materialism, it reveals rational knowledge as a higher grade of reflection of the material world, in comparison with the direct apprehension of it in sensations and representations. Thus speaking of value, Marx says wittily:

> "The reality of the value of commodities thus resembles Mistress Quickly, of whom Falstaff said: 'man knows not where to have her.' This reality of the value of commodities contrasts with the gross material reality of these same commodities (the reality which is perceived by our bodily senses) in that not an atom of matter enters into the reality of value. We may twist and turn a commodity this

---

[1] "Actually all really exhaustive knowledge is thus characterized in our thoughts, we take a single thing out of its singleness and turn it into a particularity, and this latter into a generality – that is, we find infinity in finity, the eternal in the transitory." Engels, *Anti-Dühring*.

way and that – as a thing of value it still remains unappreciable by our bodily senses."[1]

That is, you can see and touch the material envelope of different commodities but not their value, not the universal connection between the owners of commodities, not capitalism as a whole.

The same thought concerning the deeper reflection of actuality in ideas is expressed by Lenin, speaking of the reflection of movement in consciousness; "Movement of three hundred thousand kilometres per second" – he says – "is difficult for us to represent, but we can *understand* that light moves at such a speed." In another place, developing the idea of the dialectical connections of the various aspects of the material world in relation to their mutual transition one to another, Lenin writes: "The usual representation grasps the difference and contradiction, but not the transition from one to the other, and *that is very important*." And further: "Reason sharpens those differences which do not prevent ultimate reconciliation, *i.e.* the simple diversity of the appearance of things; it does not reveal irreconcilable differences, final contradictions."

How important is the thought of the development of understanding as a deepening of knowledge, as a new qualitative moment in the knowledge of an object, can be seen from this, that Engels in his criticism of the Kantian-agnostic theory of hieroglyphics, uses this new conception of knowledge as one of the essential arguments against Helmholtz. As we know, Engels saw that the fundamental mistake of Helmholtz lay in his forgetting that thought is "united" with our eyes. The "uniting" is as follows – the organ, in this case the eye, responsible for the sense data, which actually emerge in connected form, discloses something more than can be grasped by the eye alone. The "uniting" of thought, of which Engels speaks, can by no means be understood mechanistically, generalizations are not developed in any external fashion in relation to the sensed material of knowledge, but they arise and are developed in so far as the investigator *masters* his data, equipped as he is with ideas derived from the many-sided, sensed experience of mankind, and in so far as he is permeated by that experience.

The question of the transition of experience into rational knowledge, of the preservation of sense experience in the latter,

---

which occupies a most important place in the dialectical theory of knowledge, was first faced by Feuerbach, who criticized what he called the "drunken speculation" of Hegel. Hegel, although he was often formally correct in his treatment of the inherent connection of sense data and reason, did not understand the basis of that connection which remained for him therefore a fortuitous one. Thought is nothing else than sensations connectedly read, says Feuerbach. Why then was he unable to find a complete solution of the problem of the relation of sense knowledge to reason?

The matter stands thus: Even the very smallest generalization or mental conclusion is a certain activity of the subject. The *movement* of knowledge in the direction of ever deeper connections supposes an active, operative relationship of the subject to its object. By defining representations, ideas, as a mirror-like reflection of the object in consciousness, the Marx-Leninist theory of knowledge is only seeking to stress the material nature of the object and the reflection of its real aspects in representations. But from this mirror-like element in reflection, it by no means follows that human consciousness, like a lifeless reflecting surface, mirrors only that which immediately stands in front of it, nor that our consciousness, like a material mirror, always and in the same way reflects objects according to some immutable laws of its own, and consequently gives, at any given point, either absolute truth or absolute falsehood. By drawing such conclusions from the theory of reflection, opponents of the Marx-Leninist philosophy, such as Max Adler, have either deliberately or inadvertently distorted it; like Axelrod, they "forget" that this "reflecting" knowledge is an active moment of historical, evolutionary, social practice.

"The practice of man, by repeating itself millions of times, is fortified in consciousness by the figures of logic," says Lenin concerning the actual historic basis of the so-called "eternal" forms of logical thought.

Of course, being the exponent of contemplative materialism, and not understanding practical action, Feuerbach was quite unable to solve the problem of exactly *how* the sense data are synthesized, just *how* ideas come into existence. He could only *state* that which required explanation. But thence flows the perversity of his whole position; not being able to resolve the question of how this change took place he had no notion of what it consisted in. To put it simply: Instead of explaining the uniqueness of logical thought, as a higher stage of knowledge of the material world which contains sense knowledge within itself as one of its moments and depends upon it, Feuerbach reduces logical knowledge to the level of elementary sensations.

As regards the German idealists, they could never solve this problem because they persisted in treating both the subject and its activity idealistically. The Hegelian understanding of dialectic as a theory of knowledge is nothing else than the disclosure of the immanent process of the enrichment of knowledge on the basis of the activity of thought. The German idealists by endowing only thought itself with activity could not resolve the problem of the transition of the sensed to the logical, since the sensed itself was understood by them as a derivative from the logical and as possessing no basis of its own.

A philosophical system, in which the sensed is regarded as something external and foreign to the logical, where all the independence of the material of sensations vanishes into "pure" thought, was naturally incapable of finding the way out. That can only be done if the subject is regarded as the materialistic but at the same time organic centre of an active process which indissolubly unites sensation and thought. This activity of the social subject is, however, the same thing as the material practice of social man. In this we have the sensuous apprehension of the world of objects by purposeful, directed action, an apprehension which thus includes a reasoned relationship to surrounding reality. It is this concrete human sensuous activity that Marx opposed to the purely ideal activity of German philosophy.

A rational relation to the object, as a moment of sensuous human activity, distinguishes a social man's perception of the surrounding world from the passive perception of it proper to an animal. Animals passively perceive material actuality by passively adapting themselves to the surrounding environment. Man actively confronts it. This contradiction also finds its expression in purpose, which characterizes man's relation to the external world. Everyone knows the dictum of Marx on that form of labour which appertains exclusively to man. It is this, that in contradistinction to animals, man "not only changes the form of that which has been given by nature – but also realizes at the same time his own conscious aim, which, like a law, defines the means and character of his actions and to which he is compelled to subordinate his will."

And the further this or that stage of social development stands away from the period when man was still only an animal, the sharper is the distinction, and the more complete the conscious direction of his action. Instinctive man does not draw distinctions in nature. The conscious man distinguishes categories, which are the very essence of that process of distinction which is knowledge itself, which are, as it were, the knots of a net that assists man to apprehend and master reality.

This same activity of thought which is a moment in the general practical relationship of man to the surrounding world, has been turned into something self-sufficient by the German idealists. In actuality both the conscious aim of action and the understanding of the material conditions of its realization are included in the process of social practice, are brought forth by it and evolve on its basis. The recurrence in practice of various phenomena with which man comes into contact, the reproduction of phenomena, the substitution of one object for another, the union of very different objects in the reproduction of conditions of social life, etc. – all these create the basis for generalizations, conclusions.

Engels points out that the notion of the causal connection of phenomena, which expresses the objective connection of various aspects of the material world, arose from the very fact of man's active changing of nature by his activity. Man, by reproducing the conditions necessary for the occurrence of any given phenomenon, by acting upon one phenomenon and thereby evoking from it another – often something not previously met in relation to the first phenomenon – rises to the level of an understanding of causal relations.

"We not only find" – he writes – "that after a known movement there follows another movement, we also find that we are in a position to reproduce that movement by creating the conditions in which it issues in nature; we find too that we are in a position to evoke movements which are not even to be met with in nature (or at least, are not met with in that precise form) and that we can give to these movements such characteristics and quantities as we may decide on beforehand. Thanks to this, thanks to the action of man, there is created the notion of causality, the notion that one movement is the cause of another."

Sensuous human activity increases with the development of the instruments of production, with the perfecting of technical devices, by the aid of which the further study of objective processes is made possible. The instruments of production assist the extension of the reality apprehended by the senses, by lengthening the human arm, by perfecting man's eyes and ears. The microscope, the telescope, the most accurate measuring instruments, etc., assist in the enrichment of sensed material, in the human perception of the surrounding world, and by this means create a basis for ever wider and deeper generalizations.

The whole development of social-historic practice, taken in all its moments, creates a basis for theoretical generalizations. For example, one can take the development of socialistic revolution, which draws millions into political struggle and creates in the minds of millions of people premises for the Marx-Leninist understanding of reality. And the more revolutionary practice spreads and the deeper the historic crises in which the contradiction and connections of reality emerge ever more starkly, so much the wider is the *possibility* of a right understanding of the object (that possibility is not realized fundamentally without the previous mastery of the whole store of knowledge that has been accumulated by man). The analysis of the different stages in the development of social practice shows incontrovertibly that the depth and width of the theoretic generalizations that correspond to that stage are indissolubly and organically connected with the wealth of the factual world, as comprehended in direct experience at the given stage.

Theory and practice interact with one another. Were there no hypotheses, no scientific generalizations, no theoretical "plan" behind the creating of a telescope, there would not be one, and there would be no possibility of widening the field of sensed vision. Without a development of our understanding of the objective world in practice, there would be no refinement of hearing or taste, no "trained" eye, which detects the finest shades and modulations of colours.

Compel a man who is of a primitive level of culture to listen to a symphony, and he will grasp nothing in it except a chaos of sounds that deafens and confuses him. A sharp contrast is presented by the hearing of a musician, who can detect the plan of musical development in the symphony and the function of every note in the harmonious whole.

The senses of man develop and are perfected along with the development of social-historic practice, the index of whose stage of development is the ability to generalize, and the level of theoretic thought. They have, therefore, a deeply historic character. Marx in attacking Feuerbach's physiological, anti-historical understanding of sensation emphasizes that "the education of the five senses is the product of universal history." "A needy man, full of cares" – says Marx – "is not able to understand a very beautiful composition. The dealer in minerals sees only their money value, not the beauty or the special character of the minerals; he has no mineralogical sense." The historic character of the five senses is determined by the level of development of human history, by the concrete practice of social man. Marx stresses the gulf that lies between the senses of a savage and of a man in a higher stage of evolution; the senses of a man of primitive society are, in his opinion, to be radically distinguished from the senses of man as contemporary with the epoch of capitalism.

Practice, by its creation of the unity and mutual conditioning of the sensed and the logical moments of knowledge, is, at once, a verification of the correctness of both of them, and a measure of the truth of knowledge as a whole. In this same verification there is realized in its turn the mutual transition of the sensed and the logical, and we notice that the verification of any theory – the transformation of it into life – is at the same time a creation of a new objectivity that is now accessible to direct perception. Practice is the crown and completion of the ideal and, as such, unites in itself both the moment of universality, attainable at once by reason, and the great diversity of sensed material. "Practice" – Lenin emphasizes – "is higher than theoretical knowledge, because it has not only the property of generality, but also direct actuality."

In this "completion" of the ideal is shown the objective content of the latter. Ideas have as their basis human action, the attribute of man alone; they give him his uniqueness, since they have no place in any other forms of the movement of matter.

The transformation of scientific theory into life, and the possibility, on its basis, of uniting and dissociating the different forms of movement of the material world, that are found outside the human head, and of manipulating them according to previously formed aims – these disclose the close connection of theory with objectivity.

CHAPTER IV

THE DOCTRINE OF TRUTH

Marx and Lenin call objective truth that in our knowledge "which depends neither on the subject, nor on man, nor on society." The question of objective truth occupies a central place in the Marx-Leninist theory of knowledge. Plekhanov, because of his failure to understand this question of objective truth, stumbled, with his hieroglyphic theory and his "belief" in objective reality, into the paths of agnosticism and idealism.

Lenin's attitude was always unusually guarded and he was careful to check the least tendency to deviate from an objective view of truth, holding that it led inevitably to subjectivism and agnosticism. As an example of his irreconcilable hostility to such deviations, we may refer to his comments on Bukharin's *Economics of the Transition Period*. Bukharin speaks of *"considering"* certain elements in the productive progress from a particular *"point of view,"* from which they are *"theoretically interesting."* Lenin's marginal comments run: "The wrong expressions. Solecism. Subjectivism. The point lies not in who 'considers,' to whom it is 'interesting,' but in that which *is*, independent of human consciousness."

This insistence on the independence of the external world from human consciousness is the principle that distinguishes the dialectical materialist from the subjectivist in his attitude to objective truth. For Bogdanov the objectivity of a thing has only one meaning – its *"general significance."*

> "The objective character of the physical world," says Bogdanov, "lies in this, that it exists not for me personally, but for everybody and has for everyone a definite significance, which I am assured is just the same is it is for me. The objectivity of the physical order is its *general* significance."

As we see from the foregoing, Bogdanov means by objectivity the coincidence of representations in the consciousness of a number of "co-men," and only that; thus he denies a purely concrete objectivity of nature, *i.e.* its independence of man and of human existence. The Bogdanovian principle of "general significance" sets the objectivity of the material world wholly in dependence on the subject, as a result of which the distinction between science and superstition seems to be obliterated. This last point is sharply stressed by Lenin, who declares that it can be said of any religious belief you like that it possesses "general significance," because even to-day it may be found that a "great part of mankind" cling to it. The other character of objective truth, according to Bogdanov, is that it is connected with social organization; but this too, in Lenin's opinion, relates it to almost any form of social superstition.

Although not materialists, the neo-Kantians also accept the objectivity of knowledge. The favourite boast of these neo-Kantians, whom we find in the ranks of reformist socialism, is that they are thoroughly scientific in their study of objective reality. Moreover, this objectivity of scientific understanding is, in their opinion, given not from its correspondence with an object independent of the subject, but by a unity of the logical categories and by the common possession by all subjects of a simple super-subjective consciousness.

In distinction from this interpretation, scientific truth for materialists is defined as a concordance of ideas and of objective reality, "which is copied, photographed and reflected by our sensations, while existing independent of them."

However, a logical attainment of objective truth together with the power to carry the materialistic principle into life is not reached merely by granting that an object independent of human consciousness exists. It is necessary to disclose the object in all its concreteness and fullness, in the light of all its connections and relations, and in all its aspects.

"The aggregate of *all* the aspects of a phenomenon, their actuality and their mutual-dependence – that is the source of truth," Lenin points out, taking into account all the aspects of an object in their mutual relationships. The determination of the place and role of each one of them; the reckoning of the multiform connections of the given object with its surroundings; the displaying of the object in its development, with an exposition of the source of its self-movement, of those chief basic contradictions, from the overcoming of which development and forward movement ensue; the detection of the uniqueness of the forms in which the essential contradictions express themselves and appear; the disclosure of the elements of the new content that lie in the old; the struggle of the new content with the old form; these are some of the aspects of really concrete experience to which Lenin directs our attentions in the search for objectivity.

On the basis of *contemplative* materialism, which deals only with the surface of phenomena, all kinds of distortions and perversions of objective truth are possible.

For example, the materialism of Kautsky and his disciples stops short with a simple statement of what meets the eye; it ignores underlying contradictions and the necessity for discerning what is basic and essential in the phenomenon from what is secondary. The result is that the different aspects of the object emerge before the knower with but a single meaning, and facts are equated without regard to the differences underlying their unity. It is materialism of this sort that fails to understand the true meaning of capitalism because by dwelling only on the surface it ignores the ever strengthening basic contradictions; it ignores the class struggle which is the determining factor in the actual development of capitalism.

A similar distorted understanding of truth lies at the base of all opportunism. For example, in stating the general contradiction between evolving capitalism and the feudalistic order in the period of the revolution of 1905, the Menshevists excluded from their analysis the revolutionary activity of the proletariat and of the peasantry – excluded the very thing which promotes and resolves the self-creative contradictions of social development.

Lenin often reproached Plekhanov for "right-wing" tendencies due to his love of abstractions. This is what Lenin wrote in a note on the second project of Plekhanov's programme for the Second Party Congress.

> "The general and basic defect of this project, which makes it unacceptable, is this: it is not a programme of a practical fighting party but a mere voicing of principles. It is rather a programme for students (especially in the very important part that is devoted to the characteristics of capitalism) and for that matter elementary students, a programme in which capitalism in general is discussed, not even Russian capitalism."

When facts or aspects of reality are considered discretely and out of relation with one another the ground is prepared for an arbitrary selection of facts and subsequent grouping of them to support some theory. But the real situation can only be known if the facts are seen *in their actual relations*, if the whole complex is examined as it is found.

It is just the failure to do this that led to the subjective distortion of events by the representatives of the Second International in the war-period of 1914, when the imperialist, predatory character of the war was obscured by sophisms about the freeing of oppressed nationalities, about "the aggressor," about the right of every worker to defend his country. In these sophisms the particular covered the general, the fortuitous was set in the place of the law-determined, forgery was covered by the name of Marx. They cited the fact that Marx and Engels in the period of the wars of the '50's "also" stood on the side of one of the belligerent countries. They forgot that the national wars of that period were wars in which the progressive bourgeoisie was fighting against feudalism.

Eclecticism and sophistry of this sort are common in our day and form an instrument frequently used to distort objective reality and conceal it from the workers.

How often do we hear it said that it does not matter of what sort a dictatorship is, whether bourgeois or proletarian, that a dictatorship is a dictatorship. It is a "subjective hotch-potch" when Kautsky, Trotsky and others with them declare that the new business methods of Soviet industry are a return to the capitalist methods of economy, that socialist competition is the resurrection of capitalist methods of competitive struggle between producers for the stimulation of their initiative.

Whence it follows that any abstract, lifeless, contemplative understanding of objective truth so far from contradicting subjectivism, and arbitrariness, leads inevitably to them.

Suppose then that we are careful to take full account of the moving, complex nature of reality, can it be said that the fulfilment of this very important requirement guarantees a complete disclosure of objective truth at once, finally, and without mistake? In other words do we grasp objective truth in all its completeness or is its attainment a difficult, tortuous path pregnant with errors, with delusions and fantastic divagations. It is characteristic of most metaphysicians that they should fail to comprehend that the reflection of truth is an historic process. By admitting the absolute immutability of all that exists (including also truth itself), they hold that our ideas straightway grasp the object just as it is. The categories, which they use in this metaphysical fashion, are in their opinion eternal. Thus for instance the English economists, the forerunners of Marx (Adam Smith, Ricardo), considered the category "capital" as an absolute reflection of the relationship between people in the whole course of human history, beginning with primitive times and ending with bourgeois society. The researches of Marx (from the standpoint of the new social class) disclosed the complete futility of this metaphysical understanding of capitalism. Hegel's attempt in his idealistic system to express absolute knowledge is also metaphysical in this sense.

In most branches of scientific knowledge (natural science, history, philosophy, philology, psychology) there is no room for the metaphysical conception of absolute truth. The more scientific knowledge develops, the more obvious to everyone is the worthlessness of all claims to the attainment of *absolute* scientific truth at whatever stage. The old doctrine of the immutability of the species of plants and animals in the biological field has been for a long time discredited. The theory of phlogiston in chemistry has been replaced by that of Lavoisier. In the physical field the atomic theory has been replaced by the electronic; indestructibility of the chemical elements has been disproved. In art and literature one school gives place to another. In the field of philology the doctrine of an ancient Indo-European language underlying all others has been refuted. The falsity of the theory of the immutability and eternity of capitalist society (which is still even now preached by bourgeois historians) has not only been shown theoretically, but has been confirmed by the whole practice of proletarian dictatorship, the practice of constructing the basis of a classless society.

In the field of philosophy the old metaphysical view of the world has been set at nought by the science of the universal laws of the development of nature, of society and human thought – dialectical materialism. Indeed the latter, the most scientific reflection of actuality, is itself all the time being enriched and developed on the basis of our experience in the construction of socialism as well as by the latest discoveries of the different sciences. The Marxian theory of scientific socialism has been enriched by the Leninist doctrine of imperialism as the final decaying stage of capitalism; Marx's position on proletarian dictatorship has been developed and made concrete by Lenin, Stalin and the party as a whole.

But if the matter stands thus with scientific knowledge, if every theory in its time grows old and yields place to another, then are not those philosophers right who hold positions which, at first glance, are utterly contrary to our theory of absolute truth? Are not Bogdanov, Mach and other bourgeois philosophers (the pragmatists, the intuitivist Bergson) right when they assert a merely relative truthfulness for our knowledge, and its absolute conditionality?

The doctrine that regards knowledge as absolutely mutable, as deprived of any stability whatever, is not new. Such views were defended by schools of sophists and sceptics even in ancient Greece. In the new philosophy of relativism (the admission of nothing more than the relativity of processes) we witness the resurrection of Hume.

Followers of Mach have exalted relativism as one of the basic principles of their world-outlook. Petzoldt, for instance, holds that even Hume with his ideas has come to grief, by not finding his way to a systematic relativism. In him (as in his predecessor Hobbes) we find, he writes, only certain germs of relativism; it is Ernst Mach and Averarius who have revealed again this deeply buried truth *and exalted it to the position of the main factor in their world-outlook.* The relativists assert that relative truth *quite excludes* absolute truth. The "yesterday" of our knowledge is not like the "to-day," the "to-day" not like the "to-morrow." The past is *not contained* in the present at all. The present is in no degree connected with the future. All causal or rational *succession* in the evolution of scientific knowledge is denied. Such a view-point denotes nothing but subjective idealism and a complete denial of objective truth. This relativist understanding of truth is much used by subjective idealism in its conflict with materialism and the theory of reflection. How is it possible, say relativists, to assert that we reflect in our consciousness an object, if the whole history of knowledge shows that what yesterday we held to be the truth appears to-day as utter illusion? We must always be prepared, they assert, for any new scientific fact to expose all the illusions and errors of what is to-day's understanding of actuality. And, in general, the relativist continues, are we capable of attaining any degree of absolute knowledge if the instrument of knowledge, our senses and our apparatus of perception, is itself defective? Can man attain to the infinite, the unlimited, when he possesses five limited senses? Is it possible in the material of sensations, which is extraordinarily variable and transitory, to apprehend the constant, the law-directed? Is it possible to see firm contours in the variegated impressions that glitter in front of man? How can one speak of the objective grasping of an object if our sensations are utterly subjective and carry the stamp of that individual to whom they belong? How can we speak of a scientific reflection of an object or of the development of science, when even in the same epoch, at the same stage of the evolution of knowledge, every man has his own opinion, his own perception? What seems beautiful to one may appear to others as the extremity of shapelessness and ugliness; what pleases one disgusts another.

Here we see how the uprooting of sense experience from practice (in its widest sense) is responsible for relativism. "Man is the measure of things" – such is the conclusion the relativist arrives at when he denies all possibility of reaching the objectively true, the real, the eternal in what is transitory, and in principle sees no distinction between the true and the false. On the basis of such a view, truth and error, objective fact and illusion, scientific knowledge and superstition emerge as equally valid.

By breaking down the wall of division between truth and error, relativism is driven into pure superstition. A number of modern physicists have yielded to this strange aberration and as a result have lapsed into idealism, into confessing the complete relativity of scientific knowledge. They have taken the breakdown of the older notions of the physical structure of matter to justify their abandonment of all scientific belief in the reality of matter, of energy, of space and time.

The epistemological basis of such views is the isolation and exaggeration of one aspect of human knowledge, the fact that it is limited. This fact results firstly from the reflection of the *unlimited* by limited subjects and secondly from the dependence of every theory on the limits set by the historic development of social practice. The inevitable incompleteness of reflection, of every theory of objective truth, the possible errors in it, are declared by the relativists to be a proof of the complete subjectivity of any scientific theory, and any attempt to see in the truths of science the reflection of a reality independent of man is held by them to be entirely vain.

It would give a false picture if in our analysis of modern relativism we dwelt only on its philosophical errors and omitted to point out that it provides a convenient theoretical justification of the flight from reality and the class struggle. Relativism is also very much in accordance with the world-outlook of the bourgeoisie, who are limited by the horizon of the present moment and who recoil in dread before any attempt to understand the future scientifically.

Relativism in our time offers certain advantages in the struggle with dialectical materialism. It is no longer any use to attack it from the standpoint of the older and discredited metaphysics. Everything that is happening, the rapid development of science, the revolutionary changes in society, the upheavals brought about by socialist construction, all these, show to every worker that reality is in process of change, and this is the basis of a materialistic dialectic. But relativism enables the bourgeois philosophers to draw a different conclusion and to conceal, behind the appearance of admitting change and development, a denial of the objectivity of the material world and a refusal to take part in the struggle for its actual and revolutionary change.

From all this we see that the relativism which seemingly contends so zealously with the old metaphysics for the admission of movement and change is in essence a variety of that same metaphysics.

Actual change can be understood only when we regard the different moments or stages of development as organically connected with each other, as a *continuation* of each other, when in our understanding of the connection and succession of the moments of movement we proceed from a single basis or from one source of movement, but this is just what the relativists will not allow. If we argue relatively then Marx's doctrine, for instance, has no connection whatever either with English bourgeois political economy, or with Utopian socialism, or with German idealistic dialectic, or French materialism. But in actuality this is not so. Marxism included in itself all that was absolutely true in the content of the "three sources," discarding their distortions and errors, i.e. essentially remaking them from the view-point of the new revolutionary class and on the basis of the new historic data. A number of modern bourgeois physicists have lapsed into idealism because by accepting the electronic theory of the construction of matter they thought they were compelled to deny the existence of atoms. Lenin showed that the electronic theory of the construction of matter is only a further deepening of our representation of the development of physical matter, that the old representation also contained a moment of absolute truth. From the point of view of relativism science each time begins from the beginning, with a complete denial of all preceding views.

From the dialectical point of view, which rests on the actual history of scientific knowledge, each new stage of science stands on the shoulders of its predecessor and includes in itself all the absolute truth that lay in the former.

The Leninist dictum that the proletariat should master the old bourgeois culture is built on the very admission that in bourgeois culture, in comparison with the preceding formations, there is contained a very rich reflection of absolute truth. The proletariat therefore can build its own proletarian culture, and advance it beyond the development of all human culture so far attained, only by critically mastering and working over all that is positive in bourgeois culture.

The Leninist attitude to proletarian culture and its relationship to bourgeois culture is opposed firstly to Bogdanov's attempt to abandon bourgeois culture and create an entirely new proletarian culture, and secondly to Trotsky's acceptance of bourgeois culture as absolute and final and his conclusion that socialist culture can be left to grow by itself as best it can.

It is because of this very sequence of the successive grades of scientific knowledge that science can evolve. Knowledge advances by the road of contradiction. It is accompanied by errors, by deviations from the direct attainment of its object. The external appearance of things for a time hides the true content of objects from the eyes of the seeker. Thus when first we look at merchant-capitalist society the relations between people are hidden by the relations between things. But the practical mastery of the material world tears away the covering of appearance from the objects of investigation, rectifies error by transforming into actuality the true objective content of knowledge, and purges science of the illusory. Scientific experience, which is handed over by one generation to the next, and is each time enriched by some new scientific discovery, is all the time increasing the possibility of an adequate knowledge of the objective world. The experience of industrial practice, the traditions of revolution, scientific discoveries, the store of ideas, are handed over from one epoch to the next and ever more deeply disclose the infinite possibilities of human thought. In the unlimited advance of human history, at every new step of its development there is a fuller, richer, more diverse revelation of the absolute content of the material world, which content, though confined within historically limited ideas, is nevertheless absolute truth. The progressive advance of human thought, the law-governed connection of its different stages, were guessed in an inspired manner by Hegel, who criticized both the metaphysical view of knowledge (which admits only the eternity of truths), and relativism. In his *Phenomenology of Spirit* he characterizes the succession of philosophic systems in the following words:

> "The more the ordinary mind takes the opposition between true and false to be fixed, the more is it accustomed to expect either agreement or contradiction with a given philosophical system, and only to see the one or the other in any explanation about such a system. It does not conceive the diversity of philosophical systems as the progressive evolution of truth; rather it sees only contradiction in that variety. The bud disappears when the blossom breaks through, and we might say that the former is refuted by the latter; in the same way when the fruit comes, the blossom may be explained to be a false form of the plant's existence, for the fruit appears as its true nature in place of the blossom. These stages are not merely differentiated; they supplant one another as being incompatible with one another. But the ceaseless activity of their own inherent nature makes them at the same time moments of an organic unity, where they not merely do not contradict one another, but where one is as necessary as the other; and this equal necessity of all moments constitutes from the outset the life of the whole."[1]

But, for Hegel, the inevitable development which gives rise to these different ideas and successive systems arises from a merely logical unfolding, so that they are revealed finally as only moments of the "absolute idea." For dialectical materialists the unity of relative and absolute truth is based on the limitless development of social-historic practice, in which the systematic connections of the material world are disclosed.

The dialectical doctrine of the identity of relative and absolute truth makes it possible to avoid any subjectivism, agnosticism, or scepticism, which arise on the basis of either relativism or of a metaphysics which asserts the absoluteness of truth.

---

[1] Hegel, *Phenomenology of Spirit*, Preface.

"From the view-point of modern materialism, i.e. Marxism," writes Lenin, "the *limits* of the approach of our knowledge to objective absolute truth are conditioned historically, but the existence of that truth is unconditioned, the fact that we approach to it is unconditioned. The contours of the picture are historically conditioned, but the fact that this picture depicts an objectively existing model is unconditioned. In a word *every ideology is historically conditioned, but the fact that to every scientific ideology* (as distinct, for example, from the religious) *there corresponds objective truth, absolute nature is unconditioned.* You will say: this distinction of relative and absolute truth is indeterminate. I answer to you; it is just 'indeterminate' enough to prevent the turning of science into a dogma in the bad sense of that word, into something dead, frozen, shackled; but at the same time it is 'determinate' enough to keep aloof in the most resolute and irrevocable fashion from fideism[1] and agnosticism, from philosophic idealism and from the sophisms of the followers of Hume and Kant."

The conditionality, the relativity of every different step of knowledge of actuality (and only in these successive stages is absolute truth disclosed) are engendered by the limitations that are proper to each given stage of social practice and dictate our notions of the object. Wherefore thought is not able finally to grasp truth as a whole. The inevitable and necessary abstractions of thought may cause it to lose touch with actuality. Its limitations will necessarily contain the possibility of error.

The failure to understand that the given historical conditions will be superseded at a higher stage of historic development has brought those who do not master dialectic – Kantians and Machists – to a complete denial of objective truth. "This problem (i.e. the problem of unknowableness) of the 'thing-in-itself,'" writes Engels, "can have a certain sense; we can attain knowledge only in the

---

[1] *Fideism.* If scientific "truths" are only symbols or are accepted only because of their convenience it is clear that they are only true for us because we choose to have them so. Socialism itself becomes such a "truth," in other words it is a "faith." This is fideism and it is of course a form of scepticism and subjectivism.

given conditions of our epoch, only *just as far as these conditions allow.* " But the limitations of the historic conditions, the limitations of world-outlook, the relative scarcity of amassed knowledge are *historical* limitations; they are not based on any fundamental principle rendering knowledge in the very nature of things impossible; they can therefore be to a certain degree overcome at a higher level of historic development.

In just the same way the limitations of the knowledge of actuality of a separate man, with his narrow experience (as compared with society as a whole), are extended by experience through the connection of the individual with a whole class, with all society, through the mastery of that knowledge which makes up the product of all the preceding history of human thought. These limitations of social knowledge are being overcome today more than at any previous stage in the history of mankind. For in the present transition period, the period of building a classless society, millions are being drawn into conscious socialist construction, mass inventiveness is developing and the situation is offering unlimited possibilities for the free development of the creative initiative of the masses on the basis of a scientific world-outlook. The new practice – socialist construction – overcomes the limited and distorted bourgeois ideology, reveals the errors accumulated during the centuries, serves as a material basis on which the cultural heritage of the old society is worked over, and gives a great impetus to the further development and concretization of the knowledge of objective truth.

The new historic stage of development of mankind, which for the first time in history has made possible a scientific approach not only to the problem of how to control and change the physical world but also society itself, has created conditions for a most deep and fruitful knowledge of objective truth.

On the basis of this new historic stage we find that even the most complete forms of scientific thought, such as the doctrine of Marx on capitalist society, Lenin's doctrine of imperialism, or the theories of scientific socialism, are not absolute truths, but are capable of further development and precision and consequently contain in themselves moments of relativism.

The Leninist conception of the endless extension of the knowledge of any object (and consequently of the relativity of that knowledge at any given stage) refers not only to the knowledge of those objects which evolve in the period of man's knowledge of them, but also to those which remain relatively immutable during the time of man's whole existence or have already in the past finished the whole cycle of their development. Our knowledge of the nature of chemical elements, of chemical relations, becomes ever deeper and completer, in spite of the fact that the nature of the earth's chemical elements (with the exception of the radio-active) have not changed at all during the period of existence of mankind. Our knowledge of the past geological epochs is all the time becoming richer, in spite of their having finished their cycles hundreds of millions of years ago. The scientific knowledge of feudalism became possible only after the sound of knightly tournaments, of peasant wars and of insurrections in bourgeois towns had ceased to echo. And the knowledge of capitalism becomes ever fuller and deeper according as capitalism is destroyed under the pressure of its own contradictions and the blows of proletarian revolution which such contradictions bring forth. The endlessness of knowledge is based on the limitless wealth of the development of the material world and the infinite variety of aspects and connections at every step of its development. The higher the level of social practice and the more completely all the aspects of actuality are grasped by it, so much the deeper is our knowledge of actuality, both of that which is the direct object of sensed human action, and of that which is brought forward from the past and embodied in the present.

But, as we pointed out above, there exists a fundamental distinction in principle between the relativists and the dialectical materialists. For the dialectical materialist the knowledge of the *basic* law-system, if it is confirmed by the criterion of historic social practice, enters into the iron inventory of permanent scientific knowledge.

The development of practice, the enrichment of factual material and the development of scientific knowledge which is connected with these, can make our knowledge of basic law more concrete, can even show that that law-system which was regarded by us in the past stage as fundamental and universal is itself rooted in another deeper law-system and is its partial form. But all this in no measure destroys the fact that in that law-system we had reflected a "little bit" of absolute truth.

When the representatives of the Second International at the time of the imperialist war sought on a basis of incomplete study and "insufficient" discussion of national and international tactics to controvert the truth of the Basle[1] pronouncement on the imperialist, predatory character of the coming war, Lenin wrote:

"Such assertions are sophisms because they confuse a many-sided scientific analysis of imperialism, which analysis only now begins and which analysis in its essence is infinite even as science is infinite, with the essentials of socialist tactics against capitalist imperialism, which tactics have been pointed out in millions of copies of Social-Democratic papers and in the decisions of the International."[2]

The same thought on the infinity of knowledge in any realm of actuality is expressed by Lenin in many other passages in his writings; he stresses it very clearly in his discussion of trade unions. Speaking of the demands that are put forward by dialectical logic in its study of an object, he picks out the most important, the study of an object as that which sums up and is permeated by the past, in all its relations and all its fullness. He adds "We never shall attain this completely, but the demand for all-sidedness will save us from errors and deadness." We shall never get a reflection of an object that will hold good for ever, since nature, society and thought are endlessly evolving, but we shall get an ever more complete reflection.

In the development of scientific knowledge a unity of absolute and relative truth is realized. On the one hand dialectic as a theory of knowledge admits the endlessness of the attainment of knowledge, never making absolute even its truest reflection, for if it did so it would cease to express the dialectic of the material world and thus lose its power of "guidance for action"; on the other hand dialectic admits the absoluteness, the fullness of the process of scientific knowledge as a whole and the presence of "little bits" of absolute

---

[1] *Basle Manifesto.* The resolution on War adopted at the Basle Internationalist Socialist Congress of 1912. This, says Lenin, "represents the most exact and complete, the most solemn and formal exposition of the socialist views on war and on tactics in relation to war." It declares that imperialist war "cannot be justified by even the slightest pretext of being in the interest of the people." Nevertheless it was "forgotten" in 1914 when the parties to the signatures supported their national Governments.

[2] Lenin, *Works,* vol. xviii, p. 277.

truth in every scientific proposition, because it sees in it a firm basis for the assured advance of revolutionary practice.

The refusal to admit the unity of absolute and relative truth leads inevitably to the admission of one of these to the exclusion of the other, leads either to the changing of theory into dogma, or to a direct denial that theory is a reflection of actuality and therefore capable of furnishing a scientific basis for the revolutionary changing of actuality. These alternatives are different in form but identical in essence; they both refuse to allow theory as "guidance for action."

SECTION II

UNITY AND THE STRIFE OF OPPOSITES

CHAPTER I

THE LAW OF THE UNITY AND
CONFLICT OF OPPOSITES

TWO CONCEPTIONS OF DEVELOPMENT

Everything flows, everything changes; there is nothing absolutely stagnant, nothing unchangeable in the processes of actuality. This was the conclusion, the guiding principle of knowledge (already formulated by the ancient Greek thinkers) at which bourgeois science of the first half of the nineteenth century arrived, influenced as it was by the stormy social transformations of the epoch of classical bourgeois revolutions. Such a scientific conclusion was possible only after many centuries of social practice and through the accumulation of a mass of data concerning the mutability of natural phenomena. However, one ought not to think that all those who acknowledge the mutability of phenomena understand it in an objective fashion as governed by law, as an evolutionary development.

Subjective idealists, for whom actuality is nothing else than a stream of psychic experiences in the subject (which stream constitutes the primitive and therefore uncaused "given") have declared the very question of the objective law-governance of such "actuality" to be metaphysical. But even among those who have come to regard change as a law-governed development we find two different basic points of view – the materialistic, which proceeds from the development of the objective material world, and the idealistic which sees in this development the unfolding of "Idea," of spiritual essence. Within the limits of each of these basic philosophic camps there exist two more or less clearly expressed conceptions of the type and character of law-governed development; to their survey we shall now proceed.

The exponents of the first view see in development a simple increase or diminution, a repetition therefore of that which already exists. Thus qualitatively different physical processes are ascribed by them to different quantitative combinations of atoms or electrons; and transformations of physical processes one into another are ascribed to a quantitative increase, diminution or repetition of those same combinations. In the development of organic life, in the emergence and differentiation of vital forms, they see only a simple quantitative change in that which had already existed in the first living beings that appeared on earth.

And so they hold that in the capitalism of the beginning of the twentieth century and even in that of the post-war period there is nothing qualitatively new in comparison with its earlier period of development. In modern capitalism they say we are dealing *only* with quantitative developments of already existing elements and factors of capitalism – with a growth of the army of workers, with an increase in the volume of capital investments, with a lessening of the number of owners of means of production.

The exponents of this view are really quite unable to offer any solution of the actual problem of development – the law-governed emergence of the new out of the old. They merely describe the growth, the decrease, the recurrence of this or that aspect of the object.

This first conception remains on the surface of phenomena. It can describe merely the outer appearance of movement but cannot divulge its essence; it is able merely to describe the growth or diminution of different elements or factors in a process, but cannot explain the internal cause of its evolutionary movement, cannot show how and why a given process develops. The supporters of this conception, when they would attempt such an explanation, are compelled to seek for some external factor to account for the qualitatively new, since this could never be given by merely quantitative changes. It is hardly surprising that they are frequently driven to the theory of divine intervention. The supporters of this view cannot explain how a thing comes to be turned into its own opposite, cannot explain "leaps," the disappearance of the "old" and the emergence of the "new." Thus from this standpoint it is impossible to show why capitalism must inevitably grow into socialism, or why classes in the U.S.S.R. disappear as the result of sharp class struggle. The exponents of this point of view are supporters of the mechanistic conception of development.

The exponents of the second conception proceed from the standpoint that everything develops by means of a struggle of opposites, by a division, a dichotomy, of every unity into mutually exclusive opposites. Thus capitalism develops in virtue of the contradiction between the social character of production and the private means of appropriation; transitional economy develops on the basis of the struggle between developing and growing socialism and developed, but not yet annihilated, capitalism, and also on the basis of the sharpened conflict of classes in this period in the course of which classes ultimately disappear.

The second conception, not remaining on the surface of phenomena, expresses the essence of movement as the unity of opposites. It demands a penetration into the depth of a process, a disclosure of the internal laws which are responsible for the development of that process. This conception seeks the causes of development not outside the process but in its very midst; it seeks mainly to disclose the source of the "self-movement" of the process. To understand a process means to disclose its contradictory aspects, to establish their mutual relationship, to follow up the movement of its contradictions through all its stages. This view gives the key to the "leaps" which characterize the evolutionary series; it explains the changing of a process into its opposite, the annihilation of the "old" and emergence of the "new." Thus only by disclosing the basic contradictions of capitalism and by showing that the inevitable consequence of such contradictions is the destruction of capitalism by proletarian revolution do we explain the historic necessity of socialism. This second conception is the conception of dialectic materialism. In his celebrated fragment "On Dialectics," Lenin wrote:

> "Two fundamental (or is it the two possible? or is it the two historically observed?) conceptions of development (evolution) are: development as decrease and increase, as repetition; and development as a unity of opposites (the division of the one into mutually exclusive opposites and their reciprocal correlation).
>
> "The first conception is dead, poor and dry; the second is vital. It is only this second conception which offers the key to understanding the 'self-movement' of everything in existence; it alone offers the key to understanding 'leaps' to the 'interruption of gradual succession,' to the 'transforma-

tion into the opposite' to the destruction of the old and the appearance of the new."[1]

Throughout the whole course of philosophic history we meet with these two conceptions, more or less clearly and precisely formulated, or we meet with views that are occasionally muddled yet approximate to one of these two conceptions of development.

Thus the Greek philosophers Leucippus and Democritus attacking the metaphysical theory of the Eleatic school (the school of Parmenides, which held the world to be unchangeable and denied the reality of movement) declared that the world develops according to the principle of necessity; that everything in the world is found in eternal and endless motion. But their conception of development is mechanical. The world, in their opinion, consists of an endless number of atoms, different in form and moving in empty space. In the atoms there exist no internal states ; they act on one another only by collisions resulting from their mechanical movement. The difference between things is explained by the difference in the spatial attributes, the number and mutual arrangement of the aggregates of atoms which compose them. Emergence is the uniting of atoms; disappearance their falling apart.

Proceeding from this materialistic conception, the leading one of its time, Leucippus and Democritus explained the origin and development of the solar system, the movement of the human soul, etc. To this point of view, with some variations, Epicurus and his followers adhered.

In the seventeenth century a very similar philosophy was established and developed by Pierre Gassendi. His contemporary, the great philosopher and physicist Rene Descartes – idealist on the question of the origin of our knowledge, materialist in his physical researches – confirmed the idea of the universal connection of all the phenomena in nature and explained the development of the world purely mechanically, although somewhat differently from the Greek Atomists.

This conception of movement was the basis of most of the physics of that period and finds expression in the works of the great French materialists. The mechanistic attitude was not only dominant in material science but profoundly influenced the theories concern-

---

[1] Lenin, vol. xiii, p. 323.

ing the development of human society. A succession of bourgeois philosophers explained all social phenomena as due to the simple interactions of individuals seeking their self-preservation. But these philosophers failed to observe the class struggle and the contradictions in society; they were, therefore, quite unable to reveal the actual laws of social development.

In more recent times, under the influence of ever intensifying class contradictions, there has appeared a mechanistic theory which sought to explain social development by the antagonism of forces directed one against the other and their eventual equilibrium. The direction of the development of a social phenomenon is, it is said, determined at any particular moment by the quantitative predominance of the force which determines that direction. Thus, according to Herbert Spencer, "tyranny and freedom" are forces independent of each other, which strive to balance each other. By the quantitative predominance of freedom or of tyranny the resultant of this antagonism is determined. We also find this principle of development in Dühring, who attacked the dialectic of Marx and Engels, and after Dühring came Bogdanov who constructed a complete philosophy which proposed to explain every phenomenon of nature, society and thought by the principle of equilibrium.

This conception was afterwards borrowed from Bogdanov by Bukharin who saw the cause of the development of social structures not in their internal contradictions but in the relationship of the system with the environment, of society with nature.

The mechanistic theory of development permeates reformist sociology, which holds that the simple quantitative growth of monopoly and of finance-capital signifies the growing of capitalism into socialism, that the simple growth of bourgeois democracy is an ever greater winning of power by the working class, etc. These philosophers have thrown aside the theory of movement by means of contradictions as too revolutionary. A mechanistic principle of development also penetrates the views of Trotskyism; for instance its acceptance of the superficial view that capitalism was planted in Russia by the West, a view which ignores the development of capitalism that proceeded among us on the basis of the break-up of the peasant community. The Trotskyist theory of the impossibility of a socialist victory in one country alone proceeds from its ignoring of the unevenness of the development of capitalism and of the internal laws of development of the U.S.S.R. which have by the operation of new internal forces made it possible to resolve those contradictions of the proletariat and peasantry that obstruct the building of socialism. This theory holds that the external contradictions of capitalism and the U.S.S.R. are the determining factor in our development, and that the course of development of the environment (capitalism) determines the course of development of the system, i.e. the U.S.S.R.

Not only the mechanistic but also the dialectical conception of development is met in the course of philosophic history. "Movement itself is a contradiction," the Eleatics pointed out, and that is the very reason why they, as metaphysicians, denied the objectivity of movement. The greatest of them, Zeno, brought together a number of examples to refute the objectivity of movement. The basis of his proof is that movement contains within itself a contradiction and is therefore untrue, since from the viewpoint of the Eleatics a thing is true only if it is at one with itself, is identical with itself, unalterable.

The Greek philosopher Heraclitus declared: "All things flow, all changes. It is impossible to enter twice into one and the same stream." Everything is found in eternal flux, at one moment in the process of stabilization, in the next of passing away. He affirmed that everything is found in development by virtue of the strife of opposites.

In the new philosophy which grew up along with the rise of the bourgeoisie the idea of development by means of contradiction was revived by Kant and Hegel.

In opposition to the view of Newton, who held that the movement of the solar system, once it had been brought into existence as a result of the first divine impulse, remains unchanged, and that the planets preserve their primeval relative distances and distribution, Kant, in the early phase of his development, propounded a theory of the origin of the solar system from a revolving nebula without the intervention of God. He affirmed that out of the primeval nebula, as a result of the struggle arising from the repulsion and attraction of its components, was formed a system of planets, including our earth, and he predicted an inevitable collapse of that system, in the distant future. Kant's notion of development still lay as a whole within the bounds of a mechanistic world-outlook, for we see that attraction and repulsion were considered by him as opposing mechanical forces belonging to matter. It was only later in his more fundamental philosophical works that the critical Kant approached to a dialectical understanding of contradiction, which, however, he now limited by the bounds of reason, ruling out any idea of contradiction in connection with the objective world of "things in themselves."

The idealist system which most clearly and fully works out the idea of development by means of the strife of opposites was that of Hegel, and this part of his philosophy is his greatest contribution to human thought. He wrote:

"Identity is the definition only of a simple, immediate, dead being, but contradiction is the root of all movement and vitality, and only in so far as a thing has in itself contradiction does it move, does it possess an impulse and activity.

"Contradiction is not simply the negation of normality but is the principle of every self-movement, of that which indeed is nothing else than the expression of contradictions.

"All things are contradictory in themselves – this proposition expresses the truth and essence of things better than any other."

Hegel, in opposition to Kant, held that it is impossible to attribute contradiction to the subject alone. He insisted on the necessity of disclosing the contradictions in the very process of actuality (which was understood by him idealistically) because in the strife of opposites he saw the root, the basis of every self-movement.

But having set up this basic law of development, the idealist Hegel inevitably distorted and limited it. He held that the movement of the objective world is a form of movement of absolute spirit, and subordinated the development of objective processes to a system of categories, made up in his own head. Thus at every step he betrayed the law he had himself set up. Being a bourgeois idealist and a German philistine he declared that in the Idea, i.e. in the highest stage of development, contradictions are reconciled, a stoppage of development takes place. After depicting the movement of society as the development of the World Spirit through contradictions, he declared that in the Prussian monarchy – the highest incarnation of the State idea – social contradictions were reconciled. Thus Hegel subordinated the revolutionary law of a struggle of opposites to the bourgeois theory of their reconciliation. Modern neo-Hegelians like Bradley, and Gentile, the philosopher of Fascism, act as did the reactionaries of Hegel's day; they seize on this reactionary side of the

Hegelian philosophy and develop a theory of reconciliation of opposites. Marx and Engels, on the contrary, took from Hegel this same revolutionary side, reworked it critically and developed the law of the unity and conflict of opposites. Lenin wrote:

> "Consider such expressions as 'movement and self-movement,' meaning spontaneous, internally necessary movement, 'change,' 'movement and vitality,' 'the principle of every self-movement,' 'movement and action,' in contrast to 'dead existence' – and who will believe that these represent the very core of Hegel's frozen absolutism, as it has been called. It is necessary to disclose this essence, to understand it, to save it, to remove its shell, to cleanse it – and that is what Marx and Engels did."

Marx and Engels, being materialist-communists and therefore free from the half-and-half policy of Hegel, were the first to show the essentially revolutionary character of this law. In a large number of their works – Capital, Anti-Dühring, The Poverty of Philosophy, Ludwig Feuerbach, Dialectic of Mature – as well as in a number of their letters, they indicated the theoretical and practical importance of this law as a universal law of the development of nature, society and thought. They were the first logically, dispassionately and exhaustively to apply it to the analysis of all those processes and phenomena which they undertook to investigate, whether it was the analysis of the basic laws of development of social structures, the analysis of capitalism, the different historic episodes of class struggle, the politics and tactics of the workers' movement, or the development of technique and natural science. They did not constrict the investigation of concrete processes by forcing it to conform with ready-made abstract schemes, they did not subordinate it to an artificial, laboured movement of categories, as did Proudhon and Lassalle, who succumbed to the worst features of Hegelianism, but they disclosed the internal contradiction of processes and traced out their movement and mutual connection, their transitions one to another in all their concrete and unique characteristics.

In their enquiries Marx and Engels did not confine themselves to pointing to the presence of all the contradictions in this or that process as though they were of equal importance, but singled out the essential contradiction upon which the others depended. Marx applied this law of the unity and conflict of opposites with remarkable completeness and thoroughness in his *Capital,* which remains till this day the unsurpassed model of the application of dialectical materialism to the investigation of the complex process of social development. Marx showed in *Capital* the movement of the contradictions of capitalism from its rise to its decay, and established the necessity of its final downfall. He showed how the contradictions of capitalism are intensified and how all the conditions and possibility of their revolutionary solution are being prepared. He was able to show just how it was possible to prepare practically for the solution of those contradictions which are the motive force of social development. Thus he became the founder of the strategy and tactics of the workers' party. His analysis showed with great force that the unity of capitalism was relative and that the struggle of opposites within it was absolutely fundamental.

In contrast to the reformist theoreticians who discarded Marxian dialectic as an "unnecessary survival," Lenin remained faithful to it, made it concrete, developed and exalted it to a higher level. His service in working out and further developing the law of opposites was very great. In the struggle with the liberals, the reformists, the Social Revolutionary Party[1] and dissentients within the party, he applied it in just as masterly a fashion as Marx to the investigation of whatever phenomena he chose to consider. He investigated the further development of the contradictions of capitalism in the epoch of imperialism, he uncovered the basic contradictions and transitions of the contradictory forces at different stages of the class struggle and brilliantly applied this basic law of dialectic to the policy and tactics of the party. In his struggle with the Kantians, with the Machists, with bourgeois reactionary philosophy he 'showed in masterly manner the bi-polar nature of thought, the fact that it is at one and the same time relative and absolute. By developing Marxism both on the basis of the experience of the class struggle in the epoch of imperialism (from which he drew important conclusions) and on the basis of new developments in science since the time of Engels, he gave a most brilliant philosophic expression to the law of opposites as the basic law of development.

---

[1] *Social Revolutionary.* This party desired an agrarian revolution to the advantage of the peasants who were their chief support. They were extreme petty bourgeois democrats and often resorted to terrorism.

To sum up, the two fundamental conceptions of development are the mechanistic, which regards development as a simple increase, diminution and repetition, and the dialectic, which sees in development the division of a unitary process, the unity and conflict of opposites.

In the same year, 1914, that Lenin was writing his notes "On Dialectic," J. V. Plekhanov in his work *From Idealism to Materialism* sought to formulate his own understanding of the two conceptions of development. He wrote:

"Hegel's view-point was the view-point of development. But one can understand development in different ways. Even nowadays we still meet naturalists who repeat sententiously, 'Nature does not make leaps.' Sociologists too quite often repeat the same thing, 'Social development is accomplished by means of slow, gradual changes.' Hegel affirmed, on the contrary, that just as in nature so too in history *leaps are unavoidable.* 'Changes of being,' he says, 'consist not only in the transition of one quantity to another quantity, but also in the transition of quality into quantity, and the reverse process – every one of the transitions of the latter type forms a break in gradualness and gives to the phenomenon an entirely new character, qualitatively different from the former.' Development becomes comprehensible only when we consider *gradual changes* as a process by which a leap (or leaps maybe) is prepared and evoked. Whoever wishes to explain the emergence of a given phenomenon merely by slow changes must in fact unconsciously suppose *that it has' already existed but remained unnoticed because its dimensions are too minute.* But in such an 'explanation' the notion of *emergence* is replaced by the notion of *growth,* of a simple change of magnitude, i.e. the very thing requiring explanation is arbitrarily removed."

Plekhanov has correctly formulated the essence of the mechanistic conception of development, but he did not succeed in showing the dialectical essence. He speaks of leaps, of the breaking of continuity, of the transition of quantity into quality. But he has not seized the main point, the essential thing in the conception of development. He has not understood the duality which is found within the unity, in other words the unity and conflict of opposites, that fundamental conception which alone gives us the key to the understanding of leaps in evolution, of breaks in gradualness, of the transition of quantity into quality, in fact, of the whole developmental process in nature and history.

CHAPTER II

THE DIVISION OF UNITY, THE DISCLOSURE OF ESSENTIAL OPPOSITES

All processes that originate in nature and society are found in uninterrupted mutual action. In one way or another they are mutually linked up and influence each other. But in order to get to understand any one of them, to investigate the course of its development, to establish the character of its mutual action with other processes, it is no use to proceed only from the action of external forces on a given phenomenon, as do the mechanists, but it is necessary to lay bare its *internal* contradictions.

The fact that all phenomena in the world contain within themselves a number of contradictory aspects and properties was noticed long ago and is still noticed every day and reflected in people's thoughts and notions. But these opposing aspects were and are reflected in different ways. The eclectics, who see the opposing aspects of some processes but do not know how to expose their internal connection and mutual relationships, grasp at now one, now another of its opposing factors, according to their point of view or to the changing situation, and whatever aspect they select they advance as the general characteristic of the whole.

Another group of philosophers holds that contradictions belong only to the surface of processes, to their appearance; that there are none within the essence of things. Therefore from their point of view a true notion cannot contain a contradiction within itself. Thus, as we saw, thought the Eleatics, Parmenides and Zeno; thus think metaphysicians of all times. Certain liberal thinkers of the 'go's, for example, could not deny a number of contradictions in the economic order which existed in the Russian countryside and were expressed in the progressive land-deprivation of part of the peasantry, in seasonal occupations, in the contradictions between the dealer and the home craftsman, etc. But these contradictions were regarded by them, not as the expression of the development of peasant economy along the capitalist path, but as phenomena that were external and fortuitous with regard to the countryside, which had retained its primordial communal character all the time.

It is only the materialist-dialectician who does not have to give confusing answers when called on to explain how it is possible to make contradictory assertions about the same thing, who does not have to explain the contradictions of a process as lying merely on the surface of phenomena or existing merely in our thought. Only dialectical materialism proceeds from the objective contradictions of actuality, from the internal struggle of the opposing aspects of a process, proceeds as it were from the law of the change and development of actuality itself. Lenin wrote:

> "The division of the one and the knowledge of its contradictory parts... is the essence (one of the essential aspects of being, its fundamental, if not *the* fundamental characteristic) of dialectic. This is exactly how Hegel puts the question.
>
> "The condition for understanding all world processes as in self-movement,' in spontaneous development conceived in its vital and living forms – is the knowledge of the unity of their opposites. Development is in fact the conflict of opposites."

Even in a simple mechanical impulse we find this contradiction in an elementary primitive form, in the form of action and counter-action, but in this the source of self-movement is not yet revealed because mechanics seeks the cause of movement outside the object in motion. Mechanical movement is always only one aspect, one external form of the self-movement of concrete phenomena.

The class struggle in the history of society, the contradiction between productive forces and the relations of production show clearly enough the correctness of this law in relation to the development of social structures. It is the same in natural processes also.

Modern science no longer regards the atom as an unalterable, self-identical "brick of the universe," a final limit to the division of physical matter. It has shown the atom to be a unity of centres of positive and negative electricity, which by their mutual penetration determine the physical and chemical properties of the atom. Nay, more, physicists and chemists have closely and critically examined the basis of the historic view of the nature of chemical elements, which a few decades ago appeared to be absolutely fixed. They have been able to show that their nature is not fixed. Chemical elements develop and the internal cause of their development is the movement of the internal contradiction of their atoms.

The dialectical character of the processes of nature emerges with special clarity in regard to the phenomena of life. Life and death, emergence and annihilation, assimilation and dissimilation (accretion and discharge of matter and of energy) are found to be side by side and to interpenetrate each other both in the life of organisms and in the life of every component cell.

The contradictory unity of variability and heredity displayed by the organism in the struggle for existence is the mainspring of organic evolution.

In the history of technique also we deal with development on the 'basis of the internal contradictions found in any given social-economic structure, contradictions which determine the course of its self-development. Thus in the development of machinery we meet with the emergence of contradictions between the machine and the material of which it is made and the solution of these contradictions by the construction of machines out of more suitable materials – out of metal instead of wood – (originally machines were wooden), out of high quality steels, out of hard alloys, out of plastic material which can be easily moulded, etc., by the transition to new types of machines, by increasing the power of the old, etc. We have also a continual contradiction between the motive machine that provides the power, the transmissive mechanism and the machine that does the work at the "tool" end of the process.

We have contradictions between the technical bases of the different productive branches. Thus when the perfection of the loom in England at the end of the eighteenth century revealed and intensified the backwardness of spinning, the contradiction was solved by the appearance of the spinning machine, which in its turn made weaving backward; this new contradiction led to the appearance of Cartwright's loom. The contradiction between the appearance of the new machines and the handcraft methods of their production brought forth the appearance and development of a new branch of production, machine-construction. These technical revolutions in industry led in turn to a contradiction with the backward transport system (sailing ships and horse wagons) and that evoked the railway and the steamship.

Contradictions of such a type exist all the time. An invention which arises as the result of the accumulation of preceding technical and social development is grafted on to the older technique when conditions are favourable, and leads to new contradictions, to be resolved by new inventions. It is in this way that technical progress is achieved.

The unity of opposites, the division of unity is the universal law of the development of our thinking. Lenin wrote:

> "Knowledge is the eternal endless approximation of thought to the object. The reflection of nature in man's thought must not be understood in a 'dead manner', 'abstractly,' without movement, without contradiction* but as an eternal process of movement, as the emergence of contradictions and their resolution."

Our knowledge of the objective world, as we have said already, moves between the poles of relative and absolute truth. At every stage of social development our knowledge is relative, because it is conditioned by the historic degree of the development of practice. But we move on the whole towards absolute truth, reflecting at every stage of our relative knowledge more and more of the aspects of absolute truth.

Our ideas, in proportion to the development of human knowledge and its closer approximation to reality, become more and more flexible, and therefore more and more adequate to reflect the universal connection, the division of unity, the conflict of opposites in objective actuality.

Each one of the general categories of materialistic dialectic which reflect the degrees of man's knowledge of the laws of development of actuality presupposes its own opposite; thus, quality is unthinkable without quantity, content without form, possibility without actuality. Such categories are more and more seen to embody the principle of the unity of opposites.

Lenin in his fragment "On Dialectic" emphasizes the fundamental importance of the division of unity as follows:

> "This aspect of dialectics customarily received very little attention (e.g. by Plekhanov): the identity of opposites is taken as the sum-total of examples, for example 'a seed,' and in Engels's, for example, 'primitive communism.' But this is in the interest of popularization and not as the law of *knowledge* (and as the law of the objective world.)"

The "seed" is taken as an example of development through contradictions, for the seed dies that a new plant may live, then the plant dies that the new seed may live. "Primitive Communism," too, is only able to develop into civilization through the appearance within it of inequalities which are at one and the same time a forward step and a retrogression.[1]

But while Engels gave these examples in order to make the law of opposites more easily understood, Plekhanov used them because he did not understand the unity and conflict of opposites and could only deal with instances without proceeding to explain the underlying law itself.

In one of his works Plekhanov wrote:

"Now here is a point we must examine. We already know, that Überweg was right – and in what measure he was right, when he demanded from logically thinking people a definite answer to the definite question as to whether a given object possessed a given property. But imagine that we are dealing not with a simple object, but a complex one, which unites in itself directly opposite phenomena and therefore combines in itself directly opposite properties. Does Überweg's demand apply to pronouncements on such an object? No, Überweg himself – although he opposes the Hegelian dialectic – finds that here it is necessary to make use of a new principle, in fact the principle of the combination of opposites.

"One more point has to be considered. We know already that Überweg was right, and we know how right he was, in demanding that those who think should think logically, and in demanding definite answers to definite questions as to whether this or that characteristic attaches to this or that object. Now, however, let us suppose that we have to do with an object which is not simple but complex and has diametrically conflicting properties. Can the judgment demanded by Überweg be applied to such an object? No, Überweg himself, just as strenuously opposed as Trendelenburg to the Hegelian dialectic, considers that in this case we must judge in accordance with another rule, known in logic under the name of *principium coincidentiae oppositorum* (the principle of the coincidence of opposites).

---

1 See a long note by Lenin in vol. xiii of his *Works*, p. 322.

Well now, the immense majority of the phenomena with which natural science and sociological science have to do come within the category of such objects. The simplest globule of protoplasm, the life of a society in the very earliest phase of evolution – one and the other exhibit diametrically conflicting properties. Manifestly, then, we must reserve for the dialectical method a very large place in natural science and in sociology. Since investigators have begun to do this, these sciences have advanced with rapid strides."[1]

Plekhanov admits the presence of a diversity of opposite aspects or properties and of their mutual interaction in objects and processes. He knows that it is impossible to understand their mutual connection, this combination of opposites, on the basis of *formal* logic; it requires the application of *dialectical* logic. But here he remains, for he does not understand that "the combination of opposites" in processes is not only a unity but also a *conflict* of opposites, that the conflict of indissolubly connected "mutually penetrating" opposites determines the movement, is the basic law of development.

Plekhanov not only failed to recognize the problem of development by means of contradiction as the problem of development by means of division of unity but gave very little attention to the problem of contradiction itself.

He spoke of dialectic only in very general terms as of a theory of eternal development by means of emergence and annihilation. Lenin regarded the theory of the unity and conflict of opposites as the most important aspect of dialectic, but Plekhanov was more concerned with the transitoriness of forms. Thus in expounding Hegel, he said :

"The basis, the chief distinguishing feature of dialectic is indicated by Hegel as an ᶜ eternal change of forms, an eternal rejection of each form in turn, which is first brought into existence-by a particular content or tendency and subsequently supplanted by another in consequence of the further development of that same content."

Indisputably, the dialectic of content and form comprises one of

[1] Plekhanov, *Fundamental Problems of Marxism,* p. 120.

the essential elements of dialectic. But to indicate this alone is not enough. It is necessary to explain why a given content leads to the necessity of replacing a given form with another determined form. And this is only to be explained by the contradiction of form and content, by their conflict, which is only one of the concrete ways of showing the basic law of dialectic – the law of unity and conflict of opposites. That is what Plekhanov did not understand. Plekhanov understands the law of contradiction only as the statement of the transition of a form into its own individual opposite.

Ignorance of this law led him to declare that one should study, on a basis of formal logic, the moments of comparative stability in any given process.

In the foreword to the second edition of *Ludwig Feuerbach,* Plekhanov directly states that the movement of matter is the basis of all natural phenomena, and that movement is a contradiction. But he illustrates this contradiction only by the example of a mechanical movement, the shifting of a point.

It is true that even a simple movement, the mechanical shifting of a point in space, is contradictory. A moving point is simultaneously found and not found in a given spot. Here already we have the unity of opposites, but in its simplest and most primitive form. Mechanical movement originating in consequence of an impulse or impact, i.e. in consequence of external causes, is derived from some other higher form of movement and is therefore quite inadequate as an illustration of movement in general, as for instance – physical, chemical, biological and social movement. The mechanical is contained in each one of these in a certain degree, but the higher and more complex the form of the movement of matter, the smaller is the role that the mechanical plays. So it is impossible to reduce the contradictions of all these forms of movement to that of mechanical movement.

To stop short with this type of contradiction, as Plekhanov does, is to limit the significance of the law of opposites and render it incapable of explaining "self-movement" since it does not disclose the basic contradictions in the higher types.

Nay, more, he speaks out directly against the understanding of movement by way of division of unity. In his work *On the Development of the Monist View of History,* he wrote: "Whoever wished to penetrate into the essence of the dialectical process and began by expounding the doctrine of the internal opposition found within each successive phenomenon in the course of any evolutionary series, would be approaching the task from the wrong end."

To understand a process, to disclose the source of its self-movement, it is not enough to establish the diversity of the contradictions, the conflict of the many opposing aspects – it is necessary to disclose in this diversity the basic fundamental contradictions which define the movement of the process.

In opposition to the metaphysics of bourgeois ideology, which at the best limited itself to a statement of the mutual action of so-cial" factors," Marx, Engels and Lenin demanded the disclosure of the basic contradiction of every social structure, which consists in the contradiction between those productive forces and the productive relations which are found together in that particular social structure.

This basic contradiction determines all the other contradictions of the given social form and the course of the latter's development. That is the reason why the classical exponents of Marxism regarded the whole mass of contradictions found in social development from the standpoint of this basic contradiction.

Bourgeois political economy, before and after Marx, took its stand on the eternity of bourgeois relations and could not disclose the actual contradictions of capitalism, which are the law of its emergence, development and decay. Even the foremost intellects of bourgeois economic science – Adam Smith and Ricardo, who taught that value is the substantiated human labour in the article of sale and that the amount of value is determined by the amount of working expenses, that profit and ground rent are the unpaid work of the labourer – even they could not disclose the basic laws of the development of the social formation they were considering, because they had not marked its contradictions. These forerunners of classical bourgeois political economy and their successors also quite failed to penetrate deeper than the surface of the phenomena of distorted capitalist practice. Their "methodology" amounted to this – they sought to turn one of the phenomena of capitalist economy, torn from its connection with the rest, into a principle which could characterize the whole of capitalism. Thus some of them found "the law of supply and demand" to be this principle, others claimed to find it in "the costs of production," a third group in "the cost to the consumer," etc. And so they were unable to give any general picture of the development of capitalism or to disclose its governing laws. Marx opposed the metaphysics of bourgeois political economy with his dialectic of capitalist actuality itself; he wrote: "Only by setting in place of opposing dogmas, opposing facts and the real contradictions which make up their concealed basis, is it possible to convert political economy into a positive science."

Marx disclosed the basic contradictions of the bourgeois means of production and in this way explained the law of its development. He showed that the contradiction between capitalist productive forces and the relations of production determines the development of capitalism.

This contradiction, which emerges in the form of the contradiction between the social character of production and the private means of appropriation, "is also that basic contradiction which includes in itself all those contradictions which surround modern society and are specially evident in heavy industry" (Engels).

This basic contradiction finds its expression and development in a number of other contradictions of capitalism. We will mention some of them.

1. The contradiction between the effective organization of production in each separate factory and the anarchy in the general course of social production.

2. The perfection of machines and the widening of production as the compulsory law for each capitalist, on one side; the growth of a reserve army of industry, and periodically repeating crises, on the other side. Here the means of production rebels against the capitalist relations of production.

3. "For capitalism as a whole there is the peculiarity of the difference between property in capital and the application of capital to production, that is to say between finance capital and industrial or productive capital; the difference between the *rentier* who lives only by income from money capital and the *entrepreneur* together with all those people who take an immediate part in the utilization of their capital" (Lenin).

This last difference in which the social character of production distorted by capitalist relations finds its expression is clearly displayed in the joint-stock companies, in which for the mass of shareholders there remain only the functions of the *rentier* and the formal right of property in the undertaking, whereas the actual allocating of the accumulated profits, the direction of production and the income from the undertaking remain in the hands of a small group of "financial supermen" (Lenin).

Analysing the basic contradictions of capitalism, Marx showed that they lead inevitably to the necessity of revolution and to proletarian dictatorship.

Lenin traced the transformation of capitalism into the last stage of its development – into imperialism, which in a new form, in the form of monopoly, develops the basic contradictions of the capitalist system, leading them to the final crises of capitalism. By proceeding from analysis of the basic contradictions of monopoly capitalism and the whole sum of contradictions that grow up on their basis, by disclosing the inequality of the development of imperialism in different countries, Lenin showed scientifically the possibility of breaking the imperialist chain at its weakest link, the possibility of a victory of revolution, of a victory of socialism, in a single country.

Lenin and Stalin in their works have shown the basic, leading contradiction of the socialist transitional economy; it is the struggle of socialism with the remnants of capitalism.

The basic contradiction of our transitional economy was formulated by Lenin as follows:

"The economy of Russia in the epoch of proletarian dictatorship presents itself as the conflict between the first forms of the communistic unified large-scale labour-State and small-scale commodity production accompanied by the capitalism that is being preserved along with it and is always being reborn on its basis."

This concentrated Leninist formula contains the characteristic of the following three aspects of the contradiction of transitional economy.

1. The contradiction of large-scale socialist industry with the market-capitalist tendencies of small-scale commodity economy.

This contradiction was and is being resolved, not by the brutal pressure of the proletariat on the peasantry, as our enemies depict it, but in a form of union of the proletariat with the peasantry under the guidance of the proletariat, which union has as its task the abolition of classes and is directed both against the capitalist tendencies of the peasantry itself, and against those capitalist agents who ceaselessly try to play on those tendencies in order to break up this union from within.

This union is made actual firstly by means of the identification of the interests of the small producer with the interests of socialism, with the aims of developing socialist industry, and secondly by means of the socialist reconstruction of peasant economy in the form of all-round collectivization, which signifies the liquidation of that base for the continual rebirth of capitalism to which Lenin alluded.

2. *The antagonism between the interests of the proletariat, the owners of socialistic industry, and the capitalistic elements – elements which have been in part already expropriated since the October Revolution and put to rout in the civil war, but are not yet finally liquidated, and in part are being born anew on the basis of N.E.P.[1] on the basis of individualist, small-scale, peasant economy.*

This contradiction was resolved by the proletariat on the lines of the general policy of the party which was the industrialization of the country and the socialist recasting of peasant economy; different methods were required at different stages of the revolution – ranging from the policy of curtailing and expelling the capitalist elements to the liquidation of the kulaks as a class and the establishment of all-round collectivization.

The basic contradictions of the transitional period, which have been indicated by Lenin, find their expression in a number of its other contradictions. Such for example is the contradiction between our advanced socialist relations and the backward technique which is the heritage of Russian capitalism; this contradiction will be resolved by a vigorous development of socialist industry.

Another such contradiction is the contradiction between the socialist organization of production and petty bourgeois and bourgeois habits and traditions relating to production and work, which once again are the workers' heritage from the past; this contradiction will be resolved by the mass recasting of the people under the leadership

---

1 *N.E.P.* The New Economic Policy was adopted under the leadership of Lenin at the Tenth Congress of the Communist Party in 1921. It allowed considerable scope for private trading but retained a State monopoly of foreign trade, transport, heavy industry and much light industry. It allowed the rapid growth of capitalist elements in the countryside. It was in Lenin's own words, "Capitalism plus socialism."

of the Party, by the fostering of socialist discipline, by the developing of new socialist forms of work.

3. We will point finally to the contradiction between the still limited output of socialist industry and agriculture and the growing demands of the workers.

This contradiction is being resolved by the increasing productivity of labour in industry and agriculture, by the vigorous tempo of the industrialization of the land, by the development of light industry, by the mobilization of the internal resources of heavy industry for production of widely demanded goods, by the struggle for the organized economic strengthening of the collective farms and finally by the developing of collective farm trade.

In disclosing the above-mentioned basic contradiction of the transitional economy of the U.S.S.R., Lenin and Stalin showed that the proletariat of the Soviet Union under the leadership of the Communist Party, by having set up its dictatorship, by possessing large-scale industry, transport and colossal resources of natural wealth, by introducing a monopoly of external trade, by establishing a union with the middle peasantry, possesses everything necessary for the resolution of this contradiction by its own internal powers. It possesses everything necessary to industrialize the country, to lead the peasant economy into socialist forms of agriculture and in this way to abolish classes. Lenin and Stalin have shown the full possibility of a victory for socialism in our country.

Stalin wrote:

"What is meant by the possibility of the victory of socialism in one country? It is the possibility of resolving the contradictions between the proletariat and the peasantry by the internal forces of our country, the possibility of the proletariat's gaining power and making use of that power for the construction of a full socialist society in our country, accompanied by the sympathy and support of the proletarians of other countries, but without a preliminary victory of the proletarian revolution in those other countries."

This basic contradiction will be finally resolved in the U.S.S.R. at the end of the second Five Year Plan, which has as its basic problem the full liquidation of capitalist elements and classes generally, the abolition of all those causes that create class distinctions – the construction of a classless society.

After the abolition of classes, internal contradictions, in spite of the opinion of opportunists, will still be the source of the "self-movement" of society.

Although it is not our purpose here to dwell on what the basic contradiction of communist society is going to be, yet we can say with assurance, that in the first phase of communism – socialism – the determining form of this contradiction will be the contradiction between the socialist character of production (based on society's appropriation of the means of production) and the distribution of the "means of existence and enjoyment" (with the exclusion of necessary social funds) according to work done. This contradiction determines and will determine the whole diversity of the aspects of social development. It will be resolved by the growth of the productivity of labour and on that basis by such a refashioning of our people as will make possible the realization of the principle: "from each according to his ability, to each according to his needs."

And so to understand the movement of any process it is necessary to disclose, amidst the diversity of its contradictions and opposite tendencies, the basic contradiction which determines the development of the process as a whole; it is necessary to disclose the source of its "self-movement."

The internal contradictions of every process are qualitatively distinct from those of any other process. The basic contradiction of capitalism – the contradiction between the bourgeoisie and the proletariat, which can be solved only by socialist revolution, is one matter; the basic contradiction of the transitional economy, which will be solved by the industrialization of the country, by collectivization and Soviet farm construction, is another.

Trotsky did not understand the essential character and specific nature of the development of the basic contradiction of capitalism in the imperialist epoch, he did not understand the law of uneven development. This is the first reason for his denial of the possibility of a victory for socialism in one country. According to Trotsky the contradiction between the proletariat and peasantry in the U.S.S.R. is the same sort of contradiction as the contradiction between the proletariat and the bourgeoisie in a capitalist economy and, in his opinion, is to be resolved in the same way as the second – by international revolution. Trotsky also did not see the specific difference, that the peasants are small-scale commodity-producers who work with their own means of production and not bourgeois who exploit the work of other people (though it is true that from the midst of the peasants capitalism is being born every minute), that as a workman the peasant is the ally of the proletariat and that under a proletarian dictatorship conditions are created that will bring over the peasantry to socialist forms of agriculture. This is the second reason for his denial of the possibility of a victory for socialism in one country. Practice has gloriously refuted Trotsky and has shown that a contradiction which is qualitatively different must be differently resolved. The contradiction between the proletariat and the bourgeoisie in the conditions of capitalism is to be resolved by revolution, by a proletarian seizure of state-power, but the contradiction between the proletariat and the peasantry in the conditions of the U.S.S.R. is to be resolved by industrialization of the country and by the collectivization of the agricultural economy, which leads to the liquidation of classes.

Practice has gloriously confirmed the theory of the possibility of a victory for socialism in one country.

The opportunists of the right do not remark the specific character of the contradictions between the proletariat and the peasantry, and between the proletariat and the capitalist elements of a country – these two contradictions are held by them to be of the same type, on this idea rests their theory of the peaceful transition of the kulak into socialism.

The lessons we get from Trotskyism and right opportunism teach us the necessity of disclosing the specific quality of the internal contradictions of any process. And for this a knowledge of every aspect of the contradiction is necessary. Marx wrote in *The Holy Family*, "Proletariat and riches are contradictions; as such they form a united whole. Both of them are brought forth by the world of private property. The question is, what definite position does each of these two opposites occupy in the contradiction." It is not enough to say they are the two aspects of a united whole. To understand the basic contradictions of capitalism we must get to know the specific properties of the proletariat and bourgeoisie, their relations with each other, their concrete mutual independence, and the mutual conditioning factors of both classes. What the Marx-Leninist dialectic requires for the study of any process is this: the exhaustive disclosure of all aspects of the contradiction with their concrete relations, that is to say, the "definite position which each of the two opposites occupies in the contradiction."

CHAPTER III

MUTUAL PENETRATION OF OPPOSITES

Not only does every unity contain within itself polar opposites but these internal opposites are mutually connected with each other; one aspect of a contradiction cannot exist without the other. In capitalist society the bourgeoisie is connected with the proletariat, the proletariat with the bourgeoisie; neither of these two classes can develop without the other, because the bourgeoisie cannot exist without exploiting the labour of others and the hired proletariat cannot exist without selling its labour power to a capitalist, seeing that itself it does not possess the means of production.

This mutual connectedness and mutual conditioning of contradictory aspects of actuality has also been stressed by the Party in its struggle on two fronts on the question of the character of N.E.P.

"When a policy like that of the N.E.P. is adopted, both aspects must be preserved: the first aspect, which is directed against the regime of militant communism and has as its aim the securing of what is known as the free market, and the second aspect, which is directed against complete freedom of market and has as its aim the securing of a regulating role by the state over the market. Abolish one of these aspects and you will no longer have the N.E.P." (Stalin).

We see the same indissoluble connection of contradictory aspects in all the processes of objective actuality. There is no mechanical action without its counteraction. The chemical dissolution of atoms is indissolubly connected with their union. Electrical energy declares itself in the form of opposite electricities – positive and negative.

"The existence of two mutually contradictory aspects, their conflict and their flowing together into a new category," wrote Marx, "comprises the essence of the dialectical movement. If you limit yourself to the task of warding off the bad aspect (for the preservation of the 'good' aspect corresponding to it, as Proudhon demanded) then by the separation of these aspects you put an end to the whole dialectical process."

Opposites are not only found in indissoluble, inalienable connection, but they cross over and mutually penetrate each other. Thus process of production in a capitalist factory is simultaneously an aggregation of capitalist productive relations (for example the relations between the capitalist and the worker), and an aggregation of productive forces (the labour of the workers and the means of production). Development from manufacture[1] to machine production is not only a change of productive forces, but a development and spreading of new productive relations. The union of the labour force of the workers and the means of production is simultaneously a connection of productive forces and a connection of people in the process of production, which together make up the relation. The division of labour in manufacture is a relation in production and emerges also as a productive force.

On the basis of this mutual penetration of capitalist productive forces, and capitalist relations in production, the process of ever intensifying contradiction between proletariat and bourgeoisie is also developed.

The mutual penetration of opposites, the transition of one opposite into another, belongs to all processes. But to uncover and reveal this mutual penetration, a careful, concrete analysis of the process is required.

The interests of the proletariat and the working peasantry in the U.S.S.R., classes opposed to each other both on account of their historic past and their relations to the means of production, are nowadays beginning to coincide. With regard to fundamental questions of socialist construction, the peasant, as worker, appears as the ally of the proletariat. The peasant is interested in the strengthening of the proletarian dictatorship, because it guards him from having to return the land to the landlords and delivers him from exploitation by the kulak.[2] The peasant is interested in the socialist development

---

[1] *Manufacture,* strictly speaking, means "by hand" (Latin, *manus)* not by machine. It refers therefore to the period before machino-facture and steam power.

[2] *Kulak, lit.* fist. The tight-fisted, well-to-do peasant. "He may be a good manager, a man of enterprise and initiative, but as long as he ex-

of agricultural economy because this is the best method of raising agricultural economy to a higher level. The peasant is interested in the industrialization of the country because this creates a material basis for raising the level of agricultural economy and guarantees the defence of the country from the encroachment of capitalists and landlords. Here we have the coincidence of the interests of the proletariat and the peasantry. Not until conditions were favourable for the rapid expansion of socialist industry on the one hand and for a mass movement of the peasants towards collectivization on the other, was it possible to unite the private-property interests of the peasants with the general interests of socialism.

The first form of this combination was the N.E.P., which at the end of the civil war made possible the improvement of individualistic peasant economy and its co-operation on the basis of what is called the free market, under state control. In this way the raw material and provisions for socialist industry were guaranteed. The combination of peasant economy and large-scale industry became ever closer as socialist relations in industry and trade, the industrialization of the country, the development of machine-tractor stations and of the system of collective contracts with the state kept growing and were confirmed. The result of this policy is that now, on the basis of direct collectivization of individual peasant holdings, N.E.P. has become a form of combination of the private-property interests of the peasantry with the interests of socialism, and this leads to the growth and strengthening of socialist relations. The world-historical strategic significance of N.E.P. is determined by this fact, that the Party set up this policy on the basis of a profound analysis of the course and development of the contradictions of the transitional economy and the indissoluble connection of the opposite tendencies of their mutual penetration.

We have emerged into the period of socialism and we are experiencing the last stage of N.E.P. – *that is a contradiction!* We are proceeding to a final liquidation of classes and we are strengthening the financial system and credit organizations; we have adopted cost-accounting, we keep the purchasing power of the rouble stable and along with the organized economic strengthening of the collective

---

ercises his talents for his own benefit, for the benefit of individualism, he is a great danger, a great enemy and must be wiped out" (Hindus, *Humanity Uprooted*).

farms we encourage the development of collective farm trading. But we do this because the strengthening of the financial system and the state banks is at the same time helping us to take stock of our economic position, to plan more exactly and to introduce disciplined business control. The cost-accounting system, the introduction of socialist planning into the workshop, the brigade, and the collective farm. The development of collective farm trading strengthens the bond between the proletariat and the collective-farm peasants. An example of the analysis of the mutual penetration of opposites is given by Stalin in his solution of the problem of the relation of national and international culture under socialism.

"The encouragement of cultures that are national in form and socialistic in content," said Stalin, in his report to the Sixteenth Assembly, "under conditions of proletarian dictatorship in one country, with the ultimate aim of welding them into one general socialist culture (one both in form and content), with one general language, for the day when the proletariat shall have conquered and socialism have spread all over the world – in this conception we find the truly dialectical character of the Leninist approach to this question of national culture.

"It may be objected that such a way of stating the question is 'contradictory.' But do we not meet with similar contradictions in the question of the State? We are for the withering away of the State. And yet we also believe in the proletarian dictatorship, which represents the strongest and mightiest form of State power that has existed up to now. To keep on developing State power in order to prepare the conditions *for* the withering away of State power – that is the Marxist formula. It is 'contradictory'? Yes, 'contradictory.' But the contradiction is vital, and wholly reflects Marxian dialectic.

"Or for example, the Leninist statement on the right of the constituted nations of the U.S.S.R. to self-determination, even up to the point of cutting adrift from the Soviet Union. Lenin sometimes used to put his thesis on national self-determination in the form of this simple statement, 'disunity for unity.' Just think – disunity for unity! It smacks of paradox. All the same this contradictory formula reflects that vital truth of Marxian dialectic which enables the Bolsheviks to overcome the most formidable obstacles that beset this national question.

"The same thing must be said about the question of national culture; there is an efflorescence of national cultures (and languages) in the period of proletarian dictatorship in one country but the very purpose of this is to prepare the conditions for the extinction of these separate cultures and the welding of them into one common socialist culture (and one common language) when socialism shall be victorious over the whole world.

"Whoever has not understood this feature of the contradictions belonging to our transitional time, whoever has not understood this dialectic of historical processes, that person is dead to Marxism."

In the transitional period, when the masses of builders of socialism have not yet "divested themselves of the skin of the old capitalist Adam," when individualist habits and survivals are not yet outlived even in the ranks of the working class (to say nothing of the peasantry and old intelligentsia), we have to deal with many cases of the divergence of personal and social interests. But the Communist Party does not brush aside this actual contradiction and does not idealize actuality. It proceeds from the principle that the development of socialist relations for the first time in history makes widely possible such a "mutual penetration" of personal and social interests as will lead, not to the crushing of personality, but to its real and full development along the same line as the interests of all society. This "mutual penetration" is manifested in the form of piece-work, the insistence of differential wages according to the quality and quantity of the work done, the bonus system, diplomas and other awards for exceptionally good work and other forms of encouragement designed to enlist all the powers of the individual in the service of society.

"Mutual penetration" of opposites is also characteristic of the processes of our knowledge.

One of the basic contradictions of human knowledge is, as we have already seen, the contradiction of relative and absolute truths.

We have the same mutual penetration in the relationship of the particular and the general which are reflected in our ideas. The particular does not exist except in relation to the general. The general exists only in the particulars. Every generalization only approximately grasps all the particular objects. Every particular thing partly enters into the general.

The universal laws of development, reflected in the categories of materialistic dialectic, can be understood only on the basis of the mutual penetration of opposites.

"Dialectic shows," writes Engels, "that to hold that basis and consequence, cause and action, identity and difference, being and essence, are unalterable opposites, will not bear criticism. Analysis shows the presence of one pole in latent form within the other, that at the determined point one pole goes over into the other and that all logic is developed only from the moving of these two opposites in one another's direction."

Lenin used to call this "mutual penetration" of opposites – the identity of opposites. To disclose the mutual penetration, the identity of opposites in any process is the central problem of our theory of knowledge, of materialistic dialectic.

Aptly enough, Engels, in defining the three basic laws of dialectic, formulated the law of movement through contradictions as "the law of the mutual penetration of opposites."

Lenin defined dialectic as "the teaching of how contradictions may be and are identical; under what conditions they are identical; how they turn into each other and so become identical; why the mind of man must not accept these opposites as dead or frozen but as living, conditional, mobile, the one always in process of turning into the other."

To understand how opposites become identical is only possible by means of a careful, concrete and profound analysis of the process, by a study of the movement of all its basic aspects at its different stages, of all the conditions and possibilities of their transitions.

The mutual penetration of opposites, being the expression of the basic scientific laws underlying the process, becomes possible and is realized only in some particular complex of conditions.

The wage labourer is a living identity of opposites since he is the basic productive force of capitalism and all material commodities and at the same time is divorced from the means of production, possesses nothing except his hands, and is exploited by another class. Such a mutual penetration of opposites becomes possible only under the conditions of the capitalist system of production.

The development of a culture, national in form, and international in content, the strengthening of the state power for the creation of the conditions leading to its decline, become possible and necessary only under the proletarian dictatorship. The development of cost accounting in order to strengthen the financial system for the development of socialist planning is necessary in the period when it is still impossible to replace money in any way, and is possible only until the conditions for doing away with money shall have been created. The raising of the productivity of labour by enlisting the personal interest of the worker, by encouraging the more highly qualified workers, by the preferential treatment of shock-brigaders, is possible only in the conditions of proletarian dictatorship and because increase in the productivity of labour is the decisive condition for constructing a complete socialist society and for the transition to a communist society with its principle of distribution according to needs.

The understanding of this aspect of the law of the unity and conflict of opposites has made possible a correct analysis of the economic situation, of the mutual relations of classes and parties and consequently has determined the policy of our Party. Lenin wrote:

> "We have all been learning a little Marxism; we have been learning how and when it is possible to unite opposites. Even more important is the fact that the revolution has compelled us to be continually uniting opposites in practice. But let us remember that these opposites may be united so as to obtain either mere discords or a symphony."

Such a dialectical combination of opposing policies which appeared absolutely incompatible to the Mensheviks was the policy of our Party in relation to the Liberals in the period of the Zemstvo campaign[1] "to keep distinct in order to strike together." On the basis

---

[1] *Zemstvo campaign.* The zemstvos or provincial assemblies were created in 1864 and consisted of a number of elected delegates of landowners and peasants. Their powers were restricted in 1890 but in 1905 in response to public opinion they regained some of their independent

of such a combination was built the policy of the party in relation to the peasantry at different stages of the revolution, the combining of the interests of the proletariat and of the poorer peasants to bring about the socialist revolution, the policy of union with the well-to-do peasantry after the eighth assembly of the Party.

A clear model of the combination of opposites in the policy of the Party is found in the "Six Conditions"[1] of Stalin which introduced business methods and payment by results into Soviet industry and which, while giving every kind of support to the old intelligentsia, took steps to create, in the shortest period possible, numerous cadres of working-class technical experts. This "combination of opposites" in the policy of our Party is directed towards social development in a determined direction and was always worked out in practice on the basis of an accurate and concrete study of objective contradictions. That is why this combination always resulted in victory for the party line. That is why we have got from it a "symphony," not mere discords.

A combination of opposites that does not issue from a faithful reckoning with objective conditions and facts is an -eclectic combination and cannot lead to the victory of the determined trend of development, but instead to its defeat. Thus the Mensheviks constructed a whole policy of struggle for a bourgeois democratic revolution on the basis of an eclectic combination of the interests of the proletariat with those of the liberal bourgeoisie, which combination ignored the irreconcilability of those interests, ignored the concrete conditions of the development of Russia, ignored the peasantry as the basic ally of the proletariat in this revolution, and handed the hegemony in the revolution to the liberal bourgeoisie, to whose interests it subordinated those of the proletariat. Such a combination

---

initiative. The question then was to what extent revolutionary socialists should participate in these bodies.

[1] The "Six Conditions" of Stalin were laid down in his speech to the leaders of industry in June 1931. Stalin asserted that a new situation had been created by the development of industry and that this required new methods of working. He enumerated six of these including rationalization, payment by results, personal responsibility for the job, technical education, encouragement of the intelligentsia and business accounting.

led, as we said, to discord, to the defeat of the bourgeois democratic revolution.

The right opportunists in the U.S.S.R. held it necessary to combine the interests of the proletariat with those of the peasantry in such a way as neither to harm the kulak by curtailing his tendencies to exploit – rather to enable him to develop them – nor to prepare or carry out the policy of liquidating the kulak as a class. They held it was necessary to combine for many decades the small scale individualist peasant economy with large scale socialistic production. This combination is eclectic and impossible, for it fails to realize the impracticability of continuing a long drawn-out development of a double system – large scale socialist industry on the one hand, and on the other, decaying peasant economy, that economy which every hour and every minute gives birth again to capitalism. This combination ignored the irreconcilability of the interests of the proletariat and the capitalist elements. Such a combination would inevitably lead not to a victory for socialism but to a bourgeois restoration. Gradualist socialists seek theoretically to base their betrayal of the interests of the working class and their furious war against communism on an eclectic combination of the irreconcilable class-antagonists – the bourgeoisie and the proletariat – as given in the doctrine of the "evolution of capitalism into socialism."

The group of Menshevist idealists, in spite of its repeated declarations on the unity of opposites as their mutual penetration, has in its analysis of concrete problems distorted both the proposition itself and the facts under investigation. The mutual penetration of opposites has in essence been reduced by them to the more limited notion that opposites presuppose each other. It is this abstract approach, this approach "in general" without concrete analysis, that has prevented the Deborin group from rightly understanding the dialectical unity of the historic and the logical in knowledge, the unity of theory and practice in revolutionary struggle and the actual relationships between the proletariat and peasantry in revolution.

The study of mutual penetration, of the identity of opposites, demands a concrete enquiry into the contradictory aspects of a process in its movement and development, the conditioning and mobility of all its facets, their conversion into each other.

But those mechanists who hold themselves to be Marxists do not understand movement by means of contradictions. The mechanistic view has been very clearly and directly expressed by Bukharin in his *Theory of Historic Materialism.*

"In the world there exist differently acting forces directed one against the other. Only in exceptional cases do they balance each other. Then "we have a state of rest, i.e. their actual conflict remains hidden. But it is sufficient to change one of these forces, and immediately the internal contradictions will be manifest, there will ensue a breakdown of equilibrium, and if a new equilibrium is established, it is established on a new basis, i.e. with another combination of forces, etc. What follows from this? It follows that 'conflict of opposites,' i.e. the antagonism of differently directed forces, does indeed condition movement."

According to Bukharin, there exist forces independent of each other and they act on each other. It is this external collision of differently directed forces that conditions movement. While Lenin requires to know in the first place the internal contradictions of a process, to find the source of self-movement, Bukharin requires the determination of external forces that collide with each other. Lenin speaks of the division of the unity, requires the disclosure of the internal identity of opposites, the establishment of the concrete character of the connections of opposing aspects and their transitions. Bukharin requires the mere finding of independent forces. He understands the law of the unity of opposites mechanically, because he proceeds from the mechanics of a simple collision of forces independent of each other, as the general notional "model" which is suitable to explain every phenomenon. Such a reduction of an internal process to a conflict of independent forces inevitably leads to the seeking of the cause of change outside the process, in the action of its environment.

From the mechanistic understanding of the unity of opposites proceeds the theory of organized capitalism, which holds, as fundamental for the epoch of imperialism, not the internal contradictions of each country, but their external contradictions on the world arena.

On the mechanistic understanding of contradictions is constructed the Trotskyist theory that denies the possibility of a socialist victory in one country. Trotsky recognizes, as basic and decisive in this question, not the internal contradictions of our Soviet economy (which are being resolved within the country), but the external contradictions, the contradictions between the Soviet Union and capitalist countries. Trotsky holds that it is these last that determine the development of soviet economy and so only a resolution of these contradictions can lead to a complete victory of socialism in our country.

Bukharin, like all mechanists, identifies contradiction with antagonism. That is wrong. Those contradictions (carefully distinguished by Marx and Engels in their analysis of the complex forms of development of class society) are antagonistic, in which the struggle of indissolubly connected opposites proceeds in the form of their external collisions, which are directed on the part of the dominant opposite so as to preserve the subordination of its opposite and of the type of contradiction itself; and on the part of the subordinated opposite – to the destruction of the dominant opposite and of the contradiction itself as well.

The contradiction of any process is resolved, not by some external force, as think the mechanists, but by the development of the contradiction itself. This is true also in regard to antagonistic contradictions. But in the course of development of an antagonistic contradiction at its different stages, only the *premises* for its resolution are prepared and ripen. The contradiction itself at every new stage becomes ever more intensified. An antagonistic contradiction does not pass beyond the stages of its partial resolution.

Thus the periodic crises of capitalism are a violent form in which the contradictions of a given cycle of capitalist reproduction find their resolution; but in relation to the contradictions of the capitalist means of production as a whole, these crises emerge only as landmarks of the further intensification of these contradictions and of the ripening of the forces making for the violent overthrow of capitalism.

Antagonistic contradictions are resolved by the kind of leap in which the internal opposites emerge as relatively independent opposites, external to each other, by a leap that leads to the abolition of the formerly dominant opposite and to the establishment of a new contradiction. In this contradiction the subordinated opposite of the previous contradiction now becomes the dominant opposite, preserving a number of its peculiarities and determining by itself the form of the new contradiction, especially at the first stages of its development.

But in contradictions that do not have an antagonistic character, the development of the contradiction signifies not only the growth of the forces making for its final resolution, but each new step in the development of the contradiction is at the same time also its partial resolution.

Not all contradictions are antagonistic. Thus the relationships of the proletariat and the peasantry are not of an antagonistic character – in both classes we find a number of common interests. In a class society the contradictions of the basic classes are antagonistic and are resolved in antagonistic form. In developed socialist society there will be no class struggle, no class antagonism. "It is only in an order of things," says Marx, "in which there will be no more classes and class antagonism, that social evolutions will cease to be political revolutions."[1]

But Bukharin, because he identifies contradiction with antagonism, holds that in general there will be in this case no contradictions at all.

This is what Lenin wrote in answer to that assertion: "Quite wrong. Antagonism and contradiction are by no means the same. Under socialism the first will vanish, the second will remain".

If in developed socialism there were *no* contradictions – contradictions between productive forces and relations in production, between production and demand, no contradictions in the development of technique, etc. – then the development of socialism would be impossible, then instead of movement we should have stagnation. Only in virtue of the internal contradictions of the socialist order can there be development from one phase to another and higher phase.

But each step in the development of socialism will denote not only a ripening of the *forces* making for a developed communist society, but also an *immediate* partial resolution of the contradictions of socialism. Just in the same way, each new stage in the transitional period denotes not only a growth of the *forces* making for socialism (which can enter into being once the leap to a new order is made), but also an *immediate* construction of socialism, a partial resolution of the most basic contradiction of the transitional period.

The identification of contradiction with antagonism leads on the one hand to the Trotskyist assertion that the contradictions between

---

[1] Marx, *The Poverty of Philosophy.*

the proletariat and the peasantry are of the same character as those between the proletariat and the bourgeoisie, i.e. are relations of class antagonism. On the other hand, it leads to right-opportunist conclusions. The right-opportunists maintain that the relations of these classes are not antagonistic and are, therefore, not even contradictory.

CHAPTER IV

ANALYSIS OF THE MOVEMENT OF THE
CONTRADICTION OF A PROCESS FROM ITS
BEGINNING TO ITS END

Lenin wrote of Karl Marx's *Capital:*

"Marx in his *Capital* at first analyses the simplest, the most ordinary, fundamental and commonplace thing, a relation to be observed billions of times in bourgeois commodity society: the exchange of commodities. In that simple phenomenon (in that cell of the bourgeois society) the analysis reveals all the contradictions (and their embryo as well) of modern society. The subsequent exposition shows the development (both growth and movement) of these contradictions and that of society in the sum total of its fundamental parts, from beginning to end. Such must also be the method of exposition (and of study as well) of dialectics in general."[1]

Such indeed must be the method of studying any process, i.e. our task must be to find its simplest, basic relations, to disclose in it the basic contradictions, to investigate their development and their conflict; to investigate how the development of a contradiction prepares its resolution and determines the form of its resolution; to investigate the qualitative changes in the successive phases of development of a process, the relative independence of movement of contradictory aspects, their mutual connection, their transitions one into the other; to disclose in the development of the conflict of opposites in any process the necessity and also all the conditions and possibilities of its conversion into its own opposite. Such must be the course of study of any process in its emergence, development and decay.

In *Capital* Marx begins from the simplest, basic relations of merchant-capitalist society – the exchange of commodities. He at once shows the ambiguity, the contradictory characteristics of a "commodity," an article made simply for sale, as a unity of price and value, discloses its internal contradictions, the ambiguous char-

---

[1] Lenin, vol. xiii, p. 324.

acter of the labour that creates the article, the concrete labour on the one hand and on the other the abstract labour that creates the value.

Marx further shows that the internal contradiction concealed in the commodity finds the forms of its movement in the external contradiction, which emerges as the relation of the relative and the equivalent forms of value, which are polar opposites, indissolubly connected with each other. The further development of this relationship, which reflects the development of the commodity, goes through three stages of a simple, a developed and finally a universal form of value. In the last of these stages, the article takes on the double form of the commodity itself and its monetary equivalent.

The development of money, in its different functions, being the result of the extension and complication of commodity relations and at the same time the condition of the development of these relations, is the further form of development of its initial contradictions.

Marx shows further the process of the development of money into capital, the internal contradiction of the general form of movement of capital and the continual resolution of this contradiction in the buying and selling of labour power. The appearance of the latter denotes the higher development of the initial contradiction, the development of the law of value on a very universal scale. At this point development takes place more quickly and with more intensity than formerly, because by the separation of the means of production from the producer (and the stage of development of commodity relations that we are discussing inevitably leads to such a separation) the basic productive power – labour power – is turned into a commodity. Production of commodities for sale becomes capitalist. Thus we arrive at the basic means of production of a new social structure. The conversion of money into capital denotes the development of the law of value into a new qualitatively-unique law-system – into the law of Surplus Value which is the "source of the self-movement" of capitalism.

Marx shows that the capitalist organization of production "denotes the concentration in great workshops of the hitherto disconnected means of production and their conversion by this means from the productive forces of separate persons into social productive forces" but under conditions of individual appropriation. He further shows how the pursuit after a continuous increase in the rate of surplus value, which depends on the physiological limitations of the working day and the resistance of the working class, leads to the growth and intensification of the contradictions between the social character of production and individual appropriation – that basic contradiction of capitalism – leads to the growing of simple capitalist co-operation into manufacture, and thence into production by machinery. Marx showed that the increase of the rate of exploitation requires an uninterrupted expansion of production, that reproduction leads to the concentration and centralization of capital and consequently to the ruin of small-scale capitalists. From another point of view, the same process of capitalist reproduction[1] creates an industrial reserve army, and ever more and more intensifies class contradictions. Marx disclosed in all its terrible nakedness the general law of capitalist accumulation, with the absolute impoverishment of the working class as its obverse side, thus showing the inevitability of the collapse of capitalism.

In disclosing the essence of capitalism and its deep, ever changing contradictions, Marx shows the emergence, on their basis, of contradictory phenomena. To this are devoted the second and third volumes of *Capital*, where Marx shows the process of the circulation of capital and its reproduction, and the division of surplus value into the forms of profits of enterprise, interest, profits of commerce and ground rent. Marx shows here how law of value is developed in its external forms, growing into a law of costs of production. He shows how production is expanded, how the organic composition of capital grows and how under the influence of this, the rate of profit falls although the hope of its rise is the very thing which drives capitalism to develop the forces of production. He further shows how capitalist contradictions ever more and more intensify, finding their temporary solution in certain characteristic phenomena – *crisis, depression, recovery, boom* – the trade cycle, which appears as the forces of production emerge in ever more irreconcilable conflict with the social law of their development. The social structure of capitalism hampers the development of productive forces. The bourgeoisie becomes unable to control production. The movement

---

[1] *Reproduction.* A technical term in Marxian economics. In order to maintain the flow of commodities the instruments of production must be renewed; at the same time every commodity wears out or is destroyed. Industry therefore shows us various kinds of commodities being produced, used and produced again. There is a constant reproduction of things. See Marx, *Capital,* vol. i, p. 621.

of capitalist contradictions gives rise to the necessity and also to all the conditions and possibilities of the collapse of capitalism.

That is the picture unfolded by Marx in *Capital* and completed by Lenin and Stalin in their works on imperialism and the general crisis of capitalism.

The method applied by Marx in *Capital* has necessarily to be applied in the study of any process. A model of the masterly application of this method is the analysis of development of the struggle between the proletariat and the bourgeoisie given by Marx and Engels in the *Communist Manifesto*. This same method lies at the basis of the analysis of the origin, development and abolition of classes and the state given by Engels in his work *The Origin of the Family*, and by Lenin in *The State and Revolution*, and of the analysis of the origin and development of capitalism in Russia given by Lenin in his celebrated work on *The Development of Capitalism in Russia*.

An analysis of the movement of contradiction in its emergence, development and decay is the only way to a knowledge both of the basic laws of the development of a process and of the diverse concrete forms of its appearance at different stages and in different conditions.

The mechanistic conception not only cannot show the movement opposites in their emergence and development, but really inhibits such a method of getting to understand actuality, because from its point of view every process begins its movement from stable equilibrium, when either there are no contradictions or they are reconciled and balanced and therefore cannot be a stimulus to further development. Contradictions appear only at a known stage of the movement of a process, as a result of the action of *external causes;* as a result of the upsetting of equilibrium.

The group of Menshevist idealists, forsaking concrete actuality for the field of pure abstractions – of the self-movement of mere ideas, also came out with a revision of this method. The Deborin group uncritically accepted the Hegelian way of stating the question of the unity of opposites without noticing its idealistic features.

Hegel, in founding his whole philosophic system, proceeded, as we have said earlier, from the self-development of absolute spirit. However, in distinction from other idealists – and in this lies his great service – he took as a "model" for the different forms of absolute spirit the stages in the development of social knowledge, which stages he understood and interpreted in his own way. After schematizing the different forms of thought which he had observed in history, he came to the conclusion that dialectical knowledge (which contains in its own categories, and in their order, in a purely theoretical fashion, the history of knowledge) passes in its understanding of any object through stages of identity, difference, opposition and contradiction. To say nothing of the fact that Hegel wrongly represented "identity" as the first step in knowledge, the organic defect of all his philosophy was this, that he connected his scheme of the development of knowledge, of subjective mind, with the objective world as the law of development of all its subjects. In this the idealist, Hegel, stands out clearly.

Deborin did not notice that Hegel, by making absolute certain characteristic features of our thought, by declaring them to be the movement of absolute spirit, by constructing a formalistic scheme of the movement of categories, was also forcing actuality and its developments into the Procrustean bed of such a scheme.

According to Deborin (following Hegel) the development of the processes of objective actuality proceeds from abstract identity to difference, from difference to oppositeness and thence to internal contradiction. Deborin wrote:

> "When all the necessary steps of development – from simple identity through difference and oppositeness have been traversed, then begins the epoch of the 'resolution of contradictions.'"

In Deborin's opinion and that of his followers, contradiction appears in a process, not at its very beginning, but only at a certain stage of its movement; but this can mean only one thing, namely, that until this stage is reached, the development of the process is *not* by virtue of its inward contradictions. This view-point is not only a revision of dialectic at its central point, but is close to the mechanistic conception of development. Because if the development of any process begins and proceeds up to a given moment not by virtue of its internal division – assuming it be at the beginning still undeveloped – then the process, until this moment, must be due to external causes. But that is also the view of the mechanists. Deborin, by accepting Hegel's scheme, which identifies the development of knowledge with the development of matter, has, in his understanding of the basic -law of dialectic, lapsed into mechanism, against which he had waged such a desperate conflict. The only logical dialectic can be materialistic dialectic.

By applying this view on the development of contradiction to the analysis of the concrete question of the relations between the proletariat and the peasantry in the conditions of the U.S.S.R., Deborin and Luppol came to the conclusion that they are not contradictory relations but only relations of difference, Le, they came to a right-opportunist watering down of the contradiction between the two classes. Karev, proceeding from the same point of view, declared that in the Third Estate of pre-revolutionary France, there were no internal contradictions but only differences, i.e. the relations of the proletariat and the bourgeoisie were not contradictory. In actuality the interests of the proletariat and the bourgeoisie were contradictory from the very moment of the emergence of these antagonistic classes.

It is quite true that contradictions move, become intensified, go through a. number of stages in their development, forming at each one of them new qualitative properties. It is also true, that the knowledge of the contradictions of this or that process emerges most fully and visibly at the highest developed stage of the process. The proletariat, we know, becomes as a whole ever more and more conscious of the irreconcilability of its interests with those of the bourgeoisie, according as the capitalist contradictions intensify. But from these true positions it is impossible to conclude, as does Deborin, that contradictions appear only at a given stage of the development of a process. No, they belong to it from the very beginning.

Deborin's view blunts our apprehension of the contradictions of the initial stages in the development of processes, leads to a watering down of them and in this way is a perversion of dialectic, *it pursues the Menshevist line.*

The development of a process at all its stages is the movement of its contradictions.

CHAPTER V

THE RELATIVITY OF THE UNITY OF OPPOSITES AND THE ABSOLUTENESS OF THEIR CONFLICT

In the foreword to the first volume of *Capital* Marx wrote:

> "In its rational form dialectic is a scandal and an abomination to the bourgeoisie and its doctrinaire spokesmen, because, while supplying a positive understanding of the existing state of things, it at the same time furnishes an understanding of the negation of that state of things, and enables us to recognize that that state of things will inevitably break up; it is an abomination to them because it regards every historically developed social form as in fluid movement, as transient; because it lets nothing overawe it, but is in its very nature critical and revolutionary."

Dialectic "in its rational form," materialistic dialectic, is a scandal and an abomination to the bourgeoisie because, as opposed to metaphysical views which stress the immutability of existing forms or their slow uninterrupted "evolutionary" change, it demonstrates the revolutionary change of forms, the self-negation of everything existent, in virtue of the development of internal contradictions.

But whoever reduced Marx's thought, or the Marx-Leninist doctrine of development in general, to the statement "all flows, all changes," would distort the actual essence of the doctrine and would open the door to mechanism, relativism, teleology, and modern neo-Hegelianism. Indeed the mechanists also, as we know, are ready to admit that "all flows, all changes." But "flows and changes" in their understanding is only a quantitative process, the actual elements remaining unchanged. And the relativist not only admits that "all changes, all flows," but makes such change absolute, including within it our own knowledge. Thus every kind of stability in objective phenomena is swept away, becoming but a subjective appearance. Our knowledge is held to be limited and distorted in its very nature so that it does not even reflect truly the creative flow of reality.

The teleologically inclined bourgeois thinker also admits that "all flows, all changes." But he goes on to affirm that this flow, this change, is nothing else than the path to the realization of ever more perfect forms, the tendency towards which is deeply seated in life itself, that movement is determined by those ideal forms in which the imminent purposes of life reside.

There are other eclectic points of view, as, for instance, the theory that history shows an alternation of stable and revolutionary epochs, the first characterized by definiteness, stability and self-identity of the processes found in it, the second by indefiniteness, movement and change. Where there is definiteness there is no change; where there is movement, there is no definiteness – that is the essence of this eclectic wisdom!

Only a conception of development as a conflict of internal contradictions at all stages of development, gives a profound and adequate understanding of actuality and arms us against mechanism, relativism, eclecticism and other bourgeois revisionist "isms." This conception alone shows the unity of the aspects of a process and their relative identity not as an external form, not as a stage in a process, not as a basic characteristic of a process, but as a *form* of internal contradiction, of conflict of internal opposites. This form expresses the type of contradiction and is determined by it (the contradiction), emerges on its basis, develops and decays. There is no internal contradiction without a unity of conflicting aspects within,, without a general basis of conflict which expresses itself in the relative identity of opposites. But unity and identity, which are the necessary form of the movement of the contradiction, are at the same time conditioned by it as by the actual content of the development. Therefore, to regard unity, the identity of opposites, as a "reconciliation of opposites" is a direct perversion of Marxism. Yet we find this view expressed in almost identical terms by the mechanists, the reformist socialists and the Menshevist idealists.

Materialistic dialectic has nothing in common with the point of view of "reconciliation of opposites" which subordinates the conflict of opposites to a process of inevitable and pre-determined reconciliation. Materialistic dialectic which is "in essence critical and revolutionary" (Marx) understands the *resolution* of contradictions to be the replacement of one type of contradiction by another. This resolution, in which "opposites become identified" (Lenin), expresses not the "reconciliation" but the resolution of their contradiction in a new contradiction, a new type of internal conflict.

This thought was also expressed by Lenin in his celebrated proposition on the relativity of the unity of opposites and the absoluteness of their conflict, which was neglected and not understood by the Menshevist idealists. Lenin wrote:

> "The unity (the coincidence, identity, resultant force) of opposites is conditional, temporary, transitory, and relative. The struggle of the mutually exclusive opposites is absolute, as movement and evolution are."[1]

For, as we see, the conflict of mutually exclusive opposites leads to a change in the character of that unity, coincidence and mutual penetration in which they are found; this conflict determines the character of the resolution of their contradiction. Conflict makes their internal unity conditional, temporal, transitional. Conflict leads to the final resolution of the given contradictions, to their removal, creates the beginning of a new process. In a class society, every given form of society is temporal and transitory, the change of any given form of a class society and the abolition of classes are accomplished by means of class struggle. On the developing basis of the contradiction of capitalist economy, i.e. the contradiction between the social character of production and individual appropriation, only the conflict of both mutually exclusive opposites would lead to the replacing of the' original form of their unity and mutual penetration (out of which they were developing into something new) 'by another form. The growing intensity of the conflict of these opposites leads to the necessity of their final resolution and liquidation. This conflict creates also all the necessary conditions and possibilities for it.

Out of the thorough understanding of this aspect of dialectic proceeds the policy of our Party. The Party saw in the different forms of the bond between the proletariat and the peasantry, at the various stages of N.E.P., not a form of reconciliation of those opposites, but a form of resolution of the temporal, partial contradictions, characteristic of the given stage, and at the same time, a step forward in the resolution of the basic contradiction of the transitional period – the contradiction between socialism and capitalism. And so the Party did not make eternal the different forms of this bond between peasants and industrial workers (for this would have meant that we were oblivious of the basic contradictions of the transitional period – which was the mistake of the right deviation), nor did it regard the changing of slogans in relation to the peasantry as ma-

---

[1] Lenin, vol. xiii, p. 324.

noeuvres called out by the situation, allowing us to "gain time" until the final resolution of the contradiction in world socialism – which was how the Trotskyists viewed the matter. Stalin in a speech at the Fifteenth Congress said:

> "Our development proceeds, not by a smooth, unbroken movement upwards. No, comrades, we have classes, we have contradictions inside the country, we have a past, a present and a future, and the contradictions between these are still with us. We cannot therefore glide smoothly forward. Our course is one of struggle, of ever developing contradictions and of their subsequent mastery, analysis and liquidation. Never, so long as there are classes, shall we be in the position to say: Well, thank God, now all is well. Never, comrades, shall we have that state of affairs. Always in our experience something is dying out. But whatever it is, it does not like the idea of dying; it struggles to go on existing, it defends its outworn activity. Always something new is being born in our life. But whatever it is, it is not just born, it screams and cries, asserting its right to exist.... The struggle between the old and the new, between what is dying out and what is born – that is the basis of our movement."

Only in bitter class struggle with the capitalist elements, and in their eventual suppression, only in the proletariat's struggle for a socialist recasting of the small-individualist peasant economy (which is the last base upon which capitalism can rebuild itself), only in the struggle for the higher productivity of labour, in the struggle for the inculcation of socialist discipline can classes be abolished.

The policy of the Communist Party proceeds on the understanding that the contradiction between the Soviet Union and its backward technique, a struggle which takes place in the conditions of a *capitalist* environment, can be only temporary, that it will be resolved inevitably either by the Bolsheviks' mastery of technique or by the collapse of Soviet power.

A characteristic feature of our party is that we do not fear difficulties or contradictions, we do not flee from strife, but proceed to a dispassionate analysis of the contradictions of actuality, an exposure of new contradictions, a study of the course of their movement, of the course of preparation of conditions and possibilities for their mastery and solution.

Kaganovich, in a speech celebrating the tenth anniversary of the Institute of Red Professors, said in describing this feature of Bolshevist practice:

> "What exactly does the unity of opposites mean in the ordinary language of our political party? The unity of opposites in actuality means not to be afraid of difficulties. Not to be afraid of those contradictions of life which spring up on our journey, but instead to conquer them with Bolshevist energy and staunchness."

A characteristic feature of our party is its struggle for the victory of a determined tendency of development, for the victory of one of two opposite alternatives; it is a struggle that excludes any haphazard drift.

The understanding of the absolute struggle of opposites and of the relativity of their unity distinguishes Marx-Leninism from the reformist parties. Not one theoretician of social reformism, neither Kautsky nor Plekhanov, could rise to the comprehension of movement by means of the *division of unity,* of the absoluteness of the struggle of opposites and the relativity of their unity; hence their merely formal acknowledgment and lack of comprehension of these principles. The further evolution of these theoreticians, especially Kautsky, consisted of an ever greater revision of this central aspect of materialistic dialectic. It was not a matter of chance that at the end of his life Kautsky completely rejected dialectic and declared that the theory of social movement proceeding by means of contradictions was merely "revolutionary metaphysics."

The whole political theory and tactics of the right wing of the older reformism and of modern reformist socialism are based on theories of this sort and derive from the idea of the reconciliation of opposites. Thus instead of Marx's proposition on the irreconcilability of the conflict of classes, they preach a harmony of interests of the bourgeoisie and the proletariat, a compromise between both classes, they summon the proletariat to assist capitalist rationalization, or to support the national bourgeoisie in its struggle for a market, or to take part in bourgeois governments, etc. Instead of a struggle to overcome the contradictions of capitalism, a struggle for their forcible resolution by means of setting up a proletarian dictatorship and expropriating the bourgeoisie, they try to smooth over, to reconcile these contradictions and by that means to preserve capitalism.

The tactics of the Bolsheviks in relationship to the liberal bourgeoisie in the period of the Zemstvo campaign were expressed in the slogan "To keep separate in order to strike together." This common offensive with the liberal bourgeoisie at a determined stage and in a determined form was a relative, temporary, conditional moment in the tactics of socialism. But the Mensheviks attached to this relative moment an absolute significance and placed it at the base of all their strategy, and finally as a consequence played the part of the left wing of the counterrevolutionary bourgeoisie. In 1917, the Menshevists, Plekhanov in particular, came out as supporters of the bourgeoisie, preaching a harmony of class interests, and demanding the continuance of the imperialist war, and directed all their energy against everything that hindered the strengthening of capitalism and above all against the preparation for a socialist revolution. After October the Mensheviks directly supported the Whites. In the period of the developed advance of socialism on the whole front, when the Mensheviks, overestimating the importance of the capitalist elements within the country, had dreams of a bourgeois "regeneration" of the Soviet power and were finally disappointed, they transferred their activity to a direct hostility to the vital interests of the proletariat of the U.S.S.R. and to sabotage and espionage in the service of the general staffs of the imperialist powers. And all this in the name of establishing a democracy, by which they meant a society whose aim was to harmonize the interests of proletariat and bourgeoisie.

The conception of the unity of opposites as their reconciliation is also characteristic of the positions of the Right. From the Marx-Leninist position of the irreconcilability of the contradictions of the capitalist means of production they have lapsed into a theory of organized capitalism, which asserts that the contradictions within capitalist countries can be removed and transferred to an external arena, to the world market. They have formulated a theory that, all the world over, the kulak peasant economy will gradually turn into socialism. The Leninist theory of the abolition of classes by means of intensified class struggle has been replaced by a theory of the abolition of the class struggle, its peaceful dying out. They explained the intensification of class struggle in the U.S.S.R. by the "blunders of the Bolsheviks with their unwise decrees," and did not realize that the growth and advancement of socialist elements inevitably evoke the opposition of the dying capitalist elements. The Right did not see the contradictions within the peasantry itself, they represented them as a homogeneous social mass. They did not "notice" that our union with the peasantry is a union that takes account of the irreconcilability of the interests of proletariat and bourgeoisie and therefore is directed against the capitalist elements and tendencies within the peasantry.

The Right did not understand that the union of the proletariat with the peasantry is a form of the proletariat's struggle for the recasting of small-scale-commodity economy, for its transfer to -the socialist path of development. They "forgot" about the temporary character of N.E.P., about its ambiguity. The right-opportunist theory, being a theory of reconciliation of opposites, leads to the perpetuation of small-scale commodity production and therefore to the perpetuation of classes. "Bukharin, the theoretician without dialectic, the scholastic theoretician" (Stalin), did not understand the doctrine of the absolute conflict of opposites and the relativity of their unity.

The view-point of reconciliation of opposites constituted the basis for that revision of Marxian dialectic which issued from the group of Menshevist idealists. Not one of its expositors finds room to mention the absoluteness of the conflict of opposites and the relativity of their union, although they ceaselessly comment on the paragraph in Lenin's *On Dialectic* where this aspect of the "division of unity" is formulated with extraordinary accuracy and clearness. In not one of their works is a criticism of the theory of the "reconciliation of opposites" to be found. On the contrary that is the very theory from which they proceed. Thus Deborin holds that dialectical materialism "scientifically reconciles opposites, namely, freedom and necessity, subjectivism and objectivism, but reconciles them dialectically." According to him, in dialectic "subject and object, object and knowledge about the object, obtain a relative reconciliation." Deborin defines dialectic not as a doctrine of the conflict of opposites, but as a "doctrine of the merging together of opposites."

Dialectical materialism grew up in conflict with different forms of bourgeois philosophy, each of which was built upon the exaggeration and over-development of one aspect of human knowledge. But dialectical materialism did not simply cast them from the threshold, but critically worked over everything of value that had been discovered by preceding philosophy, including the rationalism and empiricism of the seventeenth and eighteenth centuries.

Deborin, however, regards this critical treatment of the bourgeois heritage as a reconciliation of opposite philosophic tendencies. He holds that "dialectical materialism reconciles, extreme empiricism with extreme rationalism in a higher synthesis of the two."

The theory of reconciliation of opposites is a *metaphysical* theory. Because it does not lead to the disclosure of the ways of egress from a given situation it perpetuates each given situation. Nor does it direct its attention to the origin of the new, to the creation of the new premises, possibilities, conditions, that will originate new processes on the basis of the contradictions of the given process.

The type and character of the contending opposites, the degree of their development, define also the character of the solution of their contradiction. It is necessary to distinguish the forms of resolution of *temporary*, partial contradictions (which make possible the development of the basic contradictions of a process) from the forms of resolution of the *basic* contradictions of a process as a whole, which lead to the removal of that process. Thus the different forms of the bond between the proletariat and the peasantry in the U.S.S.R. made possible such a development of small-scale commodity production and large-scale socialist industry as prepared the way for a final resolution of the basic contradiction. And the forms of final resolution of those contradictions, which lead to the removal of the given basic contradiction, are all-round collectivization and the conversion of agricultural economy into a branch of socialist industry. The final resolution of contradictions denotes the removal of both opposite aspects. The victory of the proletariat in the socialist revolution denotes that it ceases to be a class in capitalist society and that the elements of the bourgeoisie opposed to it cease to be the class controlling the country's economy. The construction of socialism denotes the victory of the proletariat, one of the basic classes of the transitional period, and leads to the abolition of classes as a whole, including, of course, the proletariat.

The mechanists, who hold that a process develops in virtue of externally directed forces, think that the process goes in the direction of that force which predominates quantitatively. Bogdanov wrote:

> "If this or that process – the movement of a body, the life of an organism, the development of society – is determined by the strife of two opposing forces, then, when

one of these predominates quantitatively, however little, the process goes to its side, is subordinated in its direction. As soon as another force develops and at last equalizes itself with the first, the whole character of the process changes its quality; either it comes to an end, or later (however small be the increase of the second force), it takes on a new direction."

Though this is basically true for mechanics, yet in the higher forms of movement it is impossible to attribute the direction of a process only to the direction of the quantitatively predominating aspect. Thus the capitalist elements at war with feudalism were at first feebler than the feudalistic elements, but the development went ever more and more in the direction of the former; the growth and strengthening of the capitalist elements resulted in the predominance of capitalism over feudalism, and the destruction of feudalist relations only at the end of the process.

The socialist elements in the U.S.S.R., although at the time still very feeble, yet immediately after the October revolution played the leading role in the struggle with the capitalist elements. The growth of socialist elements consolidated their position and led to their victory over the capitalist elements.

The proletariat in the U.S.S.R. takes the leading role in union with the peasantry, which quantitatively exceeds the proletariat many times. The proletariat becomes the grave-digger of capitalism, creates a new direction for the development of productive forces, creates new forms of social relations, not simply because it increases quantitatively within the framework of capitalism, but chiefly because, in the conditions of the ever intensifying contradiction between productive forces and the capitalist relations of production, it welds itself together and organizes itself, and, under the leadership of its political party, resolves by means of revolution the capitalist productive relations and establishes proletarian dictatorship.

The mechanists' view ignores all the concrete conditions of the development of a process, all the qualitative uniqueness of its laws. This leads to drift, to a falling back on natural forces, because, from this point of view, a mere simple quantitative predominance over the weaker aspect is sufficient to ensure a new direction in development. This view fully justifies the reformist theory of a peaceful transition from capitalism to socialism, which is to proceed from the fact of the predominance of the specific gravity of the proletariat in large-scale capitalist countries. It also fully justifies the Trotskyist denial of the possibility of a socialist victory in the U.S.S.R., in virtue of the quantitative weakness of the proletariat and the low level of productive forces in that country.

The character and direction of a process are defined by the character and direction of its basic moving contradictions – by their concrete mutual relations, by their conflict in the determined concrete situation. In the conflict of the mutually exclusive opposites, of the different tendencies of development, of the old with the new (as we saw above in more detail), one of the aspects, one of the tendencies, develops, becomes the leading one, and this defines the character and direction of a process. But this or that aspect or tendency of development becomes a leading one only through conflict. Thus in the conflict between the capitalist and socialist elements in the U.S.S.R., the socialist elements took the lead by virtue of the fact that the proletariat had established its dictatorship, had got possession of large-scale industry, were nationalizing the land, because it had established such mutual relations with the peasantry as guaranteed the support of the latter and thus prepared all the conditions and possibilities for the socialist recasting of the whole trading economy. If the dictatorship had weakened or the clearness of the general line of the party had become confused, if the opportunist elements had conquered, if there had ensued a long period of opposition to the peasantry, then the capitalist elements would have come "on top," would have begun to play the leading role and to annihilate the socialist elements. A less progressive tendency of development can conquer a more progressive. An old, ever more and more obstructive element, can, in fighting with a new, sustain itself for a considerable time, not allow the new to develop, and for a time even destroy it entirely. Capitalism, which hinders the development of productive forces, at the same time maintains its own existence, does not come automatically to a crash. Only the conflict of the proletariat with the bourgeoisie resolves the question of the crash of capitalism. That is why our party carries on a very fierce war against the theory of drift, which weakens the struggle of the proletariat and by this means strengthens its opponents and makes it possible for capitalism to go on maintaining itself.

CHAPTER VI

THEORY OF EQUILIBRIUM

"We have expounded the basic moments of the law of the unity of opposites – the essence of dialectic.

Bukharin does not understand this law. In his book *The Theory of Historic Materialism* he set himself the task of, as it were, transposing Hegel's idealistic mystical teaching on contradiction into a materialistic key. From Bukharin's view-point this must signify the translation of Hegelian dialectic into the language of modern mechanism. True to his position he holds that Hegel and Marx in speaking of movement by means of contradictions, implied in fact a collision of two oppositely directed forces. External forces collide and form a temporary, mobile equilibrium, which is then broken and is again set up on a new basis. Following Hegel, he called the primitive state of equilibrium "thesis," its destruction "antithesis," and the setting up of equilibrium on a new basis ("in which opposites are reconciled") "synthesis." Bukharin expounds his theory thus: Everything consists of a number of elements connected with each other, which form a certain system. Every such "system" is connected with such other systems as compose its environment. Environment and system act mutually. This contradiction of system and environment lies, according to Bukharin, at the basis of all development.

Bukharin does not deny internal contradictions. He admits that in society, for instance, there exists a number of internal contradictions: contradictions between productive forces and the relations of production, contradictions of class, etc. But these internal contradictions, according to Bukharin, are the resultant of the external contradictions of the environment and the system. Thus class struggle within society is determined, according to Bukharin, by the contradiction of society and nature. Bukharin writes:

> "Internal (structural) equilibrium is a magnitude dependent on external equilibrium, is a 'function' of this external equilibrium."

Such is Bukharin's theory of equilibrium which he advances as the only correct, "theoretically systematic exposition and basis" of the Marxian dialectic. All that has been expounded in the foregoing pages makes clear that this theory leaves out of account the determining role of internal contradictions, the indissoluble connection of opposing aspects, their transitions into each other, their identity, and replaces the conflict of opposites by their reconciliation, i.e. it distorts the law of the division of unity and has nothing in common with Marx-Leninism. Bukharin's theory of equilibrium is not new. It enjoys great popularity in bourgeois sociology and economics. The bourgeois philosopher and sociologist, Herbert Spencer, built upon just such a theory a mechanistic theory of evolution. In his opinion, there exist in nature forces directed against each other, between which an equilibrium is eventually established. The direction of movement in a phenomenon is determined by the quantitative predominance of this or that opposing aspect. Thus, for example, tyranny and freedom are, in his opinion, two independent forces, which all the time seek to balance each other, from which it follows that from the quantitative predominance of freedom or tyranny depends the movement of both these antagonists. But Herbert Spencer, in contrast to Bukharin, never called his theory dialectic. Prior to Spencer, Dühring, who directly attacked the dialectic of Marx and Engels, wrote: "Antagonism of forces that oppose each other in an opposite direction is also the basic form of all the actions and manifestations of nature." Engels, in *Anti-Dühring,* strongly criticized this view. The theory of equilibrium was most clearly formulated by Bogdanov, who sought to reconcile idealism and materialism. Long before Bukharin he set himself the task of transferring on to the soil of materialism not only the dialectic of Hegel, but also the dialectic of Marx and Engels which, in his opinion, was not completely emancipated from the idealism from which it originally sprang. The Marxian conception of dialectic, that is to say, of development, suffers, says Bogdanov, in common with the purely Hegelian conception, from lack of clarity and completeness, and for this reason the application of the dialectical method is inaccurate and diffuse. Bogdanov, long before Bukharin, translates dialectic into the "language of mechanics." Just like Spencer and Dühring he holds that movement through contradictions is a conflict between "two oppositely directed activities." But he admits at once that such a conception of the law of contradictory development parts company with the basic propositions of Marxism, and goes on to assert that Marxism by its failure to realize this truth is unable to explain the transition of quantity into quality. Bogdanov defines dialectic as "an organized process that proceeds by way of the conflict of opposing forces." Movement, in his opinion, begins first as an equilibrium which contains no contradictions; then that equilibrium is destroyed by the conflict of two opposing forces and set up anew on a fresh basis. The basic, determining contradiction, he holds to be the external, which is conditioned by the conflict of internal forces and by the preponderance of one of them at a determined stage. In his opinion the basic contradiction is between the environment and the system.

This theory of equilibrium enjoyed great popularity among various groups whose social and economic policies were in opposition to the Bolshevik line.

Bukharin was also led to argue that class contradictions are only the results of the contradiction between society and the natural environment, so that if the equilibrium of society and nature is upset then the conflict of classes is intensified; if society and nature are in stable equilibrium then the class struggle ceases.

Although Bukharin tries to combine this theory with the Marx-Leninist theory of the inevitability of the proletarian revolution in view of the internal contradictions of capitalism, yet it is perfectly clear that Bukharin, by belittling the internal contradictions and not admitting their determined role, cannot prove the inevitability of the collapse of capitalism.

Following Bogdanov he holds that society (including a Soviet economic order) develops when in return for its expended working energy it receives from nature as much or more energy. When this is the case we get equilibrium between society and nature.

The whole economic policy of Soviet society must proceed from the necessity of establishing such an equilibrium and must not allow any chance infringement of it.

Bukharin proceeds to argue that the class struggle and similar contradictions can and should be removed with all speed by establishing an equilibrium between society and nature. This can be done by balancing the different factors in the natural economy.

From this it follows that the point of crucial importance is that part of the economic plan where production has fallen behind. It may be iron, in which case engineering production generally will be held up. It may be bricks, in which case the building plan will be delayed. But these "equilibrium sociologists" deduced from their theory that the way to restore equilibrium was to cut down production and building to the level of the diminished supplies of iron and bricks. In other words we are to avoid the contradiction of the class struggle by slowing down capital construction.

They also hold that we should overcome the contradiction between decaying small-scale individualist agricultural economy and large-scale socialist industry not by bringing the development of agriculture up to the level of industry (which is possible only by its transition to socialist forms of farming), but on the contrary, by lowering the tempo of the development of industry and thus establishing an equilibrium between them. Stalin himself dealt with this theory in his speech to the Agrarian Conference.

"It is supposed," said Stalin, "that we have a socialist and a capitalist sector, side by side. These two compartments are completely isolated from one another. Each can pursue its own course without affecting the other. It is a geometrical fact that parallel lines do not meet, but the authors of this remarkable theory think that at some time or other these parallels will meet, and when they do, we shall have socialism."

Whence also arose the struggle against the Bolshevik tempo of industrial development, against rapid industrialization, and the struggle of some years ago to speed up light industry (at the cost of slowing down our plan for rapid capital development), in order to provide the individual peasants immediately with generous supplies of consumption goods, this same struggle aiming at perpetuating the small peasant economy for many years to come. This, in their opinion, would be the guarantee of a swiftly obtained equilibrium between agricultural economy and industry and of a harmonious development towards socialism without any intensification of class conflict.

Marx-Leninist dialectic does not deny external contradictions – the action of one process on another. On the contrary it proceeds from the idea of an indissoluble connection of all processes of actuality and demands a knowledge of the mutual action of processes, their influence on each other, and their mutual penetration.

But whereas mechanism and its theory of equilibrium regard any phenomenon as the result of the external action of processes on each other, and opposes one to the other as external and independent aspects of one and the same process, dialectic sees in the external only a particular form in which the internal manifests itself.

Therefore, when we speak of the mutual action of the aspect of one process the dialectician will not be deceived by the moment of independence, of "externality," of these aspects but will seek to disclose in them, as the basis of their mutual action, as the actual "source of self-movement" of the process, their unifying internal contradiction. And so the dialectician will not classify the qualitatively different and mutually interacting processes as wholly independent and mutually external "systems" and "environments." Moreover, since dialectic proceeds from the idea of an internal "unity of the world, which is contained in the fact of its being material," dialectic will see in the mutual action of external processes the mutual action of the diverse forms and degrees of matter alone, which matter is developed in these forms and through their mutual action. Therefore, dialectic will regard the external mutual action of processes as a moment of world development and will never forget that the *basic* law underlying all moments is that of the unity and conflict of opposites.

There is of course no development of a process apart from its mutual action with other processes. It is a complete distortion of Leninism to represent the doctrine of self-movement, of spontaneous development, as though certain internal principles, locked up as it were and isolated from relations with the environment, were the determining factors in self-movement and provided all the conditions of development. But the external always plays its separate part not as the basis of development, but as one of its necessary conditions, and therefore its influence on a process may be understood only on the basis of a knowledge of those internal contradictions which fundamentally determine the course of development.

Marxist-Leninist dialectic does not deny the contradiction of society and nature, but regards it as not the main, not the determining contradiction of social development. When we study history we see in a number of countries that whereas the geographic, climatic conditions, the vegetable and animal world, the natural riches, remained relatively unchanged, yet the social relations were changed, e.g. feudalism was replaced by capitalism.

In the development of any particular social structure, for instance capitalism, dialectic regards the internal contradiction between capitalist productive forces and the capitalist relations of production as the important and determining factor. The contradiction between society and nature exists of course under capitalism, but the particular form of this contradiction is determined not by the properties of the geographical environment but by the basic laws of the development of capitalism. Society, by virtue of its internal law-governance and its development of productive forces, changes the geographical environment by ways and means specific for each social formation. Especially comprehensive was this changing of geographical environment by social man under capitalism with its machine technique and with its social character of production. There is a shortage of forests – the felling of them and their replanting are regulated. There is not enough coal – they substitute "white coal," i.e. petroleum. There is not enough leather, wool, silk – they make leather, wool and silk artificially. If there is not enough moisture from the atmosphere, they irrigate. The animal and vegetable world is being refashioned, for they are creating new breeds of animals, new types of plants.

If in capitalist society the total amount of change in nature is, in spite of this, extremely limited, then once again this is explained not by the contradiction between society and nature but by capitalist productive relations, which do not permit the fullest possible development of productive forces. Only socialism guarantees such a possibility. The determining role of the social system in this matter of nature and society is clearly seen in the U.S.S.R. to-day, where the unified economic plan makes use of all the achievements of science and is changing the face of the whole country.

The contradictions between the capitalist and socialist systems do, of course, influence the development of socialist relationships in the U.S.S.R. But socialist society is developing on the basis of internal laws, on the basis of internal contradictions, and not on the basis of the external contradictions between the capitalist world and ourselves. The development of the U.S.S.R. is by no means subordinate to the development of capitalist world economy as Trotsky thinks. Economic and financial blockade, the refusal of credits, the blocking of Soviet exports, the different forms of diplomatic pressure, etc. – all are in some degree reflected in the development of socialism in the U.S.S.R., but the character and degree of the reflection are determined by the internal contradictions in our country. The degree in which the development of socialism is checked by international capitalism depends on the degree of development and relative strength of the socialist and capitalist elements within the country. The weaker the former and the stronger the latter, the lower will be the tempo of industrialization and collectivization of the country, the feebler the onslaught on the capitalist elements, and the feebler our defence of the socialist front-line trenches. The stronger the force of kulakism, of N.E.P. in our country, the wider the net of our enemies. The greater the bureaucratism, the stronger the influence of opportunism in our ranks – so much the more vulnerable are we. In fact the *degree* in which our movement can be hampered by international capitalism depends in the last resort upon ourselves, upon the internal conditions of the country, and it would be completely untrue to attribute the rate of transition or the forms of transition to the varying influences of the capitalist world upon the Soviet Union.

A clear proof of this proposition and one which upsets all the assertions of the Trotskyists, is to be found in the fact that the world crisis of capitalism has not fundamentally affected the U.S.S.R. This crisis undoubtedly brought with it a number of complementary difficulties for our task of construction (the worsening conditions of credit, the fall of prices for our export, etc.), but it has had no decisive significance for the construction of socialism.

We are constructing socialism on the basis of the internal force of the country; our development towards socialism and the stages through which we pass are determined by the internal laws of social change. Nay more, the very change in the methods of the attack upon us by imperialism can be understood fundamentally only through a knowledge of our internal development.

Even the issue of the desperate attempts of capitalism to destroy the Soviet Union is determined, in significant and ever greater degree, by the measure of our development and by the strength of the Soviet Union – because international capitalism is riven by internal contradictions, and the growth of socialism in the Soviet Union and the significant development of the forces of world proletarian revolution intensify these contradictions.

The full victory of socialism in our country has a decisive importance also for the final victory of socialism.

And so we see that external contradictions certainly influence the development of a process; that such contradictions, however, are only overcome by the internal self-development of that process itself.

The theory of equilibrium ignores the specific properties, the qualitative peculiarity, of the process and its aspects. It replaces qualitative analysis with a purely mechanistic view and mechanistically derives one phenomenon from another.

The theory of equilibrium, by ignoring the concrete content of a process and the necessity of disclosing its "source of self-movement," by belittling the latter or seeking to find the source of movement outside the given process, leads, on the one hand, to an abstract rationalistic approach to questions altogether too general to be of use, and on the other hand, to an empty schematism or to plain empiricism, which fails to penetrate to the heart of things. This ambiguity is characteristic also of our "Rights." Thus on the one hand they approach the questions of Soviet economy abstractly, they do not analyse the concrete conditions, phases and stages of its development, they cannot understand how the conditions and possibilities of a new phenomenon are created, they do not notice that a new stage of development sets questions in a new way, resolves its contradictions in a new way. On the other hand, by proceeding from the theory of establishing equilibrium, by levelling down to the weak spots in national economy, they arrive at a narrow practicality, aiming at quickly establishing some sort of balance between socialist industry and peasant production, a balance which they would attain by encouraging kulakism and restoring capitalism.

The theory of equilibrium proceeds from the view-point of the reconciliation of opposites. For the upholders of this theory the state of equilibrium is the phase when opposites are reconciled. The upholders of this theory perpetuate the unity of opposites in their old form. They hold that unity cannot be removed by internal forces, it is to be removed only by external action. For them the Leninist proposition of the absoluteness of the conflict of opposites is a door with seven seals!

The theory of equilibrium, which so greatly exaggerates the relative independence of processes and their aspects, which slurs over the internal contradiction of a process, which preaches the reconciliation of opposites, is the theoretical basis of right-opportunism and of many hostile groups and therefore in its class essence is the theory of the restoration of capitalism.

The Deborin group with their tardy criticism of the theory of equilibrium were quite unable to refute it. Apart from the fact that their criticism was too general and abstract, they did not even criticize the theory of equilibrium for its main defects; firstly for its failure to acknowledge the fact that a process is from beginning to end developed by way of contradictions, and secondly for its reconciliation of opposites. They could not finally refute the theory of equilibrium because their own understanding of the law of unity of opposites is almost identical with that theory. Like the mechanists they hold that contradiction is not part of a process at the moment of its emergence, but only at a certain stage of its development. Whence follows the conclusion, which they themselves are afraid to draw, that up till this moment a process develops as the result of external forces. Like the supporters of the theory which we have been discussing, they share the reformist view of reconciliation of opposites.

SECTION III

THE LAW OF THE TRANSITION OF QUANTITY INTO QUALITY

CHAPTER I

FROM NAIVE DIALECTIC TO THE METAPHYSIC OF PROPERTIES

Primitive man did not construct scientific theories. His knowledge was built up from a variety of concrete observations and by practical rules of living which grew out of these observations. These rules were connected together by a system of mythological representations replete with images but lacking precise and logical sequence. The connection of natural phenomena with his own primitive practice was explained by myths and legends in which thunderstorms, the rain, the sun and so forth were identified with the actions of mysterious beings. Only at a certain point in social development does knowledge become scientific and man rise to the construction of a logical, connected picture of the objective world. For this transition there was necessary a definite level of development of the productive forces at which a separation of mental work from physical was possible. From that time science has (•merged as a special aspect of social action, from that time man began to theorize and to build up a picture of the objective world in logically connected ideas.

And the first thing that confronted science was the mutual action of the infinite multitude of phenomena, their ceaseless interweaving and change, their ceaseless emergence and disappearance. Knowledge, before it turns to the study of concrete details, accepts reality as a sequence of changes and interactions. In spite of the entire naivety and superficiality of this initial view the first steps of science were at the same time the first steps of conscious dialectic. "All flows, nothing is at rest nor ever remains the same" – thus one of the greatest dialecticians in history, the ancient Greek philosopher Heraclitus, used to characterize the ever-changing face of nature. As the Greeks used to say of him, "He likens things to a flowing river and says that it is impossible to enter twice into the same stream."

In these, the first steps of knowledge, freed from direct connection with myth and religion, we find the primitive beginnings of materialistic dialectic. Lenin in his philosophical notes cites a very characteristic excerpt from Heraclitus:

"This order of things, the same for all, was not made by any god or any man, but was and is and will be for ever, a living fire, kindled by measure and quenched by measure."

Lenin, when he worked put the basic law of dialectic made direct use of the figurative expressions and clear formulations of Heraclitus.

Heraclitus was the most characteristic but not the sole representative of that period of knowledge, fresh in its primitive naivety, when the world, not yet analysed on scientific lines, was being apprehended in its general flow and change. "All the ancient Greek philosophers were born dialecticians" (Engels). However, the general picture of development which they gave in their theories suffered from a fundamental defect. Their familiarity with particulars, with separate phenomena, was very slight and inaccurate. They paid "more attention to movement in general, to transitions and series, than to the particular thing that moves, is in transition and in series" (Engels).

These philosophers variously attributed the origin of things to fire, to water or to air; they did not show in any particular case *how* matter changed its form, but spoke of these changes only in order to characterize the whole world as in an eternal process of change. In confirmation of their general theories they brought forward from time to time most illuminating examples. But they were never more than examples and did not reflect a deep systematic study of objects but only approximate and superficial representations, referring to that which is immediately visible to the eyes. Heraclitus said, for instance, that "the parts of the creation are divided into two halves, each one opposed to the other; the earth into mountains and plains, water into fresh and salt water... similarly, the atmosphere (climate) into winter and summer and also into spring and autumn...." How far removed is this poetic and superficial "concretization" of dialectic from the results of modern physics, chemistry and geology! It is obvious that the Greeks by confining themselves to a merely superficial knowledge of phenomena could have no notion of their fundamental laws of development.

However, all these positive and negative aspects of the first stage of scientific knowledge fully corresponded to that social practice on the basis of which Greek science was developing.

Indeed as slave-owners they were little interested in the development of the technique of production, material labour being the despised lot of slaves. As organizers of political power, navigators, colonizers, merchants – the Greeks did not need a detailed study of individual things. And as consumers they could confine their attention to outward appearance. The need for a profound analysis of the essential nature of things, which does arise for the craftsman, did not confront the enterprising merchant. And the political action of the Greeks amounted to a struggle between different groups of free peoples, and had no bearing on the slave-owning basis of the economic order. At the same time both for their political action and their great colonizing ventures, they needed a comprehensive and connected world-outlook in which the general outlines of an ever-changing and diverse universe might be reflected. This world-outlook was supplied by the Greek philosophy of that period. But the further development of production and of class struggle ever more and more revealed the deficiencies of such an outlook; the study of individual things became an ever more pressing problem. Within Greek philosophy itself there began the transition to the *investigatory* stage of knowledge – to the stage that dissects a whole into its parts, that discriminates individual things from their universal connections – to the stage that is, in essence, *analytic.*

Very often it is possible accurately to grasp a situation as a whole in a first rapid impression. Foreign workers arriving in the U.S.S.R., even in a first cursory inspection, can apprehend the general character of socialist construction. It may even be that in certain directions they can form a better estimate than we ourselves as to how far we have travelled from capitalism. However, to obtain a real and fruitful understanding of the working of our institutions the foreigner must penetrate into the details, must understand the special task of each separate institution and learn the special difficulties of each part of our socialist construction.

A correct grasp of the whole serves as a guiding principle in the examination of the details. The first synthetic stage of knowledge prepares one for the study of the parts, gives a general orientation for a further analytical investigation. Every good manager knows that for the direction of this or other undertaking there must be a clear general understanding of the situation. But if he does not go beyond that, does not learn the technique of the business by entering into its every detail, he is but another "tinkling cymbal."

That is just how the matter stands in all practical affairs and in all questions of knowledge. We must never rest content with achieved results, nor stagnate on what is but too familiar, nor turn what are but separate stages into a whole system; we, must press forward and strive for an ever deeper penetration into actuality and thereby be in a position to change it more rapidly and completely.

At the stage of knowledge we are discussing this deepening process was obtained chiefly by separating individual things from their general connection and by studying the peculiarities of each. For this there is necessary an accumulation of a great quantity of experimental data and observations concerning physical phenomena. There is necessary an inventory of animals, plants and minerals and then their classification – i.e. a comparison and division of phenomena into classes and a description of their properties. This task was first attempted in the later or Alexandrian period of Greek science, it was continued in the Middle Ages and considerably developed in the Renaissance.

The basic problem of knowledge in this phase consisted in diverting the attention from general connection and change in order to consider everything as isolated and at rest and thus to establish its specific, unalterable properties which distinguish it from other things, i.e. to study its *quality*. But what one says about an isolated and immobile thing amounts to a description of its different aspects and properties. The qualitative uniqueness of a thing is given in a comprehensive account of its properties. The thing as something that possesses determined properties – that is what the "object" comes to be in this period of science.

Certain groups of properties are found in a number of different things and characterize them each and all in a fundamental way. The same things differ in other, less essential properties. On the basis of these more general properties a system of classification is created and this in turn assists us in our analysis of the characteristics of individual things.

Let us take for example one of the most important branches of knowledge in the Middle Ages – alchemy (mediaeval chemistry). The alchemists turned their attention to the three basic properties (as they thought) of bodies: metallic glitter, combustibility and durability. Every substance possesses, in greater or less degree, these properties, therefore they characterized each substance by the determined degree of these properties. In their ignorance of how to disclose the laws according to which things change, the alchemists regarded these properties as independent elements out of whose combination the different bodies were formed. The pure embodiment of metallic glitter, they said, was mercury, of combustibility was sulphur, of chemical durability was salt.

Each *property* thus became an independent quality, a thing in itself, a substance, a force. The alchemists also considered that change itself was a kind of force and due to a special agent which they called the philosopher's stone, the stone of the wise men. For many centuries the exertions of the alchemists were directed to the search for this philosopher's stone, which, incidentally, was to be the means of turning base metal into gold.

The alchemists were unsuccessful, yet their failures were extremely fruitful for the development of science. In their researches an enormous mass of experimental material was obtained and also an exact knowledge of the real properties of many different chemical compounds. But the further the accumulation of such practical material went, the more clearly were the limitations of this stage of science revealed. In every department of nature investigation kept revealing more and more new properties, and every one of them was regarded as a thing in itself, a special aptitude or faculty. With such a method there was no difficulty in "explaining" any phenomenon – smoke flies upward, because it possesses the tendency to fly upward; glass cuts because it possesses a cutting force; opium sends to sleep because it possesses a soporific force; a tree has an aptitude for growing, etc., etc.... Genuine thought was submerged in an immense number of mysterious forces, properties, aptitudes and substances, of which things were supposed to consist and these explained – exactly nothing! The "explanation" simply repeated that which had to be explained, with the mere futile addition of such words as "force," "substance," or what not.

The science of the feudal period "inflated" this method of considering phenomena and their properties into a complete world-outlook, and thus created a thoroughly logical and ossified system of physics (anti-dialectic). The whole world, so thought the mediaeval metaphysicians, consists of a great number of absolutely independent forces and substances. Nothing new emerges and there is no development, since all changes amount to a simple external uniting and disuniting of unchangeable, independent forces. Change itself was to them an independent substance and was understood now in the likeness of a spiritual force, a god or a devil, now in the likeness of the philosopher's stone, etc. In contradistinction to dialectic, which regards the world as a system of flowing processes, connected internally together by the general course of development, mediaeval science saw only a mechanistic accumulation of independent unalterable things. While dialectic discloses the contradictory character of every phenomenon, of every process, mediaeval science based its thinking on the principle of empty formal identity – combustibility is a hot substance, metallic glitter is metallic glitter, i.e. mercury, etc. Every property in itself is identical, non-contradictory and unalterable, just like a solid substance. It is not surprising that this age is renowned for its elaborate and profitless scholasticism, its logic chopping and endless deductions and the chaos of words that resulted.

The metaphysical limitations of mediaeval science were wholly the result of the limitations of feudal social practice. The parcelling-out and separateness of the feudal estates and towns, the low level of the technique of agriculture and of trade, the ossification of all social relations – that was the material basis that converted the characteristic features of one of the stages of social knowledge into a finished metaphysical *system*. It is true the mediaeval trader (and in part also the feudal landowner) was more interested than the Greek slave-owner in the development of material production, but with the stagnant character of production the problems of technique were not those of creating new things but of combining and recombining the things they had and improving their traditional skill in handling materials provided practically ready-made by nature.

The class interests of the feudalists and masters of workshops, who were seeking in their world-outlook to perpetuate feudal limitations, turned this method into an ossified system.

But on the soil of feudalism and, at first, by feudal methods, there was already being prepared and developed the capitalist means of production. The development of merchant capital broke up the solidity of the feudal order and drove the alchemists on in the pursuit after gold. In these attempts – often fraudulent – was expressed the powerlessness of feudal culture to resolve the real productive problems that confronted men at the end of the Middle Ages.

However, it is not only under the conditions of feudalism that we meet with this curious metaphysical practice of creating "substances" and forces to explain phenomena.

This metaphysic of properties has shown a special liveliness in bourgeois thought. It has found one characteristic expression in the so-called theory of factors.

To the question why France in Napoleon's time carried on wars of conquest, the upholder of the theory of factors will answer that in France at that time such a factor as the idea of glory and conquest had begun to dominate, an idea which Napoleon was active in disseminating. Again, why in capitalist countries is there a "surplus" of population which cannot find employment? Because the workers are multiplying too quickly, owing to the biological "factor" of the growth of the population. Why have innumerable wars broken out between the Turks and Bulgarians? Because the factor of national antagonism was at work.

Of course in the stout volumes of learned investigators the matter looks much more complicated than as given in these examples. But if from the mass of material and pedantic exposition we pick out the essential method of stating and solving these problems we shall see that it amounts to nothing else than the "soporific force of opium" and the "cutting force of glass."

More or less successful attempts to get beyond the theory of factors have been made from time to time by bourgeois science but they have never completely succeeded. Latterly, in the epoch of the downfall of capitalism, we see a certain revival of the metaphysics of isolated properties both in social sciences and along the whole line of bourgeois ideology.

And it is perfectly clear why. When classes and parties oppose a radical change of social relations and to this end seek after a system of fixed social relations, simple, permanent and ready-made, their ideological weapon is the metaphysic of independent properties.

The ideology of reformism, that strong support of modern capitalism, gives not a few clear examples of the utter degradation of bourgeois thought, of its return to the methods of the Middle Ages.

Kautsky, for instance, asserts that in the epoch of imperialism there is at work in industrial capitalist countries a "tendency" for conquest. So as to avoid war this tendency must be opposed by such a factor as a "tendency" to peace, a propaganda for peaceful organization of the economic order.

Take away from iron its properties of combustibility, add in the right proportion metallic glitter and chemical durability and you will get gold, said the mediaeval alchemists. Karl Kautsky in the same manner proposes to "combine" the positive properties of the epoch of imperialism (concentration of production) with a positive property of the pre-imperialist epoch (peaceful economic policy). He compounds a mischievous and empty Utopia, in which this metaphysic of independent forces can only distract the working masses from a real understanding of the nature of the capitalism that oppresses them.

Lenin, criticizing the petty-bourgeois dreams of the liberals about the eternal preservations of small-scale production, wrote:

"And indeed, how simple it is. All you have to do is to take the good things from wherever you can find them – and there you are. From mediaeval society 'take' the means of production as the property of the workers, from the new (i.e. capitalist) form of society 'take' one good thing from here and another from there. This philosopher (Mikhailovsky) looks on social relations purely metaphysically, as on a simple, mechanical aggregate of these or those institutions, a simple mechanical linking up of these or those phenomena. He selects one of these phenomena – the ownership of the land by the land-holder in mediaeval society – and thinks that he can transplant it just as he finds it into our quite different form of society like transferring a brick from one building to another."

But when the peasant does not own his land you have as an essential element in the social structure the exploiting landlord. Every special feature of a given form of society is inseparably connected with the whole of which it is a part. These eclectic sociologists never see the intimate connection of social phenomena.

We find the same metaphysic of independent properties in many pages of the history of Trotskyism. Trotsky was always coming out with daring plans for combining various desirable things. At the time of the trade-union discussions he proposed to transfer the military method of handling men, which played a great part in warfare, to the work of the unions in industry.[1] By keeping politics and economics apart Trotsky again and again shows that he is under the influence of this same methodological error and is thinking in terms of separate "factors." In Russia, says Trotsky, the political factor is strong enough for the construction of socialism but the economic factor is not, therefore the construction of socialism in Russia is impossible.

In all the examples we have given, we see the same features as were analysed above:

(1) A superficial view that is content with a statement of separate properties as they stare one in the face.

(2) A way of regarding properties as if they were separated from each other.

(3) An immutability, an identity of the properties in different things, which things are considered as different external combinations of those properties.

The basic formal-logical principle of the metaphysics of independent properties is that a property is absolutely identical with itself.

---

[1] *Militarization of Labour.* At the end of the civil war Trotsky urged that the armies instead of being demobilized should occupy the industrial front. He therefore advocated compulsory labour service, making use of the apparatus of the War Department, and demanding from the workers the same discipline and executive thoroughness which had been required in the army. He felt that this form of organization was necessary if a single economic plan were to be attempted and without such a plan socialism would certainly prove impossible. The leaders of the Third Army instead of demobilizing their men transferred them to labour work and a good deal of clearing up and reconstruction was carried through. It was soon made clear, however, that flesh and blood could not stand the indefinite continuance of the unwearying effort possible in war time. The policy was abandoned and Russia adopted the New Economic Policy.

CHAPTER II

FROM THE METAPHYSIC OF PROPERTIES TO THE METAPHYSIC OF RELATIONS

The question whether this or that property belongs to a thing is not at all as simple as appears at the first glance. For most people iron is the type of a hard substance, but the polisher of precious stones says contemptuously of a bad material, "soft as iron." Compared with wood, iron is hard, compared with a diamond it is soft.

There is no absolute hardness or absolute softness in itself. The hardness of a thing appears in *relation* to other things; and according to the things to which it is related are its properties thus or otherwise. A workman may for many years be regarded as ungifted, good for nothing, but if you set him to a job that suits him he may display great gifts in relation to it. Rain may be a blessing or a curse; it depends on the situation. The deserts that surround the valley of the Nile were at an early stage a help to the development of the productive forces of Egypt, since they acted as a protection from the onslaughts of wild nomads. But at a much later stage, when Egypt was ripe for trade-relations with other lands, these same deserts became an obstacle to further economic growth.

All properties exist only in determined relations, all properties are relative – such is the conclusion to which we are led by our knowledge of mutual action.

The mediaeval alchemists studied separated properties selected at will from the general mutual action of things and therefore these properties could appear as something absolute and immutable. But once the circle of observations was widened and people began to compare a great number of properties, studying their changes as well as the changing of things themselves, science had to reject alchemistic metaphysics.

And then appeared a new question which the alchemist never foresaw: *to which of the two (or many) mutually acting things does this or that property belong?* The mediaeval scholars never doubted that glass possesses a peculiar cutting or wounding force. The English scientist, Boyle – representative of the new epoch – ridiculed this view and showed that the point of the matter does not lie in the glass but in the mutual relationship of glass with the determined properties of that which it cuts. He proved that sudorific, soporific and other medicines do not in any way possess corresponding absolute forces or qualities but that their action must be explained by their mutual action with the organism. However, it is easy to cite mutual action. It is far more difficult to determine what part *each side* plays in mutual action and wherein lies the basic cause of the fact that this particular mutual action leads to that determined result.

All relations are two-sided. If A is related to B, then B, too, is related to A. Deserts at different periods influenced in different ways the development of Egypt. But wherein lies the root of this influence – in the different geographical properties of deserts or in the change of the properties of Egyptian economics?

Things that come into relation mutually display their properties one through the other, as if they are reflected in each other. The properties of the desert were reflected differently in the different stages of Egyptian history and conversely the properties of the stages of Egypt's development were reflected in the different influence of the desert. Each side is defined through its relation to the other, each side has only a relative definiteness. To the discovery of this mutual or reflex relationship Marx and Engels, following Hegel, attributed a very great importance.

> "Such relative definitions," wrote Marx, "are, in general, something quite singular. For example, this man is a king only because other people are related to him as subjects. They however think, on the contrary, that they are subjects because he is king."

Everyone who has looked at the first chapters of *Capital* knows that Marx in his exposition of all the basic questions of the theory of value proceeds from the reflex relations of exchanged commodities, of commodities and money, and of commodity-producers between each other. Marx showed up the commodity-fetish and proved that "the property" of possessing value, which is ascribed to an article as a thing, is, in fact, the expression of a definite social relation.

The discovery of the relativity of properties was the first step of bourgeois science at the beginning of the New Age, and it must be said a very significant step. The researches of Galileo, of Descartes, Boyle and other natural scientists and philosophers dispersed like smoke the doctrine of mysterious forces and qualities held by mediaeval physico-chemical science. The "soporific force" of opium became an object of universal jest, and Moliere, in his brilliant comedies, brought its upholders on to the stage in the roles of clowns.

However, to point to the relativity of properties does not in itself explain very much. It sends us from one thing to another and from that back to the first, from geography to economics and from economics back to geography, and gives no single and complete explanation of any phenomenon or any process. It is impossible to exhaust the study of properties by the discovery of their relativity. A positive working-out of the question is needed. And bourgeois science tried to give such a positive doctrine in the theory of the so-called primary and secondary qualities.

First of all the founders of this theory selected a number. of properties of things (colour, taste, smell, sound) which we receive directly as sensations, and explained them as existing only in relation to our sense organs, as subjective.

Those are the so-styled secondary qualities. The rest – the so-styled primary qualities – were considered by them as belonging to the things themselves, as existing in objective actuality. Secondary properties appear as the relations of primary properties to our perception.

Does a tickling "force" really exist in a tickling hand? – Galileo used to ask. The hand touches our body, and this contact evokes in us a peculiar sensation, which is not at all like the hand or its movement. The movement of the hand, its making of contact, its motion along our body is a primary objective quality, the sensation of tickling is secondary, subjective.

Warmth is not a peculiar quality but a movement of particles in space, their simple motion, which is reflected in our consciousness as a secondary quality, as the sensation of warmth.

Primary qualities are quite few. They are "the spatial form and position of bodies, movement, the contact of bodies and therefore solidity. All other differences of phenomena, colour, sound, scent, taste, relate to secondary qualities. These properties are subjective and in no measure reflect processes that are found in objective actuality.

Everything in nature is made up of non-qualitative, colourless, soundless matter and every difference between phenomena may be ascribed to the mechanics of identical particles of matter and to their combinations and movements in space.

In their conflict with the metaphysics of properties the most progressive tendencies of bourgeois science in the seventeenth and eighteenth centuries took up the position of mechanistic materialism. In comparison with the mediaeval world-outlook this was a big step forward. Instead of occupying itself with a piling up of mysterious forces and isolated, utterly inexplicable properties knowledge turned to the study of movement (although in its simple form, namely the study of mechanistic movement). Instead of "explaining" the lifting of water in a pump by saying that "nature abhors a vacuum," they began to investigate the real mechanical processes of the movements of liquids, and as a result Torricelli discovered atmospheric pressure. They ceased to attribute to an organism vegetable, motive, nutrimental and all sorts of other forces and aptitudes but directed their attention to the study of mechanical movements in the life-activity of an organism even though these were, at first, only the most elementary motions in the body, and again as a result Harvey discovered the circulation of the blood.

The new point of view proved very fruitful and was the basis of a large number of valuable discoveries. Rene Descartes, one of the founders of mechanistic philosophy and the greatest of French philosophers of the seventeenth century, was right when he wrote about his methodological principles:

> "by them I perceived it to be possible to arrive at knowledge highly useful in life; and in room of the speculative philosophy usually taught in the schools, to discover a practical, by means of which, knowing the force and action of fire, water, air, the stars, the heavens, and all the other bodies that surround us, as distinctly as we know the various crafts of our artisans, we might also apply them in the same way to all the uses to which they are adapted, and thus render ourselves the lords and possessors of nature."[1]

In these words of Descartes, besides his deliberate and severe contrasting of the method of "practical philosophy" with the "speculative and scholastic philosophy" of the Middle Ages, there is reflected also the connection of the new forms of thinking with modern productive practice of the industrial type (although Descartes was doubtless unaware of this connection). The fruitfulness of

---

[1] Descartes, *Discourse on Method*, p. 49 (Everyman).

mechanistic natural science came from its close connection with this productive practice.

The industrial production of that time was pre-eminently the direct action of the workman's tool. People were interested not in the *changes* of the substance, but in those mechanical devices by which change was evoked. All the "machines" of that period were basically simple combinations of the same lever, block, windlass, inclined plane and screw which had been known from ancient times. And so the natural science of that period was preoccupied with the investigation of the movement of bodies (and of systems of bodies) under the influence of forces applied to them, with the conditions of the equilibrium of bodies, the movement of liquids, etc.

Chemical properties of matter were "explained" mechanically, vital phenomena were "explained" by analogy with the actions of mechanical automata. For instance, the following explanation of the difference in the tastes of nitre and nitric acid (which was then called "spirit of nitre") appeared "clear and evident" to Spinoza:

> "Particles of nitre, if laid on the tongue, he on it in consequence of their quiet condition with their fiat sides down and by this means the pores of the tongue are closed – which is the cause of the sensation of cold. But if these particles are lain on the tongue in a state of excitation and movement [Spinoza here has iii mind "spirit of nitre," which, in his opinion, is made up of the same particles as nitre but is found "in a state of excitation and movement"] then they will fall on it with their sharp edges, will pierce into its pores – -just as a needle if it falls on the tongue will evoke different sensations, this difference depending on whether the contact is made with the sharp or the long surface."

The passion for automatic explanations at the ruling courts of the seventeenth century was a similar reflection of the view, general in "enlightened" circles, that the properties of every whole, including living organisms, must find their explanation in the mechanical relations of its parts.

The roots of bourgeois thought in this age are to be found in the mechanical connections which underlay the manufacturing and productive processes and appeared to be fundamental. Thus mechanism became the model for all knowledge and in the philosophy of the time we have the "reproduction in thought" of the objective connections of things.

Whence the relative historic value of the mechanistic method but also its one-sidedness and its limitations. Valuable though the mechanical discoveries of Galileo, Torricelli and others were, yet their tendency to ascribe all the diverse phenomena of nature and society to mechanical relations prevented them from giving a correct solution of the problem of properties.

This new one-sidedness became a universal principle and so, inevitably, a new form of metaphysical theory. The whole world appeared as divided into two independent parts, the mechanical properties of matter, and the subjective qualities of experience. The mutability and diversity of qualities were regarded by the mechanists as secondary properties, i.e. as subjective appearance, as empty illusion.

The real world, since it exists in itself in its own primary properties, is from their standpoint ever the same and unchangeable. Elements of matter are identical and unchangeable. All their relations are attributed to external combinations in space and to simple mechanical contact.

In the real world there is no development, there is only movement in one and the same circle. There is no self-movement of matter but only a mechanical displacement of it under the influence of external impact. The metaphysic of absolutely unchangeable properties gives place to a metaphysic of absolute, quality-less particles and their mutual relations.

And what about properties? How does mechanism solve this problem?

If all particles of matter are identical, then a difference of things according to properties is possible only as a result of a different relation between the particles. Things are differentiated according to their external form in space, by the different disposition of their particles in relation to each other. Things are differentiated according to the mechanical movement of their particles, i.e. once again according to the external relations between the particles. The primary, actually objective, properties of liquidity and of solidity are determined only by the greater or lesser connectedness of their particles in their relative movements.

All things are distinguished only by their external mechanical construction. Everything consists of elements and their relations, say the mechanists, elements are without qualities, are merely carriers of relations. Relations emerge as the properties of different things. As we see, mechanistic materialism "resolves" the problem extremely simply. After showing that a property is relative it goes on to declare that a property amounts to a relation, and finally attributes all the differences of things to external mechanistic relations.

Secondary qualitatively different properties are also only relations, that is to say they are the relations of quality-less things to our sense organs. Determined movements of particles, taken in relation to our consciousness, give a sensation of warmth; other slighter movements – a sensation of light or a variety of colours. An animal is a machine and only a machine, but the relation of this machine to our perception gives an impression of a living organism, etc., etc.

And so by distinguishing two kinds of relations – firstly the relation of particles of matter among themselves and secondly the relation of their combinations to the organs of sense – mechanists divided all phenomena into primary and secondary qualities. From the point of view of mechanism the task of knowledge consists in this – to expose the fallacious appearance of secondary qualities and to attribute all the phenomena of nature to primary mechanical relations.

The French materialists of the eighteenth century applied the mechanistic method widely and were ever indicating the countless number of causes external to each other that conditioned social development. For example, the introduction of a new law is determined by a multitude of facts amongst which an important role is played by the action of the legislator, and this action depends on his disposition, which in its turn may be decided by the weather, and Paris weather has changed because a simoom was blowing in Africa and so on – endlessly.

We have taken one chain of facts, but in every social process there is an infinite number of them and they all mutually interact. Do you try, using this method, to find out in what direction the social structure of a given country is changing. The French materialists used to argue as to what was the determining factor in the mutual action of geographical environment and social development. They disputed whether the opinions of people were determined by facts, by the social structure, or, conversely, whether social structure depends on human opinions. And what emerged from their discussions was the discovery that one could draw from the mechanistic view-point an endless number of proofs both for and against any resolution of these questions.

The mechanistic doctrine of properties as relations of separate particles leads to an absolute relativism on the basis of which it is impossible to say anything definite on the properties of anything, since these properties are its relations with an infinite number of other things. "A crazy atom"[1] which has flown into the head of a lawgiver can change the course of world history – so said the materialists of the eighteenth century. The atom itself does not possess this "property," the property emerges from the relation of the atom to countless other particles, and who will say beforehand whether this "property" will emerge or not? Mechanists themselves not venturing to do so come to this conclusion – it is impossible to know anything definite about concrete things except the abstract truth that they are subordinate to the general laws of mechanics.

And pure relativism and agnosticism, as we know, are the main support of subjectivism. Mechanistic materialism, because of its metaphysical limitations, leads directly to subjective idealism. And the distance between the two is by no means so very great. The mechanists themselves show this transition to idealism in their own doctrine of the subjectivity of "secondary" qualities. Indeed by the assertion that qualitative differences of things and qualitatively different properties exist only in our consciousness, the mechanists create a gulf between objective actuality and our representation of it.

We must turn away, they say, from the illusory appearance of sensations, we must thrust it away with the help of abstract reasoning – just as we pull back a curtain when we want to know what is hidden behind it – and then only shall we make contact with the actual, objective world of pure mechanics, the world of the soundless, invisible movement of quality-less particles.

The sense data derived from an object – mechanism teaches – by no means *reflect* it, they only *correspond* to it. As a hieroglyph is a sign and bears very little resemblance to the object it denotes, so also our sense data only correspond to a determined object, are only its hieroglyph. We see a red-faced man, we see a pale-faced man. But really each is only a determined combination of quality-less

---

[1] *"Crazy Atom."* The introduction of any factor or element into a situation which leads to an unpredictable result.

particles. But evidently the motion of the particles of the one is somehow distinct from the motion of the particles of the other, and so to each of these people there corresponds a different "hieroglyph" in the likeness of our sensations. The separating of properties into primary and secondary is inevitably connected with the theory of hieroglyphs, with the theory of the symbolic denotation of objective actuality by subjective, deceptive representations.

But can we stop here? Why must we admit that the conception of so-called primary properties, of the movement and the spatial forms of bodies, reflects objective actuality exactly as it really exists? Our knowledge of these properties comes only through sensations. If we regard sense impressions as hieroglyphs, we must acknowledge the conceptions of mechanics not as exact copies, but only as signs of an unknown objective actuality.

Plekhanov, who defended the hieroglyphic theory, following certain bourgeois scientists, came sometimes in the turns and twists of his thinking to the theory that even space and time are hieroglyphs of unknown aspects of an unknown objective world.

So we see the attribution of properties to external relations leads to absolute relativism and subjectivism.

"What is truth?" the sages and prophets of bourgeois individualism ask with haughty scepticism, reflecting the "satisfaction" of the bourgeois soul with what exists at the moment and its dread of everything new and revolutionary. With a sceptical criticism of knowledge and a disbelief in objective truth they seek to defend their bourgeois objective actuality – capitalism – from every authentic revolutionary criticism. In this epoch of the domination of the capitalist forms of society bourgeois philosophy snatches at all the Weak reactionary features of mechanism, at relativism, subjectivism, at abstract metaphysics, and inflates these features into a complete subjective-idealistic world-outlook. Everything is relative, only the unalterable particles of matter that move in space are absolute – so say the mechanists.

Subjective idealism by denying the objective existence of matter itself, even of the ultimate particles of the mechanists, and by denying also the reality of space, drives the relativity of mechanistic materialism to its furthest limits.

The primary mechanistic qualities are objective. The secondary qualities are subjective; they exist only in our consciousness, only as our sensation. That is what mechanism asserts.

Subjective idealism by setting out from this very subjectivity of secondary qualities and reducing primary ones to them, in turn reduces mechanism into pure subjectivism – there exist only our sensations, all things including their so-called primary qualities are sensation-complexes combined together by the mind.

The upholders of mechanism by attributing all properties to external relations are powerless to disclose the real basis of the complex interweaving of mutual-acting things. Subjective idealists, by deepening and further developing the metaphysic of the merely external connectedness of phenomena, turn the vice of mechanism into an idealistic virtue; they assert that phenomena have no objective basis and therefore any complex can have any explanation; there are no right or wrong theories – the choice of this or that explanation depends wholly on the subjective point of view, on "mental convenience." Any explanations are good for those whom they please, and there is no truth outside arbitrary human opinions.

Between mechanistic materialism and subjective idealism there is a big difference. The one admits the existence of matter, the other denies it. The one connects things by real mechanical relations, the other acknowledges, things and connections only as "facts of consciousness." But relativism and false metaphysics make up the general features of both philosophical tendencies.

That is a fact. According to both schools properties do not flow out of the internal nature of things, they amount to external relations; the one and the same metaphysic of elements sundered from each other and of purely external connections leads both these schools (and also others) to absolute relativism, and deflects them from the struggle for a unitary, eternally developing objective truth. A close kinship between mechanism and subjective idealism is undeniable; between the two there exists a deep mutual bond.

The mechanists, by laying claim to absolute objective truth and in the name of that truth proving the deceptiveness of those qualities perceived by the senses, do themselves proceed to extreme subjectivism.

Thus the mechanists have turned the relativity of properties into an "absolute" and in contrast with the metaphysic of feudalism have identified properties with the external relations of quality-less particles to each other (primary qualities) and to our sense organs (secondary qualities). Thus they have opened the way to the blind alley of relativism and subjective-idealistic religiosity.

The further development of social practice, now within the framework of capitalism, set knowledge a new task. It was necessary to overcome the limitations of mechanism so as to open the way to the study of the qualitatively unique forms of movement in nature and society. The development of physics, chemistry, biology and the social sciences demanded a new methodological system. The problems which mechanism set but did not resolve had to be resolved on new lines. In severe pain, science began to bring to birth the dialectic method.

But only in the ideology of the proletariat, only in the works of Marx, Engels and Lenin did knowledge emerge on to the wide road of the conscious and logical working out of dialectical materialism. Only on this new level did the problem of quality and property which had been set but not resolved by the metaphysical systems of the past receive its actual solution.

CHAPTER III

QUALITY AND THE SELF MOVEMENT OF MATTER

By the beginning of the nineteenth century, it was no longer possible to see in the workshop of the craftsman and in his manual skill a model of the domination of man over the forces of nature as imagined by Descartes in the seventeenth century. The development of capitalism brought with it a radical upheaval in the entire productive activity of society.

"The bourgeoisie, during its rule of scarce one hundred years, has created more massive and more colossal productive forces than have all preceding generations together. Subjection of Nature's forces to man, machinery, application of chemistry to industry and agriculture, steam-navigation, railways, electric telegraphs, clearing of whole continents for cultivation, canalization of rivers, whole populations conjured out of the ground – what earlier century had even a presentiment that such productive forces slumbered in the lap of social labour?"[1]

The dream of the rising bourgeoisie of subduing nature, of making use of the "forces of fire, water, air, etc." (Descartes) was coming true in a remarkable degree. However, as often happens the realization was not at all like the anticipation. The new world when revealed to man in his productive action had very little in common with the colourless picture of mechanical nature given by Descartes.

The invention of engines acquainted man with the possibility of converting one form of energy, thermal, electrical, mechanical, chemical, into another, and proved in practice that movement is by no means of the same mechanical pattern as had been represented. The development of chemistry and of chemical production still further displayed the great variety of nature. The possibility of selective breeding, of producing new varieties of plants and animals, had been demonstrated in horticulture and farming. The theory of Darwin, which was largely based on these facts, showed without any of the mystical "vital forces" of mediaevalism that a living organism is not a machine, that vital phenomena can by no means be accounted

---

[1] Marx and Engels, *Communist Manifesto.*

for by mechanical laws. The earlier social theories had taken the characteristics proper to the individual craftsman type of economy and treated them as the eternal properties of society as such. But new social groups were differentiated as bourgeois production developed and their relations were ever more clearly seen to be the fundamental characteristics of the changed economic and social order.

The world was seen to be much more alive and much more diverse than the mechanists of the seventeenth and eighteenth centuries and their followers thought.

The more fundamental are the changes that we make in things, the more deeply does our knowledge penetrate into their internal nature. The recasting of nature in production is quite distinct from the external action of men on passive inert matter. In the work of a craftsman external mechanical working of the material still predominates, but the chief success of industrialization is due to its exploitation of the forces belonging to nature on a much greater scale than hitherto.

> "He (the worker) uses the mechanical, physical, chemical properties of bodies with the view of making them, as forces, act on other bodies in conformity with his own purpose."[1]

The line of the development of production under capitalism is in fact this – the capitalist seeks more and more to replace the labour of the worker by the movements of the material things themselves, the movements of the lifeless means of production.

> "Reason is just as cunning as it is powerful," wrote Hegel. "The cunning consists generally of that intervening action which forces objects, in conformity with their own nature, to act on each other and undergo a mental transformation, and while it is not directly involved in that process, none the less attains the realization of its own purpose."

What under capitalism emerges as the basic means of producing relative surplus value and is therefore always working in a primitive unconscious and somewhat disguised form, now appears in the period of proletarian dictatorship and under socialism as the conscious

---

[1] *Capital.*

guiding principle of all society, which, moreover, is liberating itself from the role of a living appendage to a dead machine.

By setting up a dam against the current of a river, we make the latter produce an electric current. The energy of falling water, the chemical energy of solid and liquid fuel convey us in a tramcar or a motor-car, or set factory wheels in motion. The automatization and mechanization of production denote man's ever increased usage of the forces of nature itself.

Everything in the world – said Descartes – is in mechanical movement. By this he meant that the source of motion is to be found in the forces that mechanically impel a thing from outside. The more developed practice of material production and of class struggle makes evident the activity of things themselves, discloses the changes within them, and reveals their *self movement*.

The principle of the self movement of matter, as we know from the previous chapter, is one of the basic principles of logical materialism, one of the basic propositions of the dialectical theory of development. The discovery of this principle and its demonstration along the whole line of science and practice puts in quite a new light the problem of our knowledge of reality and our power to change it. The changing of things is by no means the same as the recombination of things in different variants and proportions, as the mediaeval seeker after gold thought and as the alchemistic "doctors of modern capitalism" also think, nor is it a simple changing of outward relations, as thought and think the mechanists.

In the study of a thing in its changes and also in the changes wrought in it by our practical activities, we must proceed from the thing itself.

"The thing itself must be scrutinized in its relations and its development," wrote Lenin, formulating the first of the three basic elements of dialectic. This thesis was developed in detail by Lenin under the following heads:

(1) objectivity of scrutiny (not examples, not variations, but the thing in itself);

(2) the whole aggregate of the various relations of this thing to others;

(3) the development of this thing (or phenomenon), its proper movement, its characteristic form of life.

The revolutionary practice of the proletariat in contradistinction to utopian socialism is a wide application and development of this principle. All utopianism is metaphysical. Utopians in trying to recast society do not proceed from the development proper to it, or from those motive forces which are created by the capitalist order itself, but from a "good" plan, which (quite fortuitously for society) was devised one fine day by a gifted man. For the realization of their plans the utopians appeal to the representatives of the aristocratic and the bourgeois state and to different members of the exploiting classes, reckoning to evoke in them those philanthropic feelings which by no means flow out of their objective class position.

Their metaphysical and idealistic approach and their lack of contact with the movement of objective actuality make their efforts impotent and ridiculous.

"The objective world pursues its own course," and human practice which is confronted by this objective world meets difficulties in realizing its aim and even stumbles on impossibilities.

In this state of affairs "the will of man and his own practice hinder the attainment of his aims – because they separate themselves from knowledge and do not acknowledge external actuality as truly existing (as objective truth). We need a union of *knowledge and practice*" (Lenin).

If our action is not to be without result it must be included in the movement of the object itself. Only by understanding the object in its self-movement can we find the point of departure for changing it.

In this lies the revolutionary force of the theoretical studies of Marx, Engels, Lenin and Stalin. The wide range and effectiveness of Stalin's formulations of practical policy, his directives to the Soviet Government, do not merely express the clash between a revolutionary will and a resistant objective reality as some misguided socialists believe. Stalin always proceeds from a dialectical study of conditions, from an accurate summing up of each new situation, from a careful correlation of class forces. And that is precisely why his utterances show up so mercilessly the blunders of those who are continually advocating capitulation before difficulties ; that is why he is able to lay before the Party and the whole mass of workers a wide prospect of successful application of revolutionary creative energy.

The heroes of "left phraseology" show a Utopian approach to actuality. In 1927 the Central Committee of the Party, noting the perspectives of revolutionary[1] movement for the next few years and basing their considerations on the statistics of the growth of world capitalist production, recorded their conviction that there was at that time a period of relative stability in capitalism. This was indeed the case and it was not until 1929 that this period came to its close. Zinoviev was one of those who treated this analysis with contempt. He argued that it was more necessary to gauge the revolutionary spirit of the workers than the world output of coal and iron.

By closing his eyes to the objective fact of the stabilization of capitalism, Zinoviev supported the German ultra-"lefts," who were calling for immediate revolutionary action, although at that time the predisposing conditions were insufficient. One can only summon the masses to the barricades when faced by an immediate revolutionary situation, i.e. an extreme degree of economic and political crisis in the old order.

"It is impossible to 'make' a revolution.... Revolutions *grow out* of crises and culminations of history that are objectively ripened (i.e. that are independent of party or classes)."[2]

Of course a revolution does not come about without the organized activity of a revolutionary class, "the old government does not fall unless it is dropped." All history is made up of the action of people, but this action is capable of making a revolutionary change only when it reflects the self movement of the social order, the development of objective actuality itself. In all the practice of the proletariat, in all its great and "little" affairs, we find the application and confirmation of the Leninist principle: In knowledge and action we need "an objective scrutiny, not examples, not variations, but the thing in itself"; in knowledge and action is disclosed "the development of this particular thing – its own proper movement, its own life."

---

1 *Left phraseology*. Lenin exposed those "terribly revolutionary" socialists who refused any kind of compromise, were impatient with the slow-moving masses and talked of immediate revolution in spite of the immaturity of the situation. He further pointed out that their "Leftism" seldom went beyond speech-making. (See Lenin, "Left-*Wing" Communism, An Infantile Disorder*.)

2 Lenin, *Collapse of Second International*.

The disclosure of the activity of things, of their self movement, demonstrates that things are by no means fixed and constant as the metaphysicians think and as sometimes seems in experience.

"– the great basic thought that the world is not to be comprehended as a complex of ready-made *things,* but as a complex of *processes,* in which the things apparently stable no less than their mind-images in our heads, the concepts, go through an uninterrupted change of coming into being and passing away, in which, in spite of all temporary retrogression, a progressive development asserts itself in the end."[1]

In nature there are no unchangeable things, all nature is made up of processes. At first glance this thought seems strange and evokes many doubts. How are we to reconcile this formula of Engels with daily experience in which we deal with objects that are stable and unchanged for our experience? If everything is so absolutely changeable and fluid, how can we find in the world any definite stable differences? If there is no stability then there is no definiteness in any thing. Thus – says the subjective idealist – every definiteness is conditional, it is introduced by our consciousness into the flow of sensations. Our mental equipment makes us interpret sensation complexes in different ways, but all differences and distinctions exist only within our consciousness.

The mechanist, Sarabyanov, reasons in the same way. From absolute fluidity and mutability he deduces the conditionally and subjectivity of every definiteness: "Our relativity is absolute, because all flows and changes; there is no point of rest except as conditioned by us, and of course we are not scared of relativism." The daring Sarabyanov is not scared of absolute relativism and goes straight to idealistic conclusions – every state of rest, every stability is "conditioned by us," i.e. by the subject, and therefore all differences too are subjective. The Living man, the corpse, death, are processes. In these there is no stability; to distinguish them is only possible conditionally, only by introducing definiteness out of the subject. "Mankind in its practice is conditioned to understand 'living man' as a being with one kind of processes, a corpse as a being with another

---

[1] Engels, *Ludwig Feuerbach*, p. 54.

kind of processes." "Death itself is a conditioned notion," wrote Sarabyanov in another article.

All these dicta of Sarabyanov are directly connected with his negation of objective truth and are undoubtedly subjective idealism, but are not we ourselves inclining in that direction when we acknowledge all things as a process, are we not pouring water on the idealistic mill of absolute relativism? Not at all! All these subjective conclusions of Sarabyanov flow out of his purely metaphysical approach to the understanding of what comprises the stability of things.

The qualitative differences between the solid, liquid and gaseous states of a substance are perfectly definite, but this definiteness is not a stability of dead rest, as metaphysicians think, but a stability of types of movement, a definiteness of different forms of molecular movement.

Molecules in their turn consist of still smaller particles – atoms, which also are in motion, and atoms consist of constantly moving electrons. And according to the latest theory the electrons themselves are nuclear centres of special wave processes, comparable with those which give us concerts on the wireless, and with those we call light. It appears that at the basis of stable things are to be found wave processes. It is quite clear that science will not remain at this point, that the investigation into the "depth" of matter will go further. But there is no doubt that the discovery of each new qualitatively distinct stage of matter will be, as hitherto, a discovery of a new form of movement.

What is this "movement"? The mechanist, as we know, will say that movement is the displacement of a body in space and that objectively only mechanical displacements exist. It is obvious from what has been said that we disagree with this. The struggle for the mastery of the self-movement of the forces of nature and society (the latter consisting of the class struggles characteristic of the higher stages of social development) have disclosed a whole array of qualitatively unique types of movement, among which mechanical movement is only a very simple form.

> "Every movement includes in itself mechanical movement and the rearrangement to a greater or lesser degree of the particles of matter. To understand these mechanical movements is the *first* task of science, but only the first.

Mechanical movement by no means exhausts movement in general. Movement is not by any means just a 'movement,' a simple change of place, it is in hyper-mechanical realms a change of quality too."[1]

"*Movement as applied to matter, is change in general,*" which comprises an infinite number of concrete aspects of change. The movement of molecules in solid, liquid and gaseous bodies does not by any means amount to their simple change of position. This movement is latent heat, which has its qualitatively peculiar laws. The uniting and disuniting of atoms into molecules is a qualitatively unique chemical process. The movement of electrons in a metal wire gives us an electric current. Wave processes in the ether are of an electro-magnetic character.

The vital processes of an organism, the development of society, the thought of man are all qualitatively unique processes, which it is quite impossible to reduce to simple movements of particles.

However, it is wrong to suppose that all forms of movement exist independently of each other and only make external contacts. On the contrary they mutually penetrate.

"Every one of the higher forms of movement is connected always and of necessity with real mechanical (external or molecular) movement, just as similarly the higher forms of movement produce at the same time other aspects of movement; chemical action is always accompanied by changes of temperature and electrical action; organic life is impossible without mechanical, molecular, chemical, thermal, electrical and other changes. But the presence of these collateral forms does not exhaust the essence of the main form in each case."[2]

It still has in addition to these constituent movements its own unique character.

Harvey discovered the movement of the blood – circulation. This was for his time a very important discovery. Without circulation, without contraction of the muscles, an animal cannot exist. Breathing and digestion comprehend a whole range of chemical

---

[1] Engels, *Anti-Dühring.*

2 Engels, *Dialectic of Nature.*

changes. But in none of these is included the specific quality of an organism, its uniqueness. The movement characteristic for an organism is the ceaseless changing of organic substances – a process of combustion, dissolution and renovation of living matter, a process of assimilation of nourishment, whereby the fabric of the body is continuously being woven. On the basis of this process arise all other processes that are peculiar to the organism – growth, struggle with the beginnings of morbid conditions, reproduction, etc. Biological changes comprehend in themselves other forms of movement which are "collateral" to the unique vital processes of the organism.

In the interlacing of a number of distinct processes there is always a determined species of movement which embraces all the others, subordinates them to itself, and is characteristic of the thing as a whole, constitutes its uniqueness, its distinction from other things, forms the basis of its stability.

An animal will die, i.e. will cease to be an animal, will. be turned into a heap of decaying albumens if by interrupting its breathing we stop certain organic changes even for a short time. An organism is a qualitatively unique *process;* without this process there is no organism. In just the same way the various forms of society are living, fluid and qualitatively unique processes. Proletarian dictatorship exists only in the process of class struggle, in the process of building socialism, in the process of abolishing classes: Its stability and its qualitative definiteness are exactly comprehended within the definite form of class-struggle. "Proletarian dictatorship is a prolongation of class struggle in new forms," wrote Lenin. This form of movement – a struggle ever intensifying in the process of abolishing classes – makes up the inalienable definiteness of the soviet order.

The process of socialist industrialization is a form of struggle with both internal and external class enemies. The Right-opportunists did not understand that. In their fear of the difficulties of the reconstruction period they proposed to suspend the class struggle, to reduce the pressure on the kulak, to weaken the control over the middle peasantry, to slacken the tempo of industrialization. If the Party were to listen to the Right-opportunists, if the working class were to cut short its struggle against the exploiting classes and no longer to direct the peasantry, proletarian dictatorship would cease to be proletarian dictatorship and capitalism would be re-established.

It is impossible to stop the movement of matter. By stopping or delaying the socialist offensive we inevitably call into existence new forms of capitalist activity, encourage their growth and allow the offensive to pass over into their hands. Interrupting social movement in one form, we evoke it in another. The Right-opportunists did not understand the dialectic of movement and became the mouthpiece of the kulak opposition; objectively, therefore, they were counter-revolutionists.

We laid down at the beginning of this chapter that to everything there belongs internally a special type of movement. In the exposition following we drew one very important conclusion; the movement of a thing – its self-movement – defines its internal nature, is its uniqueness, its *quality*. Engels was right: the world consists of processes, of qualitatively unique movements of matter. *The quality of a thing is given by the particular kind of movement that is fundamental to it.*

This proposition of materialistic dialectic has great importance for the theory of knowledge and for the entire world-outlook. It leaves no place for mysterious isolated and unchangeable properties and forces, it rejects the representation of the world as a dead mechanism.

In spite of the metaphysic of properties the qualities of material things are now deprived of every mystery. We are enabled to study them as fully determined, exactly distinguished forms of movement.

The mechanists notwithstanding, variety and vitality exist, are. not mere subjective representations; matter by its own proper movement creates countless shades of qualitative differences. And however rich and many-sided our representations may be, the copy of the actual world in our consciousness will always be immeasurably more abstract, poorer, more dead, than the actual life of material nature.

The mechanists in their conflict with the metaphysic of properties rightly pointed out the unscientific character of representing the world as an aggregation of qualities independent of each other. But they themselves failed to understand wherein lies the unity of matter. They sought the unity of matter in identity of particles, in saying that matter is everywhere and always the same. In practice such "unity" leads to the splitting up of nature into particles externally indifferent to each other. The actual unity of the world lies in the materiality of all its qualitatively different forms, in their continual vanishing and appearance. A man, a very simple living organism, an inorganic substance – all are qualitatively different stages of one and the same ascending scale of material development.

The unity of the world exists in variety. The general connection is realized through the qualitative differences of separate things. This dialectic of the general and the particular, of unity and diversity, was unattainable by the mechanists. And yet it is just in this that we find the key to disclose the relations and connections in nature, and so provide the basis for a right understanding of the mutual connection of qualities.

CHAPTER IV

THE RELATIVITY OF QUALITIES AND THE UNIVERSAL CONNECTION OF THINGS

Quality is the inalienable and specific mark of a thing or an event. It is inalienable because without it the thing ceases to exist as that given thing. It is specific because it distinguishes that thing from other things.

The question arises, wherein lies this uniqueness, how can we give a definition of a given quality.

Moliere, with good reason, ridiculed the mediaeval savants. Their explanation of "soporific action" as due to "soporific force," and of soporific force as due to "soporificness" are indeed extremely vapid and laughable. But in what lies the root of this error of the mediaeval scholars? It lies in their determination to find a definition of an isolated quality apart from all relations. Try to define any quality without alluding to some other or implying, to however small a degree, its relation with something else, and inevitably you will find that you have fallen into the plight of Moliere's "sage."

The quality of a thing can only be understood by distinguishing it from other qualities. Thus in the very category of quality there is implied a relationship with something else, a distinction from it. It is impossible to define a thing without indicating its differences, impossible to say what a given quality resembles without indicating, however faintly, that which it does not resemble.

A lake is characterized by a certain quality, dry land has another quality. But we include in our definition of a lake the fact that it is surrounded on all sides by dry land.

If a man utters his views on any question he cannot express what he is asserting without indicating that with which he disagrees, that which he denies.

In every definition of the quality of a thing affirmation and negation are indissolubly connected. One of the greatest materialists, Spinoza, expressed this thought in the following aphorism: "Every definition is a negation." All the knowledge of one quality is indissolubly connected with its limitation by other qualities, by that which the given quality does *not* resemble – its negation. Hegel, Marx and Lenin, all stressed the correctness of this idea.

And so a definition must include in itself an indication of the discriminating relations of the given quality to another. Yet this is by no means so easy as may seem at the first glance. It so happens there exists in the world an endless number of things from which the given thing differs. And are we really expected to enumerate all these differences? Clearly they cannot all be of the same importance for the definition of the given thing, and their simple enumeration would do nothing except confuse.

What is the way to disclose the qualitative uniqueness of objective processes or things in a really complete and adequate manner?

Lenin pointed out the first steps towards this. He suggested that we should proceed from any very simple pronouncement : A terrier is a dog. Capitalism is a social formation. A planet is an element of the solar system. The proletariat is a class of capitalist society. An individual thing is a general thing – that is how we must begin. Each quality by its own peculiarity, in its uniqueness, is a part of something general and therefore contains something of the general in itself.

The terrier even in its individual peculiarities expresses the general features of a dog in general. A planet even in its particular movements expresses the general connection of the solar system. Capitalism in its own specific form expresses the general laws of society's development, the contradiction between the productive forces and the relations of production.

Thus the unity of the general and individual is not external, they mutually penetrate each other. We see this unity of opposites in the *individual thing itself* – *"the individual* is the universal. That is to say opposites are identical." "Every individual thing is in some way or other a universal."

And at the same time the individual thing as a part, as an individual aspect of a whole, expresses that whole not fully but one-sidedly. In this lies the internal contradiction of every individual thing. Capitalism, by expressing the general law of every means of production in *its peculiar way,* aids the development of productive forces, but at the same time there lies within its qualitative peculiarity its limitation : at a determined stage of development the preservation of property in the means of production becomes an obstacle to the development of productive forces. Capitalism played a definite historical role in the development of society. But if we are to understand this historical role we must relate it to the whole and find its connection with the whole line of social development. That is why Marx in expounding the theory of the capitalist means of production proceeds, after his chapter on the conversion of money into capital, to treat the question of labour and production from a universal point of view.

A planet in its movement expresses the connection of the whole solar system, but its movement is only one aspect, which outside the whole is impossible.

But the universal itself exists through the particular. Every particular is incomplete and one-sided. However, the incompleteness of one aspect is supplemented by another incompleteness, by another one-sidedness. Although they are mutually opposed yet at the same time they presuppose each other, amplify each other and are the inseparable poles of a single whole.

And so in virtue of their contradictory nature, their internal incompleteness, particular qualities cannot exist in isolation, they presuppose other opposite qualitative peculiarities and exist only in union with them. A planet exists as a planet only because there is a sun round which it revolves. Beasts of prey exist only in company with herbivorous animals. Animals as a whole can exist only because plant-life exists, whose green leaves under the influence of sun-light turn inorganic substances into organic. And in return animals exhale carbonic acid gas, which is required for the synthesis of organic substances, and so give food to plant life.

The capitalist appears as capitalist only because capitalism produces not only capitalists but also proletarians – ■ people who have nothing to sell except their power to labour. And conversely the working class, as a class of the oppressed and exploited, exists only because exploiter-capitalists confront it. Water is ceaselessly evaporating and being condensed; this maintains the flow of rivers.

> "A particular entity (an object, a phenomenon, etc.) is (only) *one aspect* of idea (truth). For truth there are needed still other aspects of *actuality*, which also seem to be independent and particular (existing peculiarly for themselves). *Only in their aggregation and in their relationship* is truth realized."

Thus wrote Lenin in his materialist working-over of Hegel's dialectic (whence, among other things, his use of the word "idea").

A particular entity, a thing, which is characterized by a definite quality, only *seems* to be quite independent. On this "seeming" are based all the metaphysical systems. Dialectic exposes this "seemingness," discloses the deep connection of particular things and demonstrates the relativity and mutual penetration of different qualities.

But are we not arriving at that same absolute relativism which we exposed and rejected in the metaphysic of mechanism? By no means! "Dialectic" – as Lenin constantly explained – "contains a moment of relativism, of negation, of scepticism, but does not *amount to* relativism." The mechanists reduce properties to relations – and external relations at that. For them there is no objective basis of relations and therefore the qualitative definiteness of things is submerged in universal relativity, in the complete indefiniteness and instability of particular phenomena. The sole issue of such a position is idealism, which enables them to introduce definiteness into the world through the agency of the subject and its "point of view." Dialectical materialism is free from these difficulties. Dialectic proceeds from the internal definiteness of a thing as the basis of its relation to another. For dialectic the relation of qualities to each other is not an external fortuitous relation, it issues from their inner nature and is the expression of an objectively existing whole which embraces both related qualities.

The second quality to which the quality of the given thing is related is not that to which the given thing is indifferent according to its inner nature, it is not an external "other" independent of it, but its own opposite, *its* other.

For animals, which all directly or indirectly feed on plant-life, the existence of plant-life is by no means a matter of indifference. Planets presuppose the sun; capitalists – the proletariat.

The mutual definition and mutual exclusion of qualitatively different things and phenomena play their part not only with things that exist contemporaneously, but also when one exists after the other and when the presence of one excludes the presence of the other. Socialism is created out of the internally necessary wreck of capitalism. Both systems exclude each other and only in a state of severe conflict can they co-exist at the same time. But in this development they are mutually connected – capitalism prepares the revolutionary transition to socialism, the emergence of a socialist society under the pressure of internal necessity is the result of the irreconcilable contradictions of the capitalist system. The irreconcilable hatred of capitalists towards the Soviet Union, similar to our irreconcilable hatred of bourgeois society, gives clear enough evidence that these systems are not absolutely external, not "indifferent" to each other. Socialism is the opposite of capitalism and in this sense we can say that socialism is the "other" of the capitalist system. Capitalism is related to socialism, as to its own opposite, as to the social formation necessary for its replacement. Socialism is related to capitalism as to the foregoing stage of social development. We shall understand nothing in capitalism or in socialism if we do not keep in view their mutual relations – the relations of irreconcilable conflict in which is expressed their historic succession and connection.

And so from different sides we have sought to show that the relations of things flow out of their inner nature. There are no isolated qualities of things. Every quality in its existence and development presupposes a number of others.

This idea was turned by metaphysicians into an absolute and thus into a source of errors, opening the door to the crudest superstitions.

The German philosopher, Leibnitz, in his philosophical enquiries stumbled on the problem of the mutual connection of qualities. In essence he was the first in the history of philosophy who stated this problem in precise terms. Leibnitz was strongly influenced by the mechanistic viewpoint, and at the same time sought to overcome its limitations on the basis of a widely extended system of objective idealism.

The mechanistic theory of the relativity of properties was understood by him more deeply than by anyone else, and he developed it to its extreme limits. Every thing, every unit of the world (or as he said – "monad") in all its content is nothing other than a reflection of all other things. All things, all properties exist only in relations. All the characteristics of each thing are the result of its relations with all other things. All things, all conceptions, possess only reflective, relative attributes.

But if each monad is *only* a reflection of all other monads then whence comes that which is reflected? The view-point of "reflective definitions" if turned into an absolute, leads to the assertion that everything in the world is a reflection without the existence of anything to be reflected, a relation without that which is related. One of the historians of philosophy characterized this view in the following way: in a room there is nothing except a multitude of mirrors which entirely cover walls, floor and ceiling; all the mirrors reflect each other, but it is perfectly clear that no definite image will be reflected in any of them. A world in which there is nothing except purely reflective relationships is as empty and as -without content as those mirrors.

To avoid the emptiness of absolute relativity, Leibnitz distinguished between those qualities in his monads which were shared in common and those which constituted their uniqueness, for they differ infinitely from one another and no two can be exactly alike. Leibnitz was so anxious to preserve the integrity of these individuals (or monads) that he refused to admit that they could affect one another. Nevertheless, each behaved as though it were part of a whole and helped to constitute that whole. The only way in which to explain such a combination is by the hypothesis that they have all been created by an exact mechanician. Every monad is, as it were, a separate time-piece, and all of them though sounding different notes strike always at one and the same time and in harmony. The concordance of things among themselves is a previously established concordance, is "a pre-established harmony." Only thus is it possible for each separate monad in itself, in its qualitative particularity, to be a reflection of the world of all monads as a whole. All is in concordance, all has been foreseen in the best possible way. All is for the best in this best of *possible* worlds.[1]

Leibnitz lived in that "happy" era when merchant capital had entered into partnership with the land-owning class, in the "happy" century of absolute monarchy. In this epoch the capitalist and landowner had made the great discovery that feudal extortion and business trickery harmonized splendidly with each other in the system of primary capitalist accumulation, and that the material and mental culture of the nobility could find itself at one with the still undeveloped culture of capitalism. Leibnitz was the spokesman of this "happy" century, and to him through the rosy spectacles of stabilized absolute monarchy, the whole world seemed to have been

---

1 By "best possible" Leibnitz did not mean "best conceivable," but the best that you can have under what he supposed to be the necessary conditions of human life and human freedom, or the necessary conditions of his own social order.

made specially to enable brilliant princesses, very rich bourgeois and royal academicians to flourish and enjoy themselves.

But one can plainly see that in the actual connection of qualities there is no "pre-established harmony."

In spite of Leibnitz's metaphysic there are no eternal qualities; qualitatively unique things are only transitory forms of unitary evolving matter. And if this is so, if qualities come and go in the unitary process of the development of the material world, then what is there wonderful in the fact that they are internally connected among themselves? And there is no need of any "pre-established harmony" to explain their internal connection within the unity of the solar system. They "only seem to be independent and separate and to be existing privately for themselves" (Lenin) whereas in actuality they exist as the result of the division of unity, each as the opposite of another.

In the same way after Darwin, we do not wonder at the internally necessary relations of the organic world. As Darwin pointed out the specialization of organisms in different directions, the emergence of qualitative differences between them, was one of the necessary conditions of their survival. In the process also of evolution the "division of unity" led to the emergence of independent species which are internally connected with each other and each of which in relation to another, is, in fact, its other.

The differentiation of an undeveloped whole, the emergence of differences between qualities by means of the division of unity proceed also in social development. The emergence of classes, the polarization which takes place in the conversion of a simple merchant economy into capitalist economy (for example the differentiation of the peasantry), the oppositeness of separate social usages – in all these examples we see always that same "immanent *emergence* of differences – the internal objective logic of evolution and the struggle of the differences of polarity." (Lenin.)

And so in the relativity of qualities there is nothing pre-established, there is nothing ready-made, no previously given concordance. The relativity of qualities is the product of never ceasing material development.

However, the connection of things is not only foreign to the idea of "anything pre-established" but also quite remote from "harmony." The relativity of qualities is not a product of a peaceful reconciliation of extremes, it arises in a harsh conflict of contradictions, it exists only in a process of eternal emergence and annihilation. It arises out of discordance, out of conflict, and having arisen is turned into its own opposite, into a source of new contradictions and of new splitting. "Reason becomes unreason, a boon is turned into a misfortune." (Goethe.)

A concordance is never wholly realized, it always exists merely as one of contradictory tendencies.

Only men isolated in their studies from all contact with the real world can dream of world harmony, "because just as this can never be in the development of nature, so too it can never be in the development of society. For only by means of a number of attempts (each one of which taken separately will be one-sided and will suffer from a certain discordance) is an ultimately victorious socialism made possible out of the revolutionary co-operation of proletarians of *all* countries." (Lenin).

Absolute concordance "cannot obtain in the development of society, just as it cannot obtain in the development of nature." Biologists who think dialectically, know quite well how important it is to estimate not only the concordance, the agreement of an organism with its environment, but also its disagreement. In the simultaneous and contradictory emergence of concordance and discordance the development of the organic world is accomplished.

And so different qualities are internally connected with each other, yet their relativity is ever changing and profoundly contradictory. In actual development, which is denied by the upholders of "pre-established harmony," concordance and discordance are interwoven and there is no stable harmony in the relations of separate things.

"The world does not consist of ready-made finished objects" (Engels), matter is in ceaseless development. And so not only are separate objects changeable and transitory, but with their changes there is indissolubly connected the change of their mutual relations. Not only do particular animals emerge and vanish, but also whole species of animals. The whole world of animals and plants arose during a definite period and has found the limit of its biological development in the formation of human society. In society the change of social structures proceeds through the change of people and their relations.

The internal contradictions of development penetrate both the general and the particular. The recasting of particular things, in the process of establishing new connections, in the process of setting up a new "general" class, is at the same time a process of destroying the old "general" class. A collective-farm worker is still a peasant, but at the same time he *already* appears as a member of an enterprise of a socialist type. The connections of the old are not yet all severed and *already* the decisive relations of the new type have been forged. Through the spreading of the new socialist relations in the country-side proceeds the breaking of the old private property connections and with it the remaking of the peasant into a worker of socialist society. The mutually relative qualities of the petty-bourgeoisie are being replaced by the new qualities of socialist workers. And until this process is consummated, the peasant collective-farm-worker will be conscious of deep internal contradictions in his position in society. In its turn the consummation of the construction of socialism will set going new problems, open up new perspectives, will require the creation of new relations and through the development of these will remake mankind.

The unity of the general and the particular is relative; their contradiction is absolute, just as movement and development are absolute. That is why always and in everything "every generality only approximately embraces all particular objects." Always and in everything the eternal development of matter and the eternal succession of its general stages of development proceed through the deep contradictions of every particular thing.

"Every concrete thing, every concrete something, stands in different and often contradictory relations to everything else, therefore it exists as itself and as something else" (Lenin).

Bourgeois thought, in the majority of cases, is unable to understand these contradictions and bourgeois scientists, to keep on the right side of bourgeois ideology, make use of two formal metaphysical devices. They either acknowledge a purely stagnant universal, in harmony with itself, into which particular things have to be forced; or they declare that general ideas are a fiction of the mind. Quite frequently they produce an alternative subjective-idealist argument against the Marxian dialectic. They point out that the general law of value never appears in its pure aspect in relation to the particular commodities on the market, and this allows bourgeois economists and revisionist theoreticians to declare that the law of value is a subjective fiction. Engels in a letter to Conrad Schmidt explained the actual dialectic of the general law and its partial manifestation.

He asked Conrad Schmidt:

"Did feudalism always correspond to its idea? – The answer is 'No.' Must we then conclude that feudalism was a fiction, that it reached full perfection only in Palestine for a short time and even so (for the most part) on paper? Or are the basic ideas in the natural sciences also fictions because they by no means always coincide with actuality? Even after we had accepted the theory of evolution our ideas on organic life only approximately agreed with actuality. For otherwise there would be no evolution. The idea of 'fish' for example includes life in water and breathing by gills. How will you progress from a fish to a land animal unless you overcome this idea? And it was overcome, for we know of fishes whose air bladder developed farther into lungs and permits them to breathe air. How can we progress from the reptile that lays an egg to the mammal that brings forth its offspring alive unless we bring one of these two ideas to a clash with actuality? Indeed, in the monotremata we have a sub-class of mammals that lay eggs, the duck-billed platypus. In the year 1843 I saw a duck-bill's egg in Manchester and in my conceited ignorance made fun of the stupid notion that a mammal could lay an egg; now we know it is a fact."[1]

In its development the world is infinitely varied. Old connections are interwoven with new and not merely in the process of emergence of the new, for even after the new type of relation has been more or less established, the old continues very often to exist *along with* the new, as another species.

The emergence of animals and plants by no means abolished inorganic nature from which the life of organisms sprang. On the contrary the very existence of animals and plants pre-supposes a definite inorganic environment – hills and plains, rivers and seas, a particular kind of soil, an atmosphere, etc. In just the same way human society needs a definite geographical environment.

---

[1] *Engels Correspondence,* published 1923.

Every universal is also only part of a system of wider connections and is in a state of internally necessary relations with other universals. Thus, all the relations of things constitute an extraordinarily complex and variegated network. Lenin in the fragment "On Dialectic," often emphasizes this complexity: "Every particular is by thousands of transitions connected with particulars of another *species* (things, phenomena, processes), etc."

Thus Lenin notes two types of relations between things; the relation within a given universal and the relation to things of another species.

The capitalist exploits the workers. This relation flows out of the internal nature of the capitalist as a social phenomenon, and is a relation not outside but within the social whole. This same capitalist may be ill from an infectious disease. His relation to the bacteria which caused the disease also cannot be regarded as a purely external phenomenon. The biological characteristics of man, although they are changed in social life, nevertheless create the internal basis for infectious disease. But if we compare these two relations we shall see that one of them is relatively external in comparison with the other. The connection of a millionaire with his workmen is an organic and direct connection; the connection of the millionaire with the germ of some disease which he might contract is (with the whole pernicious character of them both to mankind) very, very remote.

There are no things absolutely external to each other, but there exist things and events, "whose internal mutual connection is so remote or so difficult to define that we can forget it, can hold that it does not exist" (Engels).

And so in conflict with the mechanistic ascription of all connections to external relations we emphasized that the relations of things flow out of their internal nature. And at the same time, whatever the upholders of" pre-established harmony" may say, we must not forget that the mutual relativity of qualities is infinitely various, deeply contradictory and by no means absolute.

The unitary development of matter is accomplished through particular things. Their relative independence and stability in development, their contradictions and conflict, which belong to them internally and are manifested in their external relations – all these destroy the idealistic legend of an absolutely attuned harmony of nature. Thus Engels noted that with the whole unity of development there always remains "a chaotic aggregation of the objects of nature in some or other determined field or even over the whole world."

There are no absolutely external things, but also there is no absolute concordance of things. In vital development the relatively external and the relatively internal are interwoven, condition' each other, and create a vital connection of everything with everything in the unitary flow of the development of matter. Lenin, formulating one of the elements of dialectic, wrote:

> "The relations of each thing (phenomenon, etc.) are not only many and varied, but also general, universal. All things (phenomena, processes, etc.) are connected with *each other*. In development there is realized the connection (of all parts) of an infinite process, the necessary connection of the whole world... the mutual determining connection of everything."

In summing up this chapter we will recall one very essential Leninist instruction.

In order to disclose the quality of an object, to express its internal uniqueness, we must consider it in its all-round connection. But the different relations of a thing to others must be united in our knowledge and action, not arbitrarily, not externally, not haphazardly, but on the basis of that thing's own development, its own self-movement. In the self-movement of an object "its *connection* with the surrounding world is changed." When we disclose the line of this change, we reveal the actual quality of the object, we find the form of movement that belongs to it.

Lenin in the discussion on trade unions in 1921 greatly stressed the many-sidedness of the special nature of trade unions, the infinite number of relations which connected the trade unions with the other elements of proletarian dictatorship.

But in opposition to Bukharin and Trotsky, Lenin found the special functions of unions in that connection which will lead to the general, i.e. to the whole system of proletarian dictatorship, by disclosing the relativity of all the elements of that system.

To understand the trade-union question properly a whole series of questions must be faced: the *tendencies* in the field of trade unionism, the relation of classes, the relation of politics to economics, the special character of the state, of the party and of the trade unions themselves. In other words trade unions do not exist in isolation but only in relation with other organizations of the working class – with the party, the state, local state and economic organizations, the great mass of workers, etc. In these relations we see the many aspects of the role of trade unions – the defence of workers from bureaucratic perversions, the productive role in the sense of utilizing the unions for propaganda for increased production, the drawing of masses into the actual control of production, and the task of raising the political consciousness of the workers, etc.

But all this many-sidedness and relativity of the trade unions does not mean that what they really are is purely a question of the "point of view," so that they can be just as truly regarded in several different ways. On the contrary, in spite of, indeed along with, the many-sidedness of the subject under consideration, there emerges one and only one solution. In all the different functions of trade unions, in the change of these functions at different stages, we see the appearance of one line of development – the movement towards communism, the line of a "coalition" with all the other organizations of the working class, the line of drawing the backward masses up to the level of the "immediate directing advance guard," the line of promoting workers more and "more to positions of authority. In this line of development, there is also disclosed the unitary, qualitatively unique definiteness of the trade unions – which is *to be a school of communism.*

And so as Lenin has shown us, dialectical logic demands a scrutiny of all the connections of the object in the unity of its development. There are no changes in isolated things. Removed from its connection the category of self-movement is insufficient for the determining of a thing, just as an abstract proposition on "general connection" removed from actual material development will lead only to metaphysics and absolute relativism.

> "It is necessary to unite, to connect, to combine the general principle of development with the general principle of the unity of the world, of nature, of movement, of matter, etc." (Lenin).

Neither the mechanists nor the Menshevist idealists understood the unity of self-movement and general connection. For the mechanists all changes are to be attributed to the change of external relationships, and so in essence they deny development. The Menshevist idealists attribute all development to the internal self-movement of things, and thus obviate the general connection of processes. For them interference by an external influence is accidental and a hindrance to development. This tendency was for example manifested in their conception of biological development – all development was ascribed to the internal changes of the organism, independent of its surrounding environment. Thus both the mechanists and the Menshevist idealists are at one in this – neither group understood that absolutely external connections do not exist, that development by internal necessity goes on through an external relation to something else, while those relations to something else themselves flow out of the internal nature of each thing.

Only this uniting of self-movement and general connection gives us the key to the unity of quality and property.

CHAPTER V

THE DIALECTIC OF QUALITY AND PROPERTY

According to the metaphysic of properties, quality and property are simply identical with one another. A property is an independent quality, an independent force, aptitude, etc. And a thing is the external unity of these independent properties.

According to the mechanistic view a property is the relation of one thing to another, but it is an *external* relation, it does not flow out of the internal nature of the thing.

In actuality there are no independent isolated qualities. Quality exists in relation, and these relations flow out of the unique nature of each thing by an internal necessity. As a result of its contradictions a thing *must* exist in connection with others and its properties are nothing else than the manifestations of its quality in relation to other things.

"Quality is a property above all and pre-eminently in the sense of how much it shows itself in external relation as an immanent definiteness."[1]

Plants that possess chlorophyl cannot exist without sunlight; their internal qualitative definiteness manifests itself in the property of absorbing solar rays. A river does not exist without banks; it possesses the property of changing their lines, it may wash them away, it may re-establish them elsewhere. Every chemical element presupposes the existence of other elements and its chemical properties are revealed in its different relations to different elements – to one set it is neutral, with others it unites in a violent reaction. Man is a social being and his quality, the "nature" he derives from the class he belongs to (in other words his character) is revealed in his actions, in his relations to other people and things.

There is no matter without movement, and forms of movement do not exist in isolation, every quality reveals itself in its activity, which is manifested in its relations. In defining the "object" with which the natural sciences concern themselves, Engels wrote:

---

[1] Hegel, *Science of Logic*, vol. i, p. 54.

"The object is a moving substance. Again it is possible to know the different forms and aspects of the substance itself through movement; only in movement are the properties of a body revealed; there can be nothing to say of a body, that is not found in movement. It follows that out of the forms of movement flow the properties of the moving bodies."[1]

As we see, Engels distinguishes between quality and property only as two sides of one and the same definite aspect of a process. Quality and property are indissolubly connected. However, the theory of primary and secondary qualities, the hieroglyphic theory and Kantian agnosticism, all separate these categories. In knowledge – say the agnostics – we are dealing not with the "thing in itself" but only with its relation to our perception. According to the theory of hieroglyphs the "thing in itself" is knowable only in the conditional symbols of our sensations. In Kant's opinion, the "thing in itself" is absolutely unknowable, we know only the "thing for us," only a phenomenon, which has nothing in common with the "thing in itself." Further, as Hegel indicated, the Kantian "thing in itself" is an empty abstraction about which it is possible to say nothing, for this reason that by moving it from relations, from its "being for another," we ourselves destroy the bridge to the knowledge of it. In his notes on the Hegelian dialectic, Lenin wrote on this issue as follows:

"The aphorism, that we do not know what exactly 'things in themselves' really are seems to be wisdom. But the 'thing in itself' is an abstraction from every definition (from every relation to another), i.e. it is nothing.... How very profound: the 'thing in itself' and its converse – 'the thing for others.'... The 'thing in itself' as a *generality* is an empty, lifeless abstraction. In life, in movement, everything *exists* both in itself and for others, in relationship to something else, and so continually transforms itself from one state into another."

However, the arguments for agnosticism are inexhaustible and it is possible to ask, whence do you get your knowledge of the in-

---

[1] *Dialectic of Nature.*

ternal definiteness of a thing? In experience only a thing's external appearances are given to us, only its properties, and all our knowledge amounts to a description of particular properties known subjectively through the senses. We see light and we distinguish colour because we possess the organ of sight; we hear sounds because we possess the organ of hearing; we detect scents because we have an organ of smell; we discern a rough or a smooth surface because we have a sense of touch. The qualitative differences between sensations are created not by differences in the things in themselves, but by the differences of our organs of sense.

In answer to the agnostic we will admit that each particular sensation is quite one-sided and limited, but we will remind him that knowledge is by no means content with particular sensations, but is all the time correlating them and thus disclosing the unity of the properties of the objectively existing thing. And here it is easy to point out that the different organs of sense give us by no means absolutely different impressions. The organs of sense are connected, co-ordinated with each other, there is between them a known unity and up to a certain degree they amplify each other, since they themselves are the historic product of social practice in which society had to deal with a *single,* many-sided object – the world. For example:

> "Touch and sight amplify each other in such a way that you can often tell from seeing a thing what its tactile properties will be. And finally, just as always the one and the same 'I' receives and works over these different sense impressions, and gathers them into a unity, so these different impressions are conveyed from one and the, same thing, and 'appear' as its general properties, in this way making possible our comprehension of it. Therefore the task of explaining these differences, these properties, which are attainable only by the different organs of sense, of establishing a connection between them is a scientific task...."[1]

But that does not satisfy the agnostic. In the first place, he says, we do not know whether all these properties belong to one thing, as you assert, or to different things, and secondly you do not go further

---

[1] Engels, *Anti-Dühring.*

than external properties, the external relations of the thing to the consciousness.

The agnostic proceeds from the supposition that things in themselves are by their internal nature absolutely foreign to consciousness, and so in his opinion there is no bridge between the relations of a thing and its internal structure.

In this very supposition lies the basic vice of all agnostic doubts. As a matter of fact if things were absolutely foreign to us, *no* objective connection, *no* contact could be established between us and the objective world in general. As we explained above, relations between things are possible in general only because they possess in some or other relation an internal kinship. If things, as agnostics think, were absolutely external to man, we could not receive from them any sensations whatever.

In the world of reality we have sensations because both the things we know about and ourselves belong not to two quite different "substances," but are parts of one and the same world, products and stages of one and the same process of material development. During the age-long history of the animal world and of the development of human society our sense organs were formed and perfected, our capacity for knowing the objective world was developed, and this direct unity of nature and man is realized every day and every hour in our practical action.

> "We can demonstrate the correctness of our conception of a given phenomenon by the fa'ct that we ourselves evoke it, produce it from its conditions and make it serve our aims. This puts an end to the Kantian 'thing in itself.'"[1]

It is quite clear that we can evoke the phenomena of nature only in so far as we ourselves are included in its total system and only in so far as our action is a special form of material movement.

> "Primarily, labour is a process going on between man and nature, a process in which man, through his own activity, initiates, regulates, and controls the material reactions between himself and nature. He confronts nature as one of her own forces, setting in motion arms and legs, head and hands, in order to appropriate nature's productions in a

---

[1] Engels, *Ludwig Feuerbach.*

form suitable to his own wants. By thus acting on the external world and changing it, he at the same time changes his own nature. He develops the potentialities that slumber within him, and subjects these inner forces to his own control."[1]

By our work we create new things with new properties. "Labour has been united with the article of work. It has been substantialized, the article has been subjected to the labour-process" (Marx). When we perceive the external world passively the movement of a thing allows us to understand it through its properties which are reflected as sensations in our consciousness but whose objective basis we do not know. But in the process of production our action emerges as a form of movement which produces a new thing with new properties.

> "The labour has become incorporated with the subject matter of labour. Labour has been materialized, and the subject matter of labour has been elaborated. That which in the labourer appeared as movement, now appears in the product in a resting phase, as 'being' instead of 'becoming.' The worker has spun, and the product is his web."[2]

Thus in the process of material production and of class conflict, which aim at the changing of "natural" things and of social relations, there is disclosed an objective dialectic of quality and property.

In compounding a theory or scientific hypothesis we proceed from properties to the form of movement that lies at their base, but this is possible only because in *practice* – in industry, in experiment, in class struggle – we proceed by the reverse course; we create by our action determined forms of movement and arrive at new properties. The radical re-casting of things allows us to probe into the world from the inside, it opens up to us the contradictory movement that lies at the basis of things and thus creates a basis and criterion of knowledge. In our practice we ourselves make actual the development of matter, we ourselves create objective actuality.

---

[1] *Capital,* vol. i, chap. 5.

[2] *Capital,* vol. i, p. 173.

"Purposeful action is directed to this end – that, by abolishing determined aspects, features, phenomena of the external world, we may give to ourselves reality in the form of external actuality" (Lenin). Thus in practical action "the consciousness of man not only reflects the objective world, but also creates it" (Lenin).

In this creativeness we have such a close mutual penetration of man and the objective actuality that exists outside him, such an immediate unity of them, as radically refutes agnosticism and the superstition[1] that grows from it. By disclosing and developing the connection of man with the objective world, practice opens the way to a deeper knowledge of the nature of things, to an ever fuller disclosure of the internal definiteness of a thing in its properties, to an even more many-sided conversion of the "thing in itself" into the "thing for us." An impassable and mysterious gulf between the "thing in itself" and our consciousness exists only in the imagination of Kantians and their successors.

Both superficial sense impressions and very accurate scientific conceptions are reflections of actual things, copies of them, although copies of a different degree of accuracy and depth.

A thing has an infinite number of properties. In each property is reflected some one aspect of the object. We shall never exhaust all the aspects, but even in the simplest impressions, ocular, aural and so on, we are given not hieroglyphs of the thing, not subjective, secondary properties, but a reflection of it from some determined aspect. On the basis of practice we shall know ever more and more properties, ever more and more aspects, and by disclosing their internal unity, shall know ever more deeply the qualitative definiteness of the processes.

We know the quality of a thing through its properties. The diversity of properties, the diversity of aspects, in which the thing is connected directly or indirectly with all other things, is inexhaustible, infinite. Being in connection with everything, each particular

---

1 If subjective experience and states of consciousness are our only data in apprehending reality then "religious" experiences are as valid as any other and the whole world of occultism and superstition is put on a par with the world known to science. Hence this relativist agnosticism is declared to open the door to superstition.

thing is in essence just as infinite in its many-sidedness as the world as a whole. The apt expression of this thought by Dietzgen the German philosopher and worker was cited by Lenin with approval. It runs:

> "We may know nature and its parts only relatively; because every part, although it is only a relative part of nature, has nevertheless the nature of an absolute, the nature of a natural whole – which is, as such, inexhaustible by knowledge."[1]

What properties are more essential than others? Subjectivists say there is no objective distinction. In their opinion out of the multitude of particular properties we select arbitrarily those which are more interesting and important to us and pay no attention to the rest. Only one who completely disregarded actual material practice could state the question thus. To an empty "contemplator" of nature, to one whose approach to things is superficial, a mere consideration of supply and demand, the objectivity of properties is of no importance at all. A bourgeois on holiday in the country admires the bright colours of a poisonous plant, and does not bother about its more essential, harmful properties. But for the deep practical knowledge required in order to change things the most "interesting" properties are those which are objectively the most essential. "The introduction of practice into the determining of an object," of which Lenin spoke, will lead not to an arbitrary selection of properties but quite on the contrary demands the objective criteria of their essentiality or non-essentiality.

In order to transform a tree by work into paper, or to build a house from it, or to cut sleepers, or to get products by treating it chemically, it is not enough for us to know the colour of its bark or to listen to the poetical murmur of its leaves – we must know what are objectively the most essential properties of wood, etc., etc.

By what objective criteria can we tell whether properties are essential? As we have seen, every quality exists not as something discrete but only in relation to other qualities. The internal contradictions of the quality are the source of its various properties and make it possible for them to reveal themselves. Particular things are not independent – for their own existence they need other things. The

---

[1] Lenin, vol. xiii, p. 106.

connection of things consists in their difference; their unity is realized through oppositeness and conflict. The closer their connection, and at the same time the more acute their opposition, so much the more essential and characteristic are their mutual relations, so much the more are their essential properties revealed in these relations.

It is the nature of capitalists to exploit. This characteristic is expressed in their relation to natural resources, in the limitations of their interest in art, and even in their emphasized tendency to distinguish themselves by a modish costume – in all these things. But the most essential of them is their relation to the workers.

In all the habits of a beast of prey are disclosed its qualitative definiteness, but the most essential properties of a cat are manifested in the catching of mice.

An acid has many properties, but the most essential is its ability to combine with an alkali or a metal and form a salt. In a word the most essential qualities are those which a thing manifests in relation to "its other," to its opposite. Things that have little in common are for the most part "indifferent" to each other. No one examines a mechanic by playing chess with him. Just as little will be revealed by testing him on an automatic machine. A mechanic will show his essential properties in relation to "his own other," to the machine which it is his job to work, especially if he is confronted with a difficult repair job in connection with it. The most characteristic properties of a chemical element are revealed in relation with those elements which belong to the same family – a metal to a metalloid and the converse.

Chemistry at the beginning of the sixteenth century abandoned the alchemistic consideration of isolated properties and began to study properties in relation to one another. Attention was drawn at this time to the utilization of chemical preparations as medicines; this is the period of what is called *iatro-chemistry* during which the relation of chemical substance and their properties to the human organism was examined. This was mainly fruitful in increasing the knowledge of compounds but the more essential properties of chemical substances were revealed only after chemistry had begun to compare the chemical elements themselves with each other, to study their mutual "kinship."

As we have explained, the more essential properties of a thing are manifested in its relationship to the opposite thing of the same family, to the opposite particular of the same "general," to the opposite aspect of the same wider whole.

This proposition leads us to yet another quite important conclusion. Let us first ask in what are the essential features of the general itself manifested? We know that the general exists only in the particulars and through the particulars, that the whole exists only in the unity of its opposing aspects. But if this is so then clearly the specific definiteness of the whole is manifested in the relation of the opposing aspects and parts. Its essential properties are reflected in the unity of the essential properties of its opposing aspects. We begin our knowledge from relatively external, less essential properties and from them we proceed to disclose the internal relations of the thing, in which are expressed its most essential properties.

Each quality is dissected, each contains in itself a whole order of subordinate qualitative differences. Therefore each quality contains in itself a number of internal relations. It is precisely in these that the internal contradictions of quality emerge most fully and clearly and therefore in these that the most essential properties are expressed.

As long as the investigation of society proceeded along the line of its relatively external connections the knowledge of social phenomena was quite precarious and superficial. It was necessary to define the specific sphere of social phenomena, to learn to compare the different processes that lie in one and the same whole. But this could only be done by discovering the opposing sides of society, by expressing what were its specific features in a unity of opposing poles. Without this the bourgeois scientists had to be content with a description of the most superficial aspects of social life. Some of them held the essential property of social man to be his desire to imitate, others – the sex urge, a third group – the desire to accumulate, etc. Whole sociological treatises are written on all kinds of less important social phenomena, exalting them to a position of essential importance. The actual path to the understanding of social properties is revealed by approaching society as a whole, by distinguishing its opposing aspects, its opposing qualities. And as our knowledge of this unity of opposites becomes deeper, science is the more able to discover essential properties. Marx disclosed the internal contradictions in the development of the means of production, showed the inner connection of opposing classes and on this basis developed a study of the properties of society and social phenomena as no one had been able to do before him.

And so, the mechanists notwithstanding, it is impossible to ascribe properties to the external relations of things. Properties express specific definiteness, and the most essential, most characteristic properties of bodies are those which are manifested in the internal relations of the connected whole. Imperialism is a unitary system; its most essential properties are manifested in the contradictory connection of monopoly and competition. Thus in the infinite relations of a thing to other things and in the relations of its own aspects is manifested the whole diversity of its properties and in these its quality finds full expression.

Quality is necessarily manifested in properties, it can only develop itself through the unfolding of properties. "A being that exists in itself" necessarily becomes a "being that exists for another." Thus the aggregate of properties of a given thing appears by no means as something stagnant and immutable. In the development of a thing as a unitary whole its particular aspects are inevitably changed, but not in such a way that the thing should change its qualitative definiteness. "Although a thing exists only in so far as it possesses properties, yet its existence is not inseparably connected with the existence of those or other determined properties, and it can lose certain of them, without ceasing to be that which it is" (Hegel). Not every change of a trait of character changes the quality of man as a whole. But the development of this whole cannot take place except through a change of particular properties.

The unity of quality and properties, as we saw above in many examples, is a contradictory and fluid unity. It is realized not in an unchanged, quiescent relationship, but in ceaseless contradictory development. And to understand this unity the thing must be regarded not in its particular states, but in the whole line of its changes. What *is* this line of development, whither does this changing of the "being as it exists in itself" to the "being as it exists for another" lead? The mechanists hold that the development of the connections of a thing with other things is the expression of its dependence on all external circumstances. The more the relations of things are developed, the less of stability and definiteness is there in the change of each of them. The French materialists grew confused in the complex network of relations and everything seemed to them to be the sport of countless external causes. They sought the causes of change in everything in the world except in the entity that was itself changing. The collapse of the English revolution, some of them tried to explain, did not follow from its own development but from gravel that formed in Cromwell's bladder and caused his sickness and death. But this citation of gravel is purely arbitrary – it is impossible to discover all the "gravels," all the "crazy atoms."[1] And if every event is to be found in absolute dependence on external causes, it is impossible to know anything at all about its course.

We by no means ascribe movement to external causes, nor properties to external relations. We proceed from the self-movement of a thing and therefore our understanding of a being that exists for another is directly opposite to the mechanist's understanding. A thing is by no means the passive sport of external impacts. In its self-movement a thing possesses its own activity and manifests it through its properties.

Let us recall the examples which we gave at the beginning of the chapter – they exactly illustrate this active role of properties.

Even if we ourselves act on a thing, and as a consequence it takes on the appearance of a passive object of our action – even, in this case, those properties which it manifests are the expression of its own activity, its own qualitative uniqueness. In turning a piece of metal on a lathe we come up against the hardness of metal; in the chemical working of this or that material we evoke the appearance of its chemical properties. An agriculturist who despises the activity of the properties of the plants he is cultivating or the animals he is breeding will never get the results he desires. The difficulties of production and particular failures of our action on things demonstrate better than all arguments that in the development of properties, in their "being as it exists for another," things actively express their quality. The essential thing is that it is possible to evoke in the object such a change as flows out of its own nature. And if we do not apply our action to it externally or metaphysically, we shall make it "in being as it exists for us" express those properties that we need. Thus in solving the problem of properties, as in all other things, we must proceed from the self-movement of matter. And every self-movement arises on a basis of contradictions – "being as it exists for another" is one of its manifestations. Through connection with other things a thing asserts its own independence; by act-

---

1 "Crazy Atoms." See Note on p. 189.

ing on another, it develops its own definiteness; in its relationship to another a thing at the same time relates itself to itself and changes itself.

In disclosing the dialectic of the development of social man, Marx wrote:

> "By acting on the external world and changing it, he changes at the same time his own nature. He develops potentialities that slumber within him and subjects these inner forces to his own control."[1]

It is easy to note that in the proposition quoted, Marx gives a concrete picture of the contradictory development of a quality through its relations to something else. Faculties, lying dormant within man, i.e. that are found in a state of *being in themselves,* are developed through action on nature – through *being for another* – and become the proper active force of man. The developed qualitative definiteness of man, as reflected in his own consciousness, is in this way turned into his "being for himself."

The way of developing a quality lies through its many-sided connections. Here is that line of development in which quality and property emerge in their indissoluble unity.

The proletariat, until it developed its struggle against the bourgeoisie, appeared as a class in itself. It existed in the likeness of a disordered mass of workers, its qualitative definiteness as of a united, complete class with its individual properties and tasks was not yet developed, not yet unfolded. At this stage of development of the proletariat, the workers are under the thumb of the bourgeoisie in the latter's' conflict with feudalism. The way of consolidating, of rallying the proletariat, of welding it into a special class goes on through organization of the struggle against the exploiting classes.

In this relation to its "other," which is before all things its antagonist, the proletariat develops its properties. In this process it at first reveals superficial and nonessential properties, by expressing its protest in an elementary fashion and without any organization, by coming forward with particular economic demands of slight importance. But the further it unfolds its "being as it exists for another," that is to say, the more its opposition to the capitalists becomes intensified, the more deeply and widely does it manifest its

---

[1] *Capital,* vol. i, chap. 5.

essential properties, the properties of the leading revolutionary class. And when it produces its advance guard, its revolutionary party, which fosters within the proletariat a knowledge of its historical tasks and leads it on to the struggle against the capitalist system as a whole, then the proletariat emerges as an independent force of historic development, conscious of its independence – it becomes a class "for itself."

We repeat, through active "being as it exists for another" lies the way of contradictory development of every quality, the full unfolding of a given quality is the extreme intensification of its internal contradictions.

As we explained, every particular, qualitatively specific thing possesses internal contradictions. From one aspect it has the nature of a whole, includes in itself the general, from the other aspect it is limited in its uniqueness. In virtue of this contradiction it is connected with other things, is related with them. However, its "being as it exists for others," its connection with them, does not resolve its internal contradictions. On the contrary, through relation to another its quality is unfolded and thus and more fully are revealed its limitations, its finiteness. The more developed the capitalist means of production becomes, the more apparent are the signs of its end. The more an organism develops the closer is its limit, the boundary of its life – its death. From the view-point of a mechanist this limit is placed outside the quality of the thing as an external force, but actually the limit to every quality is found within it. Without a limit there is no quality, no definiteness, no distinction between one thing and another. But every end is the beginning of something new, the limit of one quality appears as the beginning of another.

The proletariat in its struggle against capitalism is turned into a class for itself, but by doing so it strives to pass beyond the bounds of capitalism, it seeks the abolition of classes and consequently points the way to its own extinction as a special class. In the full unfolding of the qualitative definiteness of the proletariat is included its self-negation. And such is the dialectic of every quality, of everything finite. In his review of Hegelian logic Lenin defined the dialectic of the finite in the following terms: "The finite is... something regarded from the view-point of its immanent limit – from the view-point of its contradiction with itself, which contradiction pushes and carries it (this something) further than its bounds...."

Thus for itself the "being" of a thing is its transition to another. Every quality, having developed all its possibilities, finds its limit, and gives rise to something new.

"So this dialectical philosophy dissolves all conceptions of final, absolute truth, and of a final absolute state of humanity corresponding to it. For it nothing is final, absolute, sacred. It reveals the transitory character of everything and in everything; nothing can endure before it except the uninterrupted process of becoming and of passing away, of endless ascendancy from the lower to the higher."[1]

---

1 Engels, *Ludwig Feuerbach*, p. 22.

CHAPTER VI

THE TRANSITION OF QUANTITY INTO QUALITY

Things in their connection are many sided and the knowledge of determined processes is not limited to the disclosure of their quality. Above all, we note that every thing along with its qualitative definiteness possesses a *quantitative definiteness*. A thing is big or little, its movement quick or slow; one collection of things may be distinguished from another by the number of its elements, by their mutual arrangement; temperature may be high or low, and so on.

At the first glance the quantity and the quality of a thing are quite independent of each other. A thing may be increased or decreased and remain qualitatively the same. Things different in magnitude may have one and the same qualitative definiteness, and conversely – one and the same quantitative definiteness may belong to qualitatively different things.

Both the huge Putilov Works and our smallest factory are socialist enterprises, just as in Germany a small factory and the gigantic Krupp's are both capitalist enterprises. We see that the socialist or capitalist quality of an enterprise does not depend on its magnitude. Here at any rate quality evidently does not depend on quantity.

So far then it would appear that quality and quantity are radically distinct from each other. If a thing changes its basic quality it ceases to be that which it was, it is turned into something else. Whereas with a change of quantity a thing does not cease to be itself. As Hegel said, quantity, unlike quality, is "indifferent" to the definiteness of the object. That is why in the early stages of scientific development the quantitative knowledge and the qualitative knowledge of things are markedly independent of each other.

Even at the most rudimentary stage of development social man came into contact with quantitative differences of things, even the most primitive practice forced him to count and to measure. The primitive savage, reckoning by means of pebbles and his fingers, was preparing the first beginnings of arithmetic. An important role in this respect was played by the emergence of private property and the development of exchange. The reckonings of the merchant were another step in the history of arithmetic, and the landowner in protecting his boundaries was revealing the beginnings of geometry. In ancient Egypt and Greece we see the first steps of mathematics as a science.

However, both among the Greeks and also among the Arabs, who developed mathematics even further, the study of mathematical relations was very loosely connected with the study of particular things and specific properties. The application of mathematics was confined to the comparatively narrow field of commercial accounts, to land measurement and astronomy. While to the alchemists, when it was their turn to investigate the properties of things, quantitative definiteness appeared a quite non-essential aspect of the matter.

They were interested in *what* substances and forces made up a given thing, and never set the question as to *what quantities* of substances were united together. And we must point out that in their way they were right – to apply an accurate quantitative measure to undefined and diffuse properties and forces was quite impossible. The study of the quantitative aspect of things was impracticable without a definite level of attainment in the knowledge of their qualities.

The more exactly and accurately we grasp qualitative distinctions, the more are we empowered to discover definite quantitative relationships. The more deeply we reveal the definiteness in which lies the relative stability and independence of a thing, the more exactly can we measure it.

Only when chemistry progressed from undefined forces and propensities to the identifying of actual chemical elements – oxygen, hydrogen, etc. – only when chemical changes were understood as the necessary mutual actions of relatively stable substances, only then was it possible to put the question – "what quantity of each substance enters into the composition of this or that body? "

The discovery of quantitative differences was very fruitful for science. The knowledge of chemical combinations was enriched by a new and extraordinarily important aspect. Our knowledge became more comprehensive and exact. The possibility of a new approach to the object permitted the solution of a large number of hitherto insoluble questions. For example, with a merely qualitative investigation of chemical changes it was not clear in all cases whether we were dealing with dissolution or combination, with a simpler or a more complex substance. Thus for a long time chemists regarded iron-rust as a simple element, and iron as a combination of iron-rust with phlogiston. The real relation of iron-rust and iron was discovered only with the help of weights, by the application of quantitative measurement to the processes under study. Iron-rust was shown to be heavier than the iron out of which it was formed – and hence iron-rust was shown to be a combination of iron and oxygen. And thus by the combination of qualitative and quantitative analysis, a huge number of simple chemical substances was very quickly revealed.

We see the same relation of quantitative and qualitative investigation in the history of every science. Only at a definite stage of the knowledge of quality does a quantitative study of concrete things become possible.

Only after the qualities of capitalism and of small-scale production, etc., were established, did it appear possible to define the degree of the development of capitalism in this or that country, by taking into account the quantity of goods produced in its factories, the magnitude of the concentration and centralization of capital, the specific gravity of the small property still unabolished in the particular country by capitalist development. According to the degree of the selection of relatively stable *qualities* from the variegated network of social inter-actions, was the application of statistics, was the enumeration of social phenomena made wider and more fruitful.

The whole history of social practice shows that only at a certain stage of development does knowledge of quantitative definiteness begin to play an essential role in man's recasting of things. Simple activity in relation to particular aspects of things gives no basis for an accurate quantitative evaluation of the changes being produced. As we know particular properties are in themselves unstable and relative. By considering them we can, in any given case, expect only an approximate, only a more or less probable, result. And only in a radical, all-sided recasting of things do we obtain the key to their stability and to their changes and are we able accurately to define the limits of the processes which we are evoking. Mastering the quality of the object in its entirety gives us the basis for reckoning the quantitative connection between our actions and the results which we obtain.

In the economy of small-scale production and with but a narrow circle of social connections, the reckoning of quantitative definiteness plays but a small part. The peasant and the small craftsmen work "by the eye" without exact measurements. The development of machine production requires a closer determination of quality and necessitates accurate measurement and the application of mathematics, both in science and production. A modern engineer can do very little without the aid of complex mathematical calculations. To construct a machine it is not enough to master its general qualitative characteristic, we must know how to produce an exact quantitative reckoning of all its details.

A peasant wishing to know the properties of a soil is satisfied by a scrutiny of it, an examination by touch, whereas an expert subjects it to a chemical analysis and finds out not only what are the ingredients of this soil, but also what quantities of them enter into its composition. Chemistry has distinguished in the composition of the soil a number of more or less stable elements, and therefore it is evidently possible to establish in each particular case their quantitative relations. In the restricted practice of a peasant it is impossible for *qualitative* study to be sufficiently highly developed to make possible an accurate *quantitative* estimate of soil composition; for this there are needed the dimensions of large-scale scientifically organized production.

In a planned socialist economy an accurate quantitative accounting plays an incomparably greater role than under capitalism. The quantitative indices of capitalist production and of trade returns reveal naked facts before which capitalists are quite helpless, whereas for us these dry figures become an active stimulus and effective guide to action. In them are incarnated our fighting slogans, from them originates intense class conflict. The percentage of the accomplishment of the Five Year Plan, the quantity of hectares under crops, the indices of the productivity of labour, etc. – in these figures we measure our successes and express the extent of the problems lying before us. The more widely and deeply socialist planning controls production, and the more we master the particular improvement of each branch of our economy, the greater will be the role that exact quantitative indices will play.

And so at a determined stage of the development of science and practice the gulf between quantitative and qualitative investigation is bridged, their closer connection is made apparent and they begin mutually to supplement each other. However, the transition to this new stage is not accomplished automatically, not of itself; before knowledge makes the transition to the study of the quantitative definiteness of things, it must go through much preparatory work.

"For enumeration, not only are the objects of enumeration necessary, but also the ability to scrutinize these objects, to disregard all their properties except their number, and this ability is the product of long historical, empirical development."[1]

We say: in such and such a factory there are so many workers. Each worker has his own characteristics – there are no two people absolutely identical. But when we express their common number we disregard their differences. Iron-rust, iron itself and oxygen are qualitatively different from each other. But when we speak of their quantitative relationships we disregard all their differences, we select only their common aspect which is expressed in their weight.

Thus for a quantitative knowledge of things we must, firstly, know their qualitative definiteness, since without this, comparison itself would be unthinkable; secondly, we must find that general thing in their qualitative definiteness which permits us to disregard their differences.

The metaphysic of properties gave no basis for quantitative investigation for the very reason that it was impossible to disclose general characteristics in propensities and forces that were sundered from each other.

As Hegel said, quantity is *definiteness* without difference. To obtain a quantitative characterization of things we must find "non-different" features in the things which we wish to compare, identical, common features that are not fortuitous or non-essential but are such as will allow us to determine by their means their quantitative relations and the qualities arising out of them.

The aspect of "non-difference," of identity, in the basic quantitative comparison of chemical elements is their weight. The great French chemist, Lavoisier, who first began consciously to apply the quantitative approach to chemical phenomena, had first of all to prove the correctness of comparing elements and their compounds by *weight,* and he did this by his discovery of the law of the conservation of matter; in all chemical changes the weight of the elements taking part remains identical, "non-different." Lavoisier's discovery depended on the great preparatory work of mechanistic natural research. Lavoisier lived in the epoch of the great French revolution

---

1 Engels, *Anti-Dühring.*

and two centuries earlier mechanism had, at the beginning of the Renaissance, insisted, as against the mediaeval metaphysic of properties, on the need of picking out the general, the identical and, consequently, the measurable in all the processes of nature.

The positive historical problem of mechanism is this – to take the first steps to the disclosure of the simplest, quantitative relations between things themselves, to create a bridge between abstract mathematics and the study of concrete processes. The natural scientists of the seventeenth century picked out velocity, mass and volume as the most simple and general aspects of all physical phenomena, to which one could apply the quantitative approach. The conversion of these aspects into unique essential properties of nature led the scientists to a complete negation of qualitative distinctions in nature, to a purely quantitative view of the world. The creation of mechanics as a science was their great service, yet at the same time, the source of their mechanistic limitations. They showed the mechanistic relations in nature and declared there were no others.

"*Mechanics knows only quantity.* It depends on velocities, masses and volume. Wherever it meets with quality – as for example in hydrostatics and aerostatics – it cannot reach satisfactory results, since it does not lend itself to the scrutiny of molecular states and molecular movement. Mechanics, therefore, *is only an auxiliary science, a propadeutic to physics.*"[1]

On the basis of mechanics, science went on to the study of qualitatively unique physical-chemical processes in their quantitative definiteness. And here was revealed that the "indifference," the "non-difference" of quantity to quality is by no means absolute – it has its limitation. The study of the different physical states of a substance, of the unique forms of energy – heat, electricity, etc., the formation of qualitatively different physical combinations – all these revealed the internal connection of quantitative and qualitative changes. At the beginning of the nineteenth century natural science laboured much to disclose this connection. Hegel gave to it, although in a distorted idealistic form, a general expression as one of the laws of development. Finally, in the materialistic dialectic of Marxism this law was revealed in all its precision as one of the ba-

---

[1] Engels, Second note of *Anti-Dühring.*

sic laws of the objective world and of knowledge and revolutionary practice.

Let us proceed. Quantitative changes at a determined stage lead inevitably to changes of quality. Solid iron may be heated in greater or less degree and still remain a piece of iron. However, when the heat reaches a certain point it causes the iron to melt and enter into a qualitatively different state. Capitalist enterprises though they may be on a big or little scale yet have their higher and lower limits of magnitude. Complete capitalist planning as between all industries is too big a task for capitalism. From the other aspect a capitalist undertaking can by no means be as small as it likes.

"Not every sum of money, or of value, is transformable into capital; before this transformation can be effected there must be a definite minimum of money or exchange-value in the hands of an individual owner of money or commodities."[1]

This minimum, adds Marx, varies at different developmental stages of capitalist production and is relatively different for each industry.

Almost every petty-bourgeois dreams of becoming a capitalist. But for him to undergo such a *qualitative* change there is in the majority of cases not sufficient *quantity* of money. The accumulation of money when it does reach the determined limit turns the petty-bourgeois into a capitalist, into an exploiter of hired labour: quantitative change leads to a change of quality.

We can show this in the changing of anything, the changing of any phenomenon. Every thing on its emergence as qualitatively unique is changed quantitatively. Up to the known limits of quantitative change it remains qualitatively the same, but at the determined stage change of quantity leads to change of quality, or, as Hegel said, "quantity goes over into quality"; instead of the former quality there appears a new one.

The transition of quantity into quality is one of the basic laws of dialectic. It is the law of emergence of the new, the law of development, which shows how in the course of gradual changes the leap from one quality to another is prepared. Every theory which ex-

---

[1] *Capital,* vol. i, chap. ix.

plains the emergence of this or that new thing has this law as one of its most essential methodological postulates.

Bourgeois scientists, though they deny or are ignorant of dialectic, are, without knowing it, absolutely forced through the influence of their own practice to base their investigations on dialectical principles. As Marx and Engels pointed out, such an elementary application of the law of transition of quantity into quality constituted a whole epoch in the history of chemistry. No sooner had this science arrived at the stage of the systematic study of the quantitative relations of the elements, than before it rose the question of the connection between the quantitative and qualitative changes of substances.

The celebrated French chemist, Lavoisier, pointed out that every chemical compound possesses a determined quantitative relation of its elements. Around this question raged a fierce controversy. Many chemists were attempting to demonstrate that "chemical compounds exist in all possible combinations of the constituent elements" and that there are no leaps, no breaking of the gradualness in chemical processes. The opponents of leaps cited solutions and fusions. They did not understand the difference between a mixture, in which no new substance emerges, and an actual chemical compound, in which a qualitatively new substance is formed. A simple mixture of oxygen and hydrogen is possible in any quantitative relation, but in the forming of the qualitatively new body – water – these two elements unite only in definite quantitative proportions. Thus between water and the other combination of oxygen and hydrogen – peroxide of hydrogen – there are no intermediate compounds whatever. In the formation of peroxide of hydrogen, exactly twice as great a relative quantity of oxygen enters into the compound as in the formation of water. Not *any,* but only a *definite* quantitative difference conditions the difference of qualities, of leaps from one chemical combination to another.

In fierce controversy with the upholders of quantitative gradualness, the doctrine of the transition of quantitative changes into qualitative developed into an harmonious chemical theory. The disclosure of the dialectical connection of quantity and quality allowed the connection of a great number of compounds into systematized orders. Discussing one of these orders Engels wrote: "We thus see a whole order of qualitatively different bodies formed by the simple adding of elements, which, however, are always in one and the same relation."[1] Marx, in his application of the law of transition of quantity into quality, cited in *Capital* these achievements of chemistry, thereby stressing the universal significance of dialectical laws.

It is, however, quite clear that in the reformulation and subsequent application of dialectic by the Marxist the content and significance of the law we are discussing emerges with incomparably greater precision and fullness than in even the most valuable dialectical attainments of bourgeois natural research, which remain at an elementary level.

The working out of the law of transition of quantity into quality reached its highest degree in Leninism. Lenin showed more deeply than anyone before him the concrete and significant appearance of this law in the course of social development; he also showed its connection with the other laws of dialectic.

As Lenin so often pointed out, dialectic demands the scrutiny of every historic moment in all its qualitative uniqueness and, at the same time, in unbroken historical relationship with the epoch preceding. The methodological basis for understanding this historical connection of the new quality with the old is the law of transition of quantity into quality. We find the most brilliant example of the application of this law to the study of concrete development in the Leninist theory of imperialism. On the basis of the dialectical method Lenin disclosed the uniqueness of the imperialist epoch as a continuation, but at the same time a qualitatively new stage in the development of capitalism.

Imperialism as monopoly capitalism is the necessary result of the development of pre-monopoly capitalism. From this historical connection, from these premises of the development of imperialism, Lenin proceeds in his investigation.

"The enormous growth of industry and the remarkably rapid process of concentration of production in ever larger enterprises represent one of the most characteristic features of capitalism."[2]

The *growth* of industry, the *enlarging* of undertakings, all these are quantitative changes belonging to capitalism. They also appear as the premises of the transition of capitalism to a qualitatively new stage. "Concentration at a certain stage of its development approxi-

---

[1] *Anti-Dühring.*

[2] Lenin, *Imperialism*, chap. i.

mates, so to speak, closely to monopoly."[1] The emergence of the new is prepared by gradual changes of the old. However, that does not mean that the transition itself, from the old to the new, is accomplished by degrees. Between pre-monopoly capitalism and imperialism there is not simply a quantitative difference – in imperialism we have a qualitatively new stage of capitalism, opposite in a certain degree to the old. In imperialism "certain basic properties of capitalism have begun to be turned into their opposite."

"Free competition is the fundamental property of capitalism and of commodity production generally. Monopoly is the direct opposite of free competition; but we have seen the latter being transformed into monopoly before our very eyes, creating large-scale production and squeezing out small-scale production, replacing large-scale by larger-scale production, finally leading to such a concentration of production and capital that monopoly has been and is the result."[2]

Free competition, the basic trait of capitalism, continues even in the new epoch to exist alongside monopolies, but the emergence of these latter creates a qualitatively new degree in the development of capitalist contradictions. A contradictory unity of monopoly and competition lies at the basis of the qualitative uniqueness of imperialism.

The transition to a new quality proceeds through a conflict, in which at a determined stage, there emerges a break, a decisive turning, a leap. At the basis of the whole process lies a conflict of contradictory tendencies, and that is just why the emergence of the new, the transition of the old quality into its own opposite, proceeds not as if due to the action of an external, alien force but as the result of growth, of the, quantitative growing of itself. Free competition through the contradictory growth of capitalism leads to its own opposite.

The enemies of dialectic, as also its false foolish "friends" depict the dialectical method as a preconceived scheme, as a master-key, with whose help it is possible to solve any problem directly

---

[1] Lenin, loc. cit.

[2] Lenin, *Imperialism*, chap. vii.

"out of one's head" – to obtain the answer to any question. The Leninist application of the dialectical laws is a brilliant rebuttal of this gross caricature of the dialectical method. Lenin regards the laws of dialectic not as a preconceived scheme but as the way to an understanding of concrete factors, a starting-point for the attentive study of objective actuality in its whole historical connection. "In order to give the reader as well-grounded an impression of imperialism as possible," Lenin cited an enormous quantity of facts. The quantitative changes of capitalism are for him no abstract phrase, but an object of detailed statistical study. He brought forward the most detailed statistical data which allow us to see "to what extent bank capital, etc., has grown, showing just how the transition from quantity to quality, from developed capitalism to imperialism, has expressed itself."[1]

And by very virtue of this concrete approach, a leap is for Lenin not an instantaneous automatic change which proceeds on such and such a day and hour, but a whole period of intense struggle. With Lenin the important thing is to determine, not the day and hour of the "final" changing of one quality into another, but the content of the break (what quality is replaced by what) and the concrete stages of the struggle in the transition to the new quality. "Needless to say, all the boundaries in nature and in society are conditional and changing, and it would be absurd to dispute, for instance, over the year or decade in which imperialism became 'definitely' established."[2]

Based on a huge mass of facts, the Leninist analysis discloses the basic line of the development of capitalism from free competition to monopolist decay and gives a concrete picture of the leap. Free competition, when it has reached the recasting stage of its development goes over into monopoly. In tense conflict through a number of *partial breaking moments* the general break in social life is accomplished – the leap from the pre-monopolist system of capitalism to imperialism.

"And so, here are the principal phases in the history of monopolies:

---

[1] Lenin, *Imperialism*.

[2] Lenin, *Imperialism*.

(1) 1800-1870. The development to its final limit of competition. Monopoly only in its smallest beginnings.

(2) After the crisis, after 1873 – extended period of the development of cartels, but these are not yet of a permanent nature. They are still a transitory phenomenon.

(3) The close of the nineteenth century and the crisis of 1900-1903 – cartels are becoming one of the bases of the whole economic life. Capitalism has turned into imperialism."

CHAPTER VII

CONTRADICTION AND THE EVOLUTIONARY LEAP

The doctrine of leaps is one of those principles of dialectic which have been subjected to severe criticism from the revisionist standpoint and also from scientists who avowedly take the bourgeois point of view. And it is easy to see why. With the question of leaps is closely connected the question of social revolution. If everything in nature and society develops by decisive qualitative changes, by leaps, then it must be admitted that capitalism too will be inevitably replaced by another social order in the process of the working out of scientific laws, and that this will take place by means of a leap, which under the conditions of capitalism can only be a socialist revolution. Such a perspective is very disagreeable to capitalists and their reformist defenders. In seeking to prove that revolutionary changes cannot advance us, that revolution is indeed the *sickness* of society, a harmful *abnormality*, bourgeois scientists and politicians are defending a theory of purely evolutionary development. "Nature does not make leaps" – that is the basic formula of this theory. All things develop by means of slow, continuous changes, by means of an increase, a quantitative growth of certain sides of actuality, and a decrease of others. In the preceding chapter we saw that this theory in essence denies that any development is an "emergence of the new," and reflects a limited, metaphysical point of view.

Indeed, if there are no leaps then there are also no radical changes, and all development amounts merely to quantitative changes of that which always existed. That which was microscopically small has now become big, that which was big has become small, but nothing new, nothing that did not exist before in some form, can appear.

Attempts to advance this view are met with in all fields of bourgeois science. We have already mentioned the view of certain early chemists on pure continuity in the formation of chemical compounds. In their view the appearance of a chemically new body is impossible – everything amounts to a mechanical mixture of particular elements. Under the pressure of fact most chemists have rejected these theories, but till this day various bourgeois natural-scientists have gone on trying, now in one form now in another, to advance the theory of the pure continuity of chemical combinations. In biology a thoroughly logical application of the evolutionary theory of development led to the "theory of preformation." How can an organism emerge from the embryonic form? Only by way of gradual quantitative changes. Therefore the embryo is the same organism, only in a folded, miniature form. The embryo of an elephant is a little elephant! This conclusion is quite contrary to fact, but the extremely logical "pre-formists" did not stop there, they set a new question; whence emerged the embryo itself? Arguing logically from the premises of pure gradualism you have to admit that it always existed, i.e. even when its mother and ancestors were themselves embryos. Thus arose the so-called "Chinese Box" theory; the embryo of every animal contains in ready-made form innumerable generations of its descendants, each one packed up in its predecessor!

The theory was confuted more than a hundred years ago. Yet none the less in our day, when it becomes very necessary for the bourgeoisie to struggle against revolutionary dialectic, bourgeois scientists return to this theory once again. According to the method of medieval alchemists they divide an organism into absolutely independent properties and declare these properties to have existed from eternity. All the development of animals and plants may thus be ascribed to the combination, the increase and the decrease of these properties. All the properties of the highest animals are already contained in ready-made but latent form within the simplest organisms. With certain refinements this is the same "Chinese Box" theory, the same metaphysic of pure evolution, the same denial of the possibility of the new and the same "rejection of leaps." In essence such a "theory of development" is a bald denial of actual development.

In so far as the bourgeoisie is interested in the development of technique it has to take account of facts, and under pressure of these facts a number of bourgeois scientists in their special departments arrived in an elementary fashion at dialectical results. But in their general world-outlook they are still opponents of dialectical materialism. And the more profound the decay of capitalism, the more do reactionary and even superstitious theories swamp the positive achievements of scientific investigators. The older metaphysical notion of fixed properties is merely carried to a further logical stage in evolutionary gradualism, in which form it becomes the methodological basis of the bourgeois reaction in science and in practice.

The place of honour in this reactionary metaphysic is taken by the social reformists. They also assert that the real road to social development lies along the path of slow gradual amelioration, i.e. along the -path of reform rather than revolution. Capitalism is sick, we must heal it – is all they have to say in the world economic crisis (1929-1932). It is quite clear that this ancient policy of patching the holes of the capitalist system is not the path to socialism, but a means of defending capitalism from the revolutionary indignation of the workers. That is why an irreconcilable struggle for the dialectical understanding of development, a pitiless showing-up of the hypocrisy of gradualism (the acknowledgment of development in words, the denial of it in action) – is the actual political task of our philosophic front.

However, we should be quite wrong if in our struggle against gradualism we reconciled ourselves with those "theorists" who seek to ascribe all development to leaps alone. We are against gradualism, but we by no means deny that evolutionary, gradual changes play a big role in development. As we saw above, a leap is impossible without a previous quantitative change within the bounds of the old quality.

The ultra-"left," representing the position of extreme "revolutionism," want at once to leap out of capitalism into communism, without any previous preparation, without prolonged struggle. These politicians, who express the psychology of "a petty-bourgeois driven mad by the terrors of capitalism," understand revolution as a sudden explosion, which at one blow destroys the old society.

Like the evolutionists they cannot find in the object itself the motive force of its development and are, therefore, compelled to seek it outside. They see in such a leap an absolute separation of the new from the old, they mechanistically distinguish between gradual preparation of the new and a leap. Therefore, they either wait passively for a revolution, not knowing how to prepare a revolution by an active participation in social struggle, or they seek the source of revolution in a subject, in the impulse of a person, in the intoxicating inspiration of some miraculously gifted revolutionary leader.

Such an understanding of leaps is purely idealistic, and like all idealism, leads directly to superstition. This theory which declares the long task of organizing the masses for actual revolutionary action to be superfluous and even harmful, and distracts the masses from its tasks of preparing for the leap, is in essence just as reactionary as the theory of evolutionism. It is not without significance that the Trotskyist opposition marked its real counter-revolutionary character by making use of similar ultra-"left" phrases. "Permanent revolution" for all lands without exception, according to one recipe; a socialist conversion at one blow, "of planetary dimensions," etc., etc. – what are these but ultra-"left" phrases, the only effect of which is to hamper real revolutionary activity?

For Lenin a correct view on this question involved a struggle on two fronts simultaneously. As early as 1910 he was writing:

> "The revisionist regards as mere phrases all arguments about 'leaps' and about the opposition (on principle) of the workers' movement to the old society as a whole. They accept reform as a partial realization of socialism. On the other hand, the anarchist-syndicalist repudiates 'petty tasks,' especially participation in parliament. As a fact, this latter tactic amounts to a mere waiting for 'great days' without any knowledge of how to marshal or prepare the forces that create great events.
>
> Both the 'right' and 'left' grasp at only one aspect of development and, by turning it into a whole, create reactionary metaphysical theories.
>
> But real life, real history, includes in itself these different tendencies in just the same way that life and development in nature include in themselves both slow evolution and sudden leaps, sudden interruptions of gradualness" (Lenin).

Thus it is impossible to separate evolution and revolution from each other. They are necessarily connected together and actual development appears as their unity. However, we must guard ourselves from a simplified formal understanding of this unity. If we follow the method of the Deborin school we shall interpret this unity as follows: the Right Wing takes its stand on evolutionism, the Left Wing on revolutionism. Dialectic reconciles these opposites, reaching a synthesis of them both. All is well and everyone is satisfied!

In a previous chapter we met with this eclectic understanding of the unity of opposites on the part of the Menshevist idealists. As we saw, they put forward, in place of a contradiction to be resolved in conflict, the principle of the reconciliation of "extremes," and took their stand on the position of a moderate and careful "golden mean." The utter futility of this eclectic method is quite evident even in application to the given question. By "synthesizing" evolutionism and "revolutionism" we shall not reach a dialectical unity of evolution and of leaps. Evolution, for the very reason of its procedure by leaps, as dictated by internal necessity, bears no resemblance at all to the peaceful gradualism of the evolutionists. Just as revolution, too, is not at all like its representation by the heroes of "left-revolutionary" phrases. Neither these nor others nor even the Menshevist idealists understand that what is important in this question is that all sides and phases of an evolving whole in the course of their development reveal irreconcilable contradictions.

Such a dialectic is very like that caricature of it which its bourgeois opponents draw. The founders of Marx-Leninism never turned the dialectical method into a simple scheme but used it as a basis for the concrete study of actuality itself – and in particular for the concrete study of the relation of quantity to quality.

Engels wrote: "Mere qualities do not exist. Only things exist which possess qualities, and moreover an infinite number of qualities."[1]

As a whole a thing is characterized by a certain basic, single quality. But this wholeness, this unity of the thing, is always split up into a number of different aspects, parts, moments – and this number is in the final reckoning infinite.

> "If production in general does not exist" – wrote Marx, showing up the empty abstractions of bourgeois economists – "then also general production does not exist. Production always represents a special branch of production, for example, agriculture, cattle-breeding, manufacture, etc., or some aggregate of them as a whole."

In its turn every branch of production includes in itself a number of subdivisions and parts, a number of technical and economic peculiarities and details.

And so each quality contains in itself a vast number of partial qualitative differences, in each of which the basic quality, the general definiteness of the thing is reflected. That is why we do not understand the evolutionary preparation for a leap merely as a mat-

---

[1] Engels, Foreword to *Anti-Dühring.*

ter of continuity. The gradualness of the evolutionary process cannot be represented as continuous and it too consists wholly and continuously of partial reverses – breaks – leaps, in which the separate
partial qualities that are included in and reflect the general quality of
the thing are changed. The transition from pre-monopoly capitalism
to imperialism is a genuine leap in the general course of the development of capitalism because in it there is a direct and leap-like
change, not of capitalism as a whole, but of the previously dominat-
ing form of the organization of capitalist enterprises and capitalist
subdivisions. But also these same stages of capitalist development,
and this same transition between them, include in their turn an infinite number of leap-like changes of opinions, of yet more partial,
more derivative aspects of the qualities of capitalism as a whole.
Every phase of crisis and revival, of war and peace, of the seizing of
a new market by this or that country and, to speak of smaller things,
every formation of a new trust, every new demand, every "deal,"
etc., *ad infinitum* – is characterized by a definite qualitative uniqueness and is connected through a leap with the other correspondingly
larger or smaller parts of the whole. In nature there is no emergence
of new qualities that does not contain in itself an infinite number of
qualitative changes and leaps of subordinated aspects.

There is no purely uninterrupted development of a whole process in its entirety; the change of a basic quality of a thing is infinitely subordinated to interrupted changes of its aspects. In this continuous interruptedness of the infinite number of qualitatively definite aspects of a thing, proceeds that relatively uninterrupted development of its general, basic quality which thus prepares for its leap.

"These middle links show merely that in nature there are no
leaps for the very reason that it consists only of leaps."[1] The process
of socialist construction is uninterrupted for the very reason that in
the countless number of separate improvements, of breaks, right
down to the mastery of the production of a determined detail in a
factory, there proceeds the unfolding and strengthening of the one
socialist quality of new social relations.

Superficially, inexactly understood, the unity of quantity and
quality appears thus: at first there are quantitative changes – *then* a
change of quality; in other words, at first there are uninterrupted
changes – *then* a leap. There you have the unity of opposites, the

---

[1] Engels, *Anti-Diihring.*

unity of evolution and of the leap, of interruptedness and of uninterruptedness. But Engels's approach is far more concrete and profound. Engels shows the mutual penetration of these opposites – firstly the interruptedness in evolution and then the relative uninterruptedness in the connection of the separate links of a leap.

But does not this view approximate by a roundabout way to this same gradualism? As a matter of fact, the social-reformist will say, the transition from capitalism to social ism does proceed by way of separate small changes, by way of partial improvements of reforms of different aspects of the capitalist system. So to what end proletarian revolution and proletarian dictatorship? The gradual growing of capitalism into socialism must proceed by "slow steps," diffidently, in a zigzag. Little drops of socialism must, by way of partial changes, trickle into the capitalist system until it is all turned into a socialist system. Capitalism grows into socialism, because socialism grows into capitalism.

The reformists slur over what is the main point – the irreconcilable oppositeness of capitalism to socialism. Capitalism, as a whole, as a system, is opposed to socialism and therefore in the limits of this capitalist system no real socialist improvements are possible. And yet capitalism itself, by changing its aspects, is actually preparing its own downfall and transition to socialism. As a qualitatively unique whole, capitalism possesses a relative stability. Partial changes of its properties do not change its basic character; nevertheless they make ready the conditions of its general crash. Through partial qualitative changes proceeds the intensification of the contradictions of capitalism, the growth of these contradictions. The qualitative changes of the aspects and properties of capitalism are thus the expression of the quantitative change of capitalism as a whole, of its basic quality, of that quantitative change which prepares its general leap.

Such is the profound internal contradiction of capitalist evolution, as of all evolution generally. Engels wrote on this issue as follows:

> "If oppositeness belongs to a thing (or to a conception), then in it and also in its expressions in thought, we find a *contradiction with itself.* For instance, in the fact that a thing remains the same and at the same time is uninterruptedly being changed, in the fact that it possesses within itself

an oppositeness between 'stability' and 'change,' there lies a contradiction" (*Anti-Dühring*).

Not only in the question of the development of capitalism does the doctrine of the contradictoriness of quantitative and qualitative changes play a big theoretical and practical part. In every process an internally necessary negation of quality is brought into being by the development and strengthening of that process. The more fully and far a given quality has been developed and the higher the stage of quantitative development it has reached, the more clearly are its final limits revealed, the more quickly does its negation, does its transition to a new quality, draw near. The dialectic of the transitional period shows this contradiction at every step. In socialist construction we pass through a number of qualitatively unique steps. In order correctly to denote the political line of the transitions of one into the other we must evaluate the uniqueness of the contradiction of the qualitative and quantitative changes of each of them. Through the present (1932) "artel" form of the collective farms we are passing to a higher logical-socialist form of agricultural organization. The more fully developed the "artel," the quicker the realization of this transition. Through the strengthening of the existing stage of socialist construction to its negation at a higher stage; that is the contradictory formula of our forward movement. One of the most important examples of the establishment and working out of this formula is its application by Stalin to the dialectic of the transitional period in the U.S.S.R.

Our state is struggling for the abolition of classes. For this purpose, by attracting ever wider masses of workers to posts of authority, it seeks to wipe out the distinction between society and state and approaches ever closer to the epoch when, according to Engels's expression "society will put the whole state machine in its proper place – in the museum of antiquities along with the distaff and the axe."

But does this mean that in our conditions there is going on an uninterrupted and gradual withering away of the state, that the successes of socialist construction must lead to the gradual weakening of the apparatus of proletarian dictatorship? Wiseacres have been found who understood the matter like that, who proposed, along with the development of all-round collectivization, to set about liquidating the village soviets. These wiseacres, like social reformers under capitalist conditions, did not understand the contradictoriness of quantitative and qualitative changes.

The Soviet state is a state of a special type. In so far as the power in it belongs to the majority, i.e. the workers, in so far as it was created for the suppression of exploiters, for the abolition of classes, it is already not a state in the strict sense of the word, it is a half-state, as it was called by Lenin. But as long as classes are not yet completely abolished, so long as the remains of class distinctions among the people are preserved, it does not lose its basic character, nor in any measure ceases to be a proletarian state, an instrument of proletarian dictatorship. As long as the bitterness of class contradictions continues to grow the state must be preserved and strengthened as a "truncheon in the hands of the ruling class" (Lenin). The vitality of the soviets, the attraction of the workers to positions of authority, etc., are aids to the strengthening of the proletarian state. And only through this strengthening can there be progress to its ultimate extinction.

"We are for the withering away of the State. And yet we also believe in the proletarian dictatorship, which represents the strongest and mightiest form of State power that has existed up to now. To keep on developing State power in order to prepare the conditions/or the withering away of State power – that is the Marxist formula. It is [c] contradictory '? Yes, 'contradictory.' But the contradiction is vital, and wholly reflects Marxian dialectic....

"Whoever has not understood this feature of the contradictions belonging to our transitional time, whoever has not understood this dialectic of historical processes, that person is dead to Marxism."[1]

In its struggle for the abolition of classes the Soviet state both strengthens itself as a state and prepares its own extinction. And until the decisive goal is reached (the complete abolition of classes and of the remains of class distinctions), it preserves itself as a state.

"The completer the democracy, the nearer the moment when it will become unnecessary. The more democratic the state (which is made up of armed workers and is 'already

---

[1] Stalin, speech at Sixteenth Congress.

not a state is the strict sense of the word'), the more rapidly does every form of the state begin to decay."

This moment when every form of the state begins to decay is the moment of the decisive turn, the beginning of the new quality – of society without a state, the beginning of the highest phase of communism. This leap is radically distinct from the leap between capitalism and socialism. There, the leap is accomplished as a revolution, as a pitiless conflict of classes. Here, the society of socialist workers is freed basically from the marks of its larval stage and progresses to a new and higher stage of development. In the one the antagonistic contradictions of capitalism are resolved in antagonistic conflict. In the other the non-antagonistic contradictions of a socialist society already subordinated to a plan are resolved by way of development in a conflict of the new forms of life. But in both the one and the other we see the final limit of the determined quality, the decisive turn to the new line of development, in both we see the resolution of contradictions. In a word, with all the difference of the types, forms and length of leaps, everything in the world, both in nature and in society, resolves its internal contradictions by way of change of quality, by way of a leap.

The reaching of the final limit is the moment of deepest contradiction and at the same time the beginning of its solution.

And so, as we see, the unity of "gradualism" and "the leap" is a contradictory unity that emerges at different stages of the development of quality.

However, the gradualist has in reserve yet another objection. Granted, he argues, that a new stage of development arises out of the old, yet since nothing arises out of nothing, it follows that in the evolutionary changing of the old there are already being created the basic elements of the new and therefore the transition from one degree to another is an uninterrupted process, a process of the gradual growing of one quality into another. The stupid Bolsheviks, say the reformists, are smashing capitalism and wish to construct a socialist society without creating the elements of socialism within the shell of the capitalist system, and since out of nothing, nothing arises, the Bolshevist "experiment" is foredoomed to failure. As a matter of fact this promised failure is not evident, and the gradualists in the camp of the enemies of the U.S.S.R. are like bad jugglers, whose tricks, promised to the public, have not been a success. They would like to create the "failure" of the Bolsheviks before the eyes of this same "public" with the aid of direct injury and even intervention. It is true, of course, that nothing emerges from nothing. The properties which become elements of the new quality are actually created in the old. But until the basic connections of the old quality are broken these properties belong wholly to the old and in no measure denote the gradual growing of one quality into another. These properties are contradictory. Within the bounds of the old they include in themselves only premises for the emergence of the new, and are only a *condition* of the leap, and only through a radical break, through a leap, do they become elements of the new.

The raising of the temperature of water is accompanied by the quickened movement of its particles. In this way the free movement of the particles of steam is prepared. But until the boiling point is reached the movement of particles remains within the bounds of the old connection.

Capitalism, by creating big-scale industry, by giving to it an ever more clearly expressed social character, is preparing the premises of socialism and, in spite of the hypocritical assertions of the reformists, had already prepared them a long time ago. But until the decisive limit is reached, until private property in the means of production is abolished, this large-scale industry remains capitalist. In this process of socializing production the capitalistically exploited working class is formed and united. It appears as the carrier of the progressive tendency, the tendency to socialization, which leads capitalism to negation, to a revolutionary leap. That was why Lenin spoke of the "opposition (on principle) of the workers' movement to the old society as a whole."

The process of the development of capitalist production "develops, organizes, disciplines the workers." But at the same time, capitalism "crushes, oppresses and leads them to debasement and poverty," corrupts them with bribes, separates them by the forces of capitalist competition and national conflict. The working class develops its socialist qualities within the frame of capitalism, *not* by creative "flowerets" of ready-made socialistic culture, as the reformists suppose, but by organizing itself for decisive struggle against the capitalist system as a whole. Only by such a struggle can it purify itself from the vices and contradictions of capitalism and only in the epoch of its domination can the socialist traits of the workers become actual elements of socialist culture.

"Capitalism itself creates its own grave-digger, itself creates the elements of the new order, and yet without a 'leap' these different elements change nothing in the general position of things, do not begin to touch the domination of capital."[1]

The changes of different aspects in the bounds of capitalism do not change capitalism as a system, yet they create conditions for the emergence of the new social order.

Does this mean that all partial changes are non-essential, that the working class must refuse to struggle for them? By no means. If we deny any significance to partial changes, we should pass to the other extreme and deny the contradictoriness of development and thus occupy the position of the heroes of the "left" phrases.

Conducting the struggle on two fronts, Lenin stressed the ambiguous, contradictory character of reforms and all partial changes within the bounds of capitalism.

The reformists by clutching at different fragments of so-called socialist relationships that emerge under capitalism, for example, democracy, co-operatives, etc., create a whole order of theories of socialist growth – "constructive," "co-operative," and many other kinds of." socialism."

At the first glance they appear to be right. In fact, co-operation surely is for us an element of socialism. Do we not say that the growth of co-operation is identical with the growth of socialism? Yet, as Lenin shows, co-operation within the system of capitalism arid co-operation within the system of proletarian dictatorship – are two quite different qualities.

"A co-operative is a shop-counter and let there be whatever changes, perfectings, reforms you will, the fact remains that it is a shop-counter. That lesson has been taught to socialists by the capitalist epoch. And there is no doubt that it was a correct expression of the essence of the co-operatives as long as they remained as an insignificant appendage to the mechanism of the bourgeois order. But it also follows that the position of the co-operatives is radically and in principle changed, from the time that the proletariat wins state power, from the moment when the prole-

---

[1] Lenin, *Dissensions in the European Workers' Movement.*

tarian state power advances to a systematic creation of socialist laws and regulations. Here quantity goes over into quality. A co-operative, in the form of a little island in a capitalist society, is a shop-counter. A co-operative, if it embraces all society in which land has been socialized and factories and works nationalized, is socialism" (Lenin).

As we see, without a revolutionary leap in the ownership of the means of production, co-operative organizations in no degree begin to encroach upon the domination of capital. Yet at the same time workers' co-operatives, even in the conditions of capitalism, are a school that teaches the workers solidarity and organization. But in the conditions of proletarian dictatorship, co-operation emerges as an "element" of the new order. How is this contradiction resolved?

The correct resolution of the question lies only in conflict, in the inclusion of the workers' co-operation as a link in the general chain of the conflicts with capitalism, in using it as one of the organizations for preparing revolution. We must look on it not as the beginning of socialism, but as a school to teach the workers solidarity in conflict, and as a means of economic support of the proletariat in the time of strikes.

Thus, once again, we are persuaded of the correctness of the Leninist thought that only the theory of irreconcilable conflict of mutually exclusive opposites, only the dialectical law of contradiction "gives the key to 'leaps,' to the 'interruption of gradualness,' to the 'conversion' into an opposite, to the abolition of the old and the emergence of the new."

Our citation of co-operation enables us to draw yet one more conclusion. As we pointed out, a workers' co-operative under capitalism can at times better the position of a particular group of workers. Thus it resolves a certain partial contradiction in the lives of some of the proletariat. However, is this partial victory in any degree a resolution of the general contradiction of capitalism – i.e. of the contradiction between the proletariat and the bourgeoisie? It is not. On the contrary, this partial success intensifies this general contradiction even more. In fact it inevitably increases the pressure from the side of the capitalists and with its limitations and lack of permanence reveals to the workers that the basic root of their growing impoverishment and oppression lies in the existence of the capitalist ownership of the means of production.

Those who would interpret these fundamental principles in such a way as to find in the partial successes of the workers a path to the reconciliation of capitalism and socialism create the illusion that these successes lead to the reconciliation of class contradictions. But sooner or later, under the leadership of the revolutionary party, the workers become conscious of the actual objective result of partial successes, a result which mercilessly shows up the reconciliatory hoax.

In fact the resolution of partial contradictions within the framework of capitalism and the struggle for their resolution are the way to intensify and deepen the general contradiction of the capitalist system.

And the more quickly the communists succeed in joining up the struggle for partial aims with the single line of preparing the masses for the decisive leap, the sooner will this leap arrive.

Lenin wrote:

> "The relation of reforms to revolution is rightly determined by Marxism alone. Reforms are the collateral product of the revolutionary class conflict of the proletariat. For the whole capitalist world this relation is the fundamental ground of the revolutionary tactic of the proletariat – the A.B.C. which the venal leaders of the Second International distort and obscure."[1]

---

[1] Lenin, *On the Importance of Gold.*

CHAPTER VIII

THE DIALECTIC OF THE "LEAP"

Hegel, in his exposition of his idealistic dialectic as a theory of the development of absolute spirit, characterized the transition of quantity into quality in the following terms:

"It is indeed never at rest, but carried along the stream of progress ever onward. But it is here as in the case of the birth of a child; after a long period of nutrition in silence, the continuity of the gradual growth in size, of quantitative change, is suddenly cut short by the first breath drawn – there is a break in the process, a qualitative change – and the child is born. In like manner the spirit of the time, growing slowly and quietly ripe for the new form it is to assume, loosens one fragment after another of the structure of its previous world. This gradual crumbling to pieces, which did not alter the general look and aspect of the whole, is interrupted by the sunrise, which, in a flash and at a single stroke, brings to view the form and structure of the new world."[1]

In spite of all the profound idealism of Hegelian thought there has been correctly indicated one of the wholly essential aspects of the leap, namely that moment of the radical change in the course of development, in the course of the break, which shows the completeness of the new quality.

In the birth of a child such a moment is its first inhalation, when for the organism as a whole begins a new stage of vitality.

The moment of break in the agitated conversion of a given mass of water into steam is the boiling point, when as small an addition of heat as you like will create at once the beginning of a qualitatively new process.

"Water through cooling does not become hard gradually, i.e. by becoming cold first and then gradually hardening to the consistency of ice, it becomes hard all at once; when it reaches the freezing point it can still remain in its

---

[1] Hegel, *Phenomenology of Spirit.*

fluid state if kept in a state of rest, but the slightest jolt will convert it into a solid."[1]

In socialist revolution such a movement is the grasping of power by the proletariat and the approach to the organization of socialist economy. In the "years of the great break" such a moment is the beginning of the liquidation of the kulaks as a class.

However, is the transition of one quality into another fully explained by this moment? Can one ascribe the leap to this moment of break alone? Menshevist idealists answer this question affirmatively. Pushing Hegel's thought to its extreme, they regard a leap as momentary, as essentially timeless, as an act which brings forth a new quality at one stroke. In this conception of the leap they have united themselves with the ultra-revolutionists of the "Left," with anarchists and all those other "left" phrase-mongers, who express the leap as a sudden emergence of the new, without any complexity. The specious "leftness" and revolutionariness of this view conceals within itself, however, a quite opportunist negation of the contradictoriness of development. In fact, as we explained above, the transition from one quality to another, the leap, is a process of resolving contradictions, a process of the destruction and breaking of the old system and of emergence of the new. It is quite clear that this process is impossible without a more or less lengthy conflict, without a complex task involving destruction and creation.

The "left" communists of the Brest Litovsk[2] epoch, in proposing to carry on a revolutionary war against imperialist Germany, proceeded from the following position: If the time for the leap from capitalism to socialism had arrived, then the swift victory of revolution all over the world was assured; if not, then in any case the ruin

---

[1] Cited by Lenin from Hegel's *Science of Logic.*

[2] *Brest Litovsk.* Early in 1918 the Soviet delegates met the representatives of the Central Powers at Brest Litovsk. It was soon made clear that the Germans wished to conclude an oppressive peace. Trotsky, who led the Russians, refused to sign and the Germans denounced the armistice and marched into Russia. After a series of debates Lenin got a majority in the Central Executive for signing the treaty even though the conditions then imposed were worse than before. The treaty was signed on March 3rd, 1918. It was annulled after the armistice of November 11th, 1918.

of Soviet power was inevitable. That is the defeatist conclusion at which the "Lefts" arrive when they regard the leap as an automatic instantaneous act. Either, in a flash of "poetic" revolutionary lightning, to conquer the whole world at one stroke, or – all is lost! The resolution of actual contradictions is by no means so easy to accomplish, is by no means so decisive.

In the first months of the revolution Lenin wrote concerning this view:

> "The whole originality of the position we are living through from the point of view of many who wish to be regarded as socialists is this, that people have become accustomed to oppose capitalism to socialism and between the two have in the profundity of their thought set the word 'leap' (some of them, remembering snatches of Engels they have read, have added with still more mental profundity: 'The leap from the kingdom of necessity to the kingdom of freedom'). Of the fact that the teachers of socialism denoted by 'leap' a break as regarded from the angle of the changes of world history and that leaps of such a type occupy periods of years – ten or even more – of this fact the majority of so-called socialists, who have studied their socialism in a 'little book' but have never seriously penetrated into the matter, have no inkling."

The first breath of a child is the first manifestation of his independent vitality, but the act of giving birth is much more than that. "The birth of a child is such an act as turns a woman into a tortured, rent, pain-maddened, bleeding, half-dead piece of flesh." As Lenin indicated in the same passage, "one ought to compare revolution with the act of birth. Births are sometimes easy, sometimes difficult. Marx and Engels, founders of scientific socialism always spoke of the long birth pangs inevitably connected with the transition from capitalism to socialism."[1]

A leap is a profoundly contradictory process. A leap by resolving the contradictions of the old quality denotes the prolongation of the same conflict in a new, far more intensified form. In a leap we find the immediate unity, the immediate coincidence of destruction of the old and creation of the new, of negation and affirmation. The

---

[1] Lenin, *Incidental Questions of the Soviet Power*.

conflict of the contradictions of the old system brings it to a crisis, and in the crisis the new is born. The birth originates out of destruction, the very act of the birth and the process of the development of the new are the destructive work of an enormous force. Without an irreconcilable, pitiless negation nothing new can emerge; in this lies the dialectic of every revolutionary change. Gorky characterizing Lenin's attitude to actuality, wrote: "Life is made up with such diabolical ingenuity, that if you cannot hate, it is impossible sincerely to love."

This spirit of implacable negation, proper to all revolutionaries and creators of the new, excites the deep displeasure of the modern "healers of capitalism" – the social reformists. Revolution leads to destruction, revolution is barbarism, they declare.

The fact that revolution is allied with destruction, with a temporary decline in the development of productive forces, is not denied by any authentic revolutionary. But whoever has not the manliness to take part in this destructive labour, the same is inevitably destined to become a defender of what is dead and decomposing.

Revolution is not empty, thoughtless destruction. On the contrary, it is for the very reason that revolutionaries follow an objective line of social development and pursue the path towards the emergence of a new quality, that their action possesses a force destructive to the old system.

The real threat to the capitalists is not in the supposititious bombs and the Tcheka but in the successes of socialist construction in the U.S.S.R.

And so the birth of the new takes place in the contradictory mutual penetration of destruction and of the new quality that issues during this destruction. In itself the birth of the new far from exhausts the transition of one quality into another. When the first molecules of water fly out into the air this by no means yet denotes the conversion of water into its gaseous state. The decisive turn has begun, the new connection of particles has been indicated, but this new connection, at the moment of birth, exists only in embryo. In October 1917, we witnessed a decisive change which opened the way towards a new system of social laws transforming the entire world, but before every department of world society is completely dominated by this new quality, before this new quality is completely actualized, there must be a long period of fierce conflict with what is being destroyed.

"The transitional period cannot fail to be a period of struggle between dying capitalism and nascent socialism, or in other words, between conquered but not annihilated capitalism and nascent but still feeble communism."[1]

Again,

"When a new thing has just been born, the old always remains for some time the stronger. It is always thus both in nature and social life."[2]

At the moment of its birth the new is feebler than the old; its feebleness depends on the *degree* of its immaturity.

"It is to be expected, that the achievement of the new cannot at once give us those firm established, almost stagnant and rigid forms, which were long ago created, have grown to strength, been preserved through the centuries. At the moment of birth the elements of the new are still found in the period of fermentation and utter instability."[3]

The feeble new enters into conflict with the stronger old. But is it possible that the strong should be conquered by the weak? – asks the formalist-metaphysician, for whom every contradiction is an absurdity. This contradiction and this victory are both facts of living dialectical development, and cannot be brushed aside by formal arguments.

The point of the matter lies in this, that socialism at the beginning of its development is weaker only in the *degree* of its development, only because it is immature, but from the very first day of its existence it is stronger according to *type,* stronger as a new, more progressive quality, free from those contradictions before which the capitalist system has already showed itself powerless.

That is why the new order appears finally as the victor, that is why it can conquer only by concentrating on its elements of real superiority and developing them with the utmost speed. That is why every step of socialist advance makes the fate of capitalism ever

---

[1] Lenin, *Economics and Politics in the Epoch of Proletarian Dictatorship.*

[2] Lenin, *The Great Beginning.*

[3] Lenin, sketch for the article *"Incidental Tasks of the Soviet Power."*

more hopeless, notwithstanding the ever more intense opposition of the capitalists.

The basic slogan for the conflict of the two systems – "in the shortest historical period to catch up and excel the leading capitalist countries in technique and economic development" – means nothing else than the task of making socialism stronger than world capitalism, not only in type, but also in the level of development, in the degree of the developing of its latent possibilities.

A socialism that is at its beginning weaker than capitalism cannot conquer with one blow. It conquers by the fact that at every particular moment it reveals its qualitative advantages, in that portion of the conflict which is decisive at that moment. Whence there is a certain irregularity in its advance, whence the number of qualitatively unique stages in its conflict with the old system.

> "The actual interest of an epoch of great leaps is this, that the ruins of the old are sometimes far more numerous than the new, often barely visible beginnings, and this situation demands skill in picking out what is most essential in the line of development. There are historic moments when for the success of a revolution it is more important than any other consideration to accumulate the, greatest possible number of ruins, i.e. to blow up as many of the old institutions as possible; there are moments when enough has been blown up, and it is time for the 'prosaic' ('boring' is the term for the petty-bourgeois revolutionary) task of clearing the ground of the debris; there are moments when a careful tending of the first beginnings of the new, which is growing among the ruins of the old on a soil still badly cleared of its rubble, is more important."[1]

That was how Lenin in 1918 characterized the particular stages of the transition to socialism.

The transitional period *is* the "great leap" itself and contains a number of transitional periods, a number of breaks, of leaps from stage to stage: the transition from war communism to N.E.P., the transition from the N.E.P. to the period of reconstruction, the "great break" of the countryside to the side of collectivization in 1929, the

---

[1] Lenin, vol. xxii.

entry into the period of socialism, these are all clear examples of those leaps in which our epoch of the "great leap" is so rich.

Moreover the last stage of the transition period is at the same time the first stage of victorious socialist society. By assuring the victory of socialism in our country along the whole line,

> "we have already issued from the transition period in the old sense of the word, and have entered into the period of a direct and developed socialist construction along the whole front. We have entered into the period of socialism, because the socialist sector now holds in its hands all the economic levers of the whole popular economy."[1]

Socialism has ceased to be an embryo. It has become, in a remarkable degree, a developed analysed quality that rules in the social life of our country. And as the Seventeenth Party Conference showed, we shall in the course of the second Five Year Plan abolish classes and construct a full socialist society.

As we see, the concrete picture of a leap bears no resemblance to petty-bourgeois, idealistic, Utopian, "leftist" revolutionism. In each leap we distinguish the particular stages of the conflict, we find in it a unique mutual-penetration of the interruptedness and uninterruptedness of development. The dissolution of the contradictions of the old system in the conflict of the new quality with the old makes up the basic content of such a leap.

---

[1] Stalin, concluding remarks of speech at Sixteenth Congress.

CHAPTER IX

THE TRANSITION OF QUALITY INTO QUANTITY

To attain to concrete knowledge we must not ascribe everything in the world to quality or to quantity but must explain the mutual connection and mutual transitions of the qualitative and quantitative definitenesses in every process. As Lenin showed, the dialectical law that connects quantity with quality is only an example, a partial case of a more general principle which he formulated as follows: "Not only is there unity of opposites, but there are *transitions* of every definition, quality, trait, aspect, property into *each* other (into their opposites)." In this formulation it is easy to recognize the concretization and development of this same unity and the mutual-penetration of opposites. The relation of quantity and quality is mutual, "each side passes over into each other."

In actuality there is no such thing as quantity in general. There exists only the quantity of a determined quality. A mere number in itself says nothing to us about a thing until we know what this thing is and from what aspect and how it was measured. Two tons of iron and two motorcars are by no means equal, although for the purpose of mathematical operations which are abstracted from concrete things two is unconditionally equal to two. Number unaccompanied by a knowledge of quality conveys nothing. But that which is clear to all in any example taken from life is by no means so evident to scientists and upholders of pure mathematics with their complex theoretical constructions.

It is by no means by chance that only at a determined stage of knowledge of qualities can every science put the question of the quantitative aspect of the processes it is studying. We saw above that chemistry could disclose the fruitfulness of the qualitative approach to elements only when these elements themselves were to a certain degree known and distinguished from each other. But as soon as the means of measuring chemical processes were discovered, chemists who had formerly been indifferent to quantity turned the quantitative approach into an absolute. In the majority of works on the history of chemistry everything that was done before this change of attitude is treated with the greatest contempt. Before Lavoisier people never dreamed about quantitative definiteness; if only they had done so two or three centuries earlier the history of chemistry would have been very different. That is the attitude and it is injudicious. Anyhow it is quite clear that by becoming worshippers of pure quantity chemists were cutting down the trunk by which they were climbing up. Contempt of quality became an obstacle to the future development of knowledge; it deprived the quantitative method of its necessary qualitative basis. The study of the quantitative aspect of things is in direct dependence on the depth and accuracy of the knowledge of their qualities. The physics of recent times was able to widen the application of mathematics, as it has done, only by accurately distinguishing between the qualitative uniqueness of the elements of matter and energy – atoms, electrons, quantum, etc. But at the same time owing to an unfortunate lapse into a metaphysical point of view on the part of bourgeois scientists this "great success of science, its discovery of the homogeneous and simple elements of matter, whose laws of motion are subject to formulae, caused matter to be forgotten by the mathematicians."[1]

Except by ignoring the material and its qualities, it is impossible to turn the application of mathematics into a basic method of investigation. Mathematical calculations and formulae play in the actual study of an object a subordinate role, because they must always be secondary to the known quality of the thing. By turning mathematics into a basis of knowledge we adopt a procedure that leads only to a barren play of figures that mean nothing, a sophistry that enables us to prove anything however absurd. This secondary importance of mathematics is specially stressed in the difference of the role which it plays in the various sciences. The more simple the qualities that are being studied by this or that science, and the more apparent and external the relations between the elements of the process, and furthermore the greater the consequent ease with which these elements can be distinguished from each other, the wider is the scope of mathematical application.

Mathematics studies quantity, i.e. external definiteness. Mathematical operations presuppose a certain stability and independence of those things whose number and measurement is required. And the less their stability and independence are, the more complex are those mathematical operations which are needed for the study of the quantitative definiteness.

---

[1] Lenin, *Materialism and Empirio-Criticism*, chap, v, sec. 8.

It is very easy and quite necessary to apply mathematical calculations to machines, which work according to a definite, exactly established pattern, whose separate parts have been made and assembled in a purely external fashion. But try to submit the life of an organism to the mathematical analysis and you will see that the fluidity and continuous mutual connectedness of vital processes convert your calculations into an empty play with mathematical symbols.

In astronomy and physics the application of mathematics has from ancient times held a very important place. Chemistry from Lavoisier's time has studied quantitative relations, but the application of mathematics was limited to simple arithmetical processes. Only in recent times on a basis of studying the deeper aspects of chemical processes has the field of mathematical calculations in chemistry been extended. But in one way or another the application of mathematics in this science occupies a place distinct in principle from its place in physics; it plays here a far more subordinate role. Chemical processes are more complex and the complete connection of their different aspects has been expressed in a much clearer manner than is possible by mathematical means.

Even more subordinate and restricted is the role of mathematics in the biological and still more in the social sciences.

Marx made use of mathematical formulae, but he never substituted them for an investigation of the quality of economic processes. On the contrary, these formula served him only as an auxiliary means of illustration and for a more accurate expression of basic economic ideas.

Quantitative definiteness is just as essential in social development as in anything else, but among social phenomena the connection of quantity and quality is markedly more complex and close and therefore the abstract and complex formulae of modern mathematics, which have been devised for the solution of physico-mechanical and technical problems, are less applicable for dealing with the quantitative side of social processes. That is why the philosophy of pure mathematics is especially artificial in the realm of social sciences.

In bourgeois political economy and sociology, mathematics emerges very often as the tool of plain political charlatanism.

One of the favourite methods of bourgeois scientists is the calculation of the average magnitude of a collection of different items.

For example, if they want to know whether the standard of living of the peasantry is improving or not, they find out and add up the incomes of all the peasant economic units, and so work out the average income of a peasant's farm. They compare such magnitudes for different years and demonstrate that capitalism in small-scale agriculture is not developing. It is easy to show that the root of this false conclusion lies in a wrong approach to the unit under consideration.

"It is supposed that by uniting together into a unit the workers and the master farmers and thus arriving at an average income-budget it is possible to demonstrate a condition of 'moderate satisfaction' and of a 'moderate net income.' But the average is quite fictitious. It merely covers up the utter poverty of the mass of lower peasantry" (Lenin).

Figures obtained like that only obscure and confuse the picture of the actual position of the countryside.

"Instead of a study of the types of peasant economy (the day-labourer, the middle peasant, the big landowner) they study, with the ardour of lovers, endless columns of figures as if it were their aim to astound the world with their arithmetical zeal" (Lenin).

This empty "play with ciphers" this "arithmetical zeal" expresses the definite class setting of those who like to underestimate the development of kulakism in the countryside.... It is not without significance that critics of Soviet policy made considerable use of this method when they openly voiced the interests of the kulaks. Statistics play a great part in science and in practice, but in order correctly to make use of numerical data we must proceed from the qualitative differences of the enumerated phenomena.

As we have seen in all the material we have been analysing, the only way to knowledge is first carefully to study quality, then quantity, and finally to restudy quality on the basis of all the data. The dialectical way of knowledge is a reflection of the law of objective development. In the development of material actuality quality and quantity are inseparable. They presuppose and penetrate each other and their unity is expressed in continual mutual transitions. Not only does quantity go over into quality, but also the reverse – quality goes over into quantity, the quality of a process defines the line, the character and the tempo of its quantitative changes.

Let us return to concrete facts. In the transition from small-scale production to capitalist manufacture there took place at first the union of many tradesmen within one workshop. "The workshop of the guild master only widens its dimensions.... At first there is only a quantitative difference" (Marx).

However, at a determined stage quantity goes over into quality – the joint work of many workmen in a capitalist undertaking is qualitatively distinct from small-scale craft. And this new quality creates a new quantity. The cooperation of many persons, the fusion of many separate forces into one common force creates – as Marx puts it – a new "force," which is essentially distinct from the summation of the particular forces that compose it. Whence does this new force appear, wherein lies the source of the magnification of the productivity of work? Quite evidently in that new quality which belongs to large-scale production. The new quality has created a new quantity, quality has gone over into quantity.

We see this same dialectical transition in the example of our collective farms.

> "The simple concentrations of the peasants' implements within the collective farms has had an effect not contemplated on the basis of our earlier experience. How was this effect manifested? In the fact that the transition to collective-farming methods gave an increase of the area under crops of from 30 per cent to 40 per cent and even 50 per cent. How do we explain this astounding result? By the fact that the peasants, who were powerless under the conditions of individualistic work, have been converted into a very great power by the concentration of their implements and by uniting into collective farms."[1]

Metaphysicians separate quantity and quality, whereas in vital developments these categories are all the time making transitions into each other. Opportunists on the question of the transition of quality into quantity, as in everything else, take up a metaphysical view-point. Both the counter-revolutionary, Trotsky, and the Right-opportunists united themselves in defence of the theory of the de-

---

[1] Stalin, on the question of agrarian policy in U.S.S.R.

clining curve of our economic growth. They asserted that with the transition from the restoration period to the period of reconstruction[1] the tempo of the development of industry would be continually lowered and would at last fall to the "normal" rate of increase, namely, that at which industry in capitalist countries develops. We have seen how drastically actual experience has treated this theory. Our tempo is determined by the qualitative advantages of planned socialist economy; the course of the qualitative changes of socialist production cannot fail to be different in principle from the growth of capitalism. The methodological root of the theory of the declining curve lies in the negation of the dialectical transition of quality into quantity.

A correct understanding of this transition plays a big role in the practical tasks of constructing a socialist economic order. In addressing the directors of Soviet industrial undertakings Stalin has pointed out a number of cases where the plan of developing industry has been unfulfilled because of inability to understand what new systems of working are possible under socialist construction. In his slogan of mastering technique in his Six Conditions[2] he showed the actual way to fulfil the quantitative indices of our plans, the way to achieve a Bolshevist tempo in socialist construction. Our successes have created a qualitatively new state of affairs, the new position demands a new quality of work, a new quality of direction, a qualitatively new approach to the organization of work on production, to the training of specialists, to the function of the old type of specialists, to the sources of accumulation in industry, etc. The way to raise the tempo is to master this new quality of work.

Meanwhile, certain metaphysicians and simple-minded directors think that the whole matter can be settled by a clamour about tempo, by simple, mechanical administrative pressure, by a campaign successfully conducted to the end of the month or quarter, etc. Nothing is obtained by such an approach except the exchange of practical work for cheap and empty exhortations. Anxiety over high

---

[1] *Restoration period – reconstruction period.* From the end of the "war communism" period, during which foreign intervention had to be faced, down to the beginning of the Five Year Plan the national economy was undergoing restoration assisted by the New Economic Policy. The Five Year Plan initiates the period of socialist reconstruction.

[2] *Six Conditions.* See note on p. 141.

tempo if it is not based on a concrete study of the quality of the given production, if it is not based on a thoughtful and serious organization of the business side of production, is abstract, empty and impotent, like the numerical conjurings of mystics, like the "arithmetical zeal" of the bourgeois economists.

We repeat, the key to actual Bolshevik tempo lies in that change of the quality of work which is to be brought about by fulfilling the six conditions of Stalin, by studying the qualitatively unique conditions and possibilities of every branch of production, by showing a creative initiative in the organization of every qualitatively unique matter. "Write what resolutions you will, swear by what words you like, if you do not master the technique, the economics, the finances of the works, the mine, the factory – all will be fruitless."[1]

Stalin in his masterly and profound treatment of the question of the tempo of socialist construction, has over and over again showed the great importance of the dialectical materialist method in the proletarian revolution. Directors must learn the dialectic of Marx, Engels, Lenin and Stalin, for without dialectic Bolshevik direction is impossible. And so in the reverse transition, in the transition of quality into quantity, we have approached from a new side the unity of quantity and quality, thus making concrete once again the unity of opposites. The problem of knowledge is not limited by the disclosure of the quality of a thing, just as it is not exhausted by the establishing of its quantitative characteristic – the point of the matter is in the transition of quality and quantity into each other. Only by disclosing the peculiarity of the transition in every phenomenon do we know an object in its self-movement, in its vital and concrete development.

The resolution of the contradictions between quality and its particular level in the evolutionary process, its degree of development, is at the same time an intensification of that contradiction, which reveals the final limit of the quality and leads to a new leap. The higher the degree of the development of the given quality, the more clearly is its limitation revealed, the more clearly the premises and tendencies of the new emerge in it, tendencies which cannot develop within its confines and are preparing the leap to the new quality. The overcoming of the remnants of the old in the new, the unfolding of a given quality as a whole, single system are at the same

---

[1] Stalin, speech on the mastery of technique.

time a process "of dividing the unity into its mutually-exclusive opposites" and the intensification of the conflict between them. The more capitalism is developed, the more strongly are revealed the contradictions between the socializing of work and private ownership, between the proletariat and the bourgeoisie, between the "changeableness" of capitalism and its "stability." The highest stage of the development of a quality, which it reaches in its evolution, is at the same time the highest stage of the intensification of its contradictions, is its limit, its end. The highest stage of capitalist development – imperialism – is, at the same time, its last stage, the eve of the leap to socialism.

By examining quality first of all in its emergence and then in the process of its evolutionary development, as a transition of quality into quantity, we showed that this quantitative change is at the same time the preparation for the transition to a new quality. In our investigation we returned to the transition of quantity into quality. And this circle expresses the continuous course of development. Development can never stop still; in the birth of a quality there is already included the seed of its decay, the decay of the one is the inevitable beginning of the new and so on, endlessly.

We are evolving into communism, but the attainment of our aim by no means excludes its further development.

> "Utterly false is the usual bourgeois representation that socialism is something dead, frozen, given once and for all; it is a fact that *only* from socialism will begin the advance in every realm of social and personal life – an advance that will be a rapid, genuine, real mass advance, in which first the *majority* of the population and later the whole population will take part."[1]

As Marx said, the transition to communism will end the prehistory of human society and will begin its real history. We do not yet know through what qualitatively unique stages this future historic process will go, but we are assured that communism will never in any way be a system of sleep and stagnation.

The double, mutually contradictory transition of quality into quantity expresses the eternal cycle of development in which matter, through the ceaseless emergence and annihilation of the forms

---

[1] Lenin, *State and Revolution,* chap. 5, section iv.

of its movement, keeps on reproducing itself in ever new movement and in ever new qualities.

> "Matter moves in an eternal cycle in which every particular form of the existence of matter – be it the sun or a nebula, a particular animal or biological process, a chemical combination or decomposition – is equally in transition, and in which there is nothing permanent except eternally moving matter and the laws of its movement and change."[1]

It is impossible to understand actuality with any degree of fullness, it is impossible to understand an object in its self-movement, until you disclose in it the cycle, the connection of its beginning and end.

The law of transition of quantity into quality and its converse show us the way to the understanding of this connection, to the study of the cycle of emergence and annihilation in all the phenomena of nature and society.

---

[1] Engels, *Dialectic of Nature*.

CHAPTER X

THE PROBLEM OF "LEVELLING DOWN"

In the struggle of the different tendencies in science which we touched on in our previous exposition, the question of the connection of quantity and quality plays an important role. The fierce controversies on this question have by no means been confined to philosophy. They penetrate into the special forms of science and may even become the methodological basis of direct political conflict.

Discussions on the relation of quantity to quality both in objective actuality and in knowledge are in large measure concentrated around the problem of reduction or analysis. In what direction must the knowledge of each phenomenon of nature and society proceed – along the line of the study of it as a complete whole, possessing a specific quality that determines all its features and properties and is expressed in them – or along the line of the analysis of it into its component parts and properties, of the reduction of the whole to the relations of its simple parts and properties?

The second alternative is one of the basic principles of mechanism. The mechanists think that a phenomenon is explained if we succeed in *reducing* it, in levelling it down to its simple elements and their external mechanical relations. In the whole there emerges nothing new in principle as compared with what was in its particular parts. Each thing only *seems* to be something indivisible, something unique, seems so from a superficial, subjective approach to it. The wholeness of a thing exists only as its secondary property. The task of science is to leave this superficial appearance and to probe deeper, to analyse the thing into its components. In this and this alone do mechanists see the task of knowledge.

Society is made up of people. To understand it one must learn the nature of man as such, his character and his desires. When these are known it will be easy to understand society as a whole. But a particular man torn out of his social connection is an animal organism and that is all. Therefore to understand society we must study man as a biological being. We must study his brain, his instincts, the physiological mechanism of the formation of the conditioned reflexes, etc. Moreover we must reduce the conduct of man to the simpler phenomena which we observe in the conduct of animals biologically lower than man. Certain physiologists following Pavlov are profoundly persuaded that those reflexes which they study in dogs can explain all wars and revolutions, all class conflicts and the subordination of one set of people to another.

But if society is reduced to a simple aggregate of animals of the species "man," then it becomes possible to explain social phenomena on the basis of the Darwinian theory. Every man carries on a struggle for existence. In this struggle the biologically stronger and better survive – the worse and weaker are doomed to extinction. This selection of the best also operates in the social process. If the weaker workers are doomed to extinction, especially in time of unemployment, then all the better for the human race. If the rich and noble are "on top," it must be because natural selection has raised them there as the strongest and best. The reactionary role of such theories is perfectly evident. By ascribing social effects to purely biological causes they are able to prove that the class order of society is the product of biological forces that inalienably belong to the human race. The reduction of sociology to biology is one of the philosophical instruments of the bourgeoisie. It is not surprising to find that "social Darwinism" is used for the justification of fascist dictatorship. And our mechanists, by defending the theory of reduction, are, whether they like it or not, pouring water on the fascist millwheel.

However, the reduction of sociology to biology is by no means the final point, it is only an intermediate station on the road of the mechanistic explanation of nature. An animal or vegetable organism is such a whole as must be explained by the physio-chemical processes that make it up. An animal is a machine, proclaim the mechanists. True the machine is more complex than any motor, but yet there is no *qualitative* difference between a man and a Diesel engine. The task of biology lies in the analysis of vital processes into their physio-chemical parts, in analysis and only in analysis, in levelling down. Biology is preserved as a particular science only because there has been as yet no successful analysis of all the biological processes that -Seem to be independent phenomena. In their turn chemical processes are ultimately physical and physical processes are at bottom the mechanical relations of "final," unanalysable, simple, identical particles of quality-less "matter as such." A few decades ago mechanists declared this "final" particle to be the atom. To-day, after still further reducing the atom they declare it to be the electron. But, as in the past, so now, this straining after something "final," eternal, immutable, simple, is the unmistakable characteristic of the metaphysical method.

Their dream is to reduce all sciences to one, to a final science concerned solely with the mechanical movements of the simplest parts. If Marx in *Capital* speaks of economic phenomena and of their peculiar laws, it is only in accordance with the imperfection of the science of his time. In the future, no doubt, we shall come to transpose the categories of *Capital* into those of electrons, and to explain the October Revolution as a definite form of electronic motion. This, then, is the final truth!

According to this there exist in nature no qualitative differences; all differences between things are ascribable to the number and distribution in space of quality-less particles, i.e. all differences are only *quantitative differences.* The differences of qualities are only a subjective appearance which we must accept until we reach the real explanation. Our mechanists have used the phrases "the untying of qualitative knots," "the elimination of all qualitative aspects." It is easy to recognize in these phrases the philosophy of the most commonplace bourgeois evolutionism. Qualitative knots and, consequently, "leaps" are only "subjective appearance." Mechanism of this type is obviously one of the forms of gradualism, the first of those theories of development examined by Lenin, the one which ascribes all changes to simple increase and decrease of magnitude. In essence such a theory of "development" is a negation of all actual development, a negation of the possibility of emergence of the new.

Our mechanists love to stress the fact that their views are strictly material. Yet the metaphysical nature of their views, independently of their wishes, takes them far away from logical materialism. All aspects of the mechanistic theory lead by one way or another to idealism and superstition. The impossibility of finding any real way of accounting for the world as we know it by attributing all phenomena to mechanical motion brings them to the subjective viewpoint, forces them more and more to admit the impossibility of getting beyond "secondary," "subjective" properties, leads more and more to the subjective-idealistic attitude to knowledge. By ascribing every form of definiteness to quantity they are led in the end to a Pythagorean numerical mysticism which is only another road from mechanism to idealism. In fact what is there to say about the particles of "mechanized" matter? Only "how many"? "how they are distributed"? and "how large and whither directed are the forces that connect them"? In this way all matter is reduced to geometrical and arithmetical relations. "The essence of the world is number." The mechanist Zeitlin, tried to "trim" Marx to the shape of a mechanist, and demonstrating (as well as he could) that Marx sought in *Capital* to ascribe all and sundry to quantitative differences, wrote: "When we asserted that Marx's *Capital* is mathematical *in its internal content*, we meant only that Marx's qualitative analysis is strictly materialistic." So according to Zeitlin, materialism is identical with mathematism; the more completely we reduce theory to mathematics, the greater the materialism.

> "As Hegel has shown already, this view, this 'one-sided mathematical view-point,' according to which matter is determinable only quantitatively and has been qualitatively the same from time immemorial, is a return to Pythagoras who long ago regarded number, quantitative definiteness, as the essence of things."[1]

The most logical mechanists do not attempt to conceal this. One of the leaders of the mechanists, E. E. Stepanov, wrote:

> "Must we not actually conclude that the electronic theory of the structure of matter brings us back to Pythagoras, who saw the essence of things in number, in quantitative definiteness? If, indeed, it brings us back, then it is on the basis of all the scientific attainments of the great period that follows on after Pythagoras."

"On the basis of all scientific attainments" modern physico-idealists return to Pythagoras; it is inevitable that everyone who denies the objective existence of qualities will ultimately find himself doing likewise. And so as we see, the different aspects of the mechanistic world-outlook reveal in the theory of reduction their unity as aspects of one and the same metaphysical philosophy, one and the same route to idealism.

The time has long gone by since mechanistic materialism, by its conflict with the mediaeval metaphysic of properties, by its investigations of the simplest mechanical movements, by its exposure of the grossest forms of superstitions, played an historically progressive role. Mechanism in our day is essentially bourgeois and has

---

[1] Engels, second note to *Anti-Dühring.*

become the weapon of bourgeois reaction both in science and in political practice. On the mechanistic theory of "levelling down" are based reactionary views as to gradual world progress by means of partial changes of the whole, are based all sorts of other bourgeois ideas that serve as a cover for the counterrevolutionary action of the modern "healers of the capitalist system" – the social reformists.

In our conditions this form of metaphysic with its abstract mathematical approach, with its "deeply philosophical" basis of gradualism and drift, has become the methodological basis of kulak ideology and its spokesmen – the Right-opportunists. Opportunistic narrow practicality that forgets about the complex connections of all the tasks of socialist construction (not seeing the wood for the trees) has as its own basis the same mechanistic reduction of the whole to the parts.

The lamentably celebrated theory of Bukharin on the peaceful transition of all the different phases of our economy into socialism substitutes for the contradictory process of a class struggle that is passing through a number of qualitatively unique stages, an even and continuous quantitative growth. On the basis of a purely quantitative approach, Bukharin has set on the same plane our socialist farms and the kulak estates.

Similarly, Frumkin asserted that we needed such and such a quantity of wheat, regardless of the sectors in which it was produced. Here was the same reduction of qualitative differences to pure quantity.

Bukharin, not without serious significance, bade us transpose the "language of Hegelian dialectic to the language of modern mechanics." This Right-opportunist practice was the logical realization of his mechanistic philosophic views.

And so mechanism, by reducing the whole to the parts, vulgarly distorts the tasks of knowledge and practice, arrives at an absolute monotony of nature and opens the door to subjective idealism.

However, in bourgeois ideology there exists yet one more resolution of the problem of the whole and the parts, a resolution which at the first glance seems absolutely opposed to mechanism. It is the stand-point of objective idealism, which rests on the wholeness of phenomena and turns this into an absolute. The upholders of this view observe the weak spots in the mechanistic theory of reduction. It is really out of their criticisms of mechanistic materialism that they construct their own philosophy of science. They point out that an organic whole is always more than the simple sum of its parts. A living organism is something more than an aggregate of physico-chemical processes; similarly the development of society is accomplished on quite a different principle from that which operates in the world of animals and plants; a man's thought is something quite other than the motion of the particles of his brain. The task of knowledge is not to analyse a whole into its parts, but to note the characteristic features of the entire phenomenon as a whole. Biology, they say, must study that which belongs only to the organism, it must confine itself to *that which distinguishes* a living organism from inorganic processes – the organic relations proper to the living body, nourishment, growth, reproduction, adaptability to its environment, the process of restoring destroyed tissues, etc. This strict regard for the whole is in flat opposition to the crudities of mechanism, yet it can fall into an even worse crudity itself.

This abstract concentration upon the wholeness of living processes tends to separate an organism from inorganic nature and to create a gulf between the living and the nonliving, between "spirit" and matter. Indeed, if life is *only* something peculiar to the whole, then how is one to explain the emergence of life from physico-chemical processes that originate on the earth's surface? The theory of absolute wholeness excludes the development of nature.

But the transition from the non-living to the living proceeds in a certain sense all the time. An organism is fed and grows. In this process it is all the time assimilating non-living substance, and turning non-living matter into living. It is easy to say that an organism possesses an "aptitude" for growth, but it is necessary to disclose *how* this growth proceeds. It is easy to say that an organism is capable of restoring destroyed tissues and fighting against disease, but it is necessary to investigate *how* these specific properties of the living organism arose in matter and how they actually developed. Moreover, in actuality the organic principle is by no means always realized. The wholeness of a living organism exists in conflict, replacement and destruction and is by no means absolutely harmonious. It becomes clear that the theory of absolute wholeness is a different aspect of the theory of "pre-established harmony," and, like it, closes its eyes to the sharp breaks, the destruction of the old, the conflicts, that take place in development. Thus to account for an evolved whole that is now in a static condition it is necessary to invoke some kind of miraculous intervention.

An organism is a ideologically constructed whole. There is none of this teleology in the particular physico-chemical processes that go on inside the organism, therefore – the upholder of "wholeness" concludes – the teleology of vital processes is a manifestation of a special beginning, of a special force, which exists outside the particular parts, which subordinates them to itself and joins them into a single whole. Since it is purposeful and is separate from inorganic nature, it appears essentially as a spiritual force. This is the "élan vital" (*vis vitalis*), whence in biology this theory bears the name of *vitalism*. This theory of absolute wholeness is obviously a profoundly idealistic doctrine.

It is easy to recognize in this doctrine the old, long familiar features of the mediaeval metaphysic of properties. That theory too acknowledged the reality of a whole as a special property that existed *along with* the properties of the particular parts. It also explained life by citing a life force. In just the same way in the "latest" idealistic doctrine separate qualities exist side by side as absolutely independent forces.

In criticizing the mechanists the upholders of absolute wholeness themselves arrive at another, a still grosser form of metaphysics; they expound undisguised superstition. The vitalists criticize the mechanists, the mechanists criticize the vitalists; each of these doctrines makes capital out of criticism of the other. And therefore they both exist in unbroken unity, each one possesses in the other "its other." In their conflict is disclosed their internal kinship.

The philosophy of absolute wholeness does not exist in biology alone. In the course of recent years it has made great strides in all the fields of bourgeois ideology. A nation is a whole, say the fascist philosophers, the life of a people is determined by its "national idea," its "national spirit," "its spirit of wholeness and of desire for power." This "idea" is higher than the interests of separate classes; workers and peasants must bow before this "idea," in its name they must abandon their demands and humbly submit themselves to Mussolini and Hitler. The direct coercion exerted by bourgeois dictatorship over the workers – the majority – is justified by the bourgeois philosophers with their idealistic theory of an absolute whole realized in the "national spirit." They depict the bourgeois State not as a cudgel in the hands of the ruling class but as an expression of the idea of a whole. Resurrecting the Hegelian idealism, the Hegelian teaching on the unity of absolute spirit, modern bourgeois philosophy creates the ideological weapon of fascism. We see a tendency to move in this direction among certain reformist theoreticians also.

The Menshevist idealism of the Deborin school took essentially the same line when it uncritically took over and began to use the whole of Hegel's idealistic dialectic. Especially in Deborin's treatment of the problem of quality do we find a distinct manifestation of an idealistic deviation. Deborin contends against idealism, he keeps aloof from vitalist superstition. But in criticizing the mechanistic theory of reduction he proceeds from abstract conceptions and therefore reaches a conception of quality as something isolated in its uniqueness. Whence his kinship with a number of semi-vitalist and sometimes even purely vitalist currents of thought.

The tendency of Menshevist idealists to understand a leap as an independent act shows that they too separate qualities from each other and fail to understand the mutual penetration of continuity and discontinuity, the internal unity of quantitative and qualitative changes.

And so objective idealism propounds, instead of the continuity of the purely quantitative changes of the mechanists, a break between qualities, a conversion of them into isolated, absolutely whole systems, separating qualitative changes from quantitative. Both forms of metaphysics are two mutually amplifying methods of the ideological struggle of the bourgeois for supremacy. Both currents, though proceeding from opposite directions, deny actual development, distort the tasks of knowledge, hinder the disclosure of the contradictions of bourgeois actuality; both encourage superstition.

The idealistic philosophy of a break between qualities is very often used by fascists for the purpose of setting one nation in opposition to another; by reformist theoreticians to buttress a purely fascist view of the State; and even by the heroes of the "Left" as the basis of the idealistic doctrine of a leap from the "kingdom of necessity to the kingdom of freedom." In the methodology of Trotskyism, which is distinguished by its extreme eclecticism and ambiguity, mechanistic reduction exists alongside an idealistic emphasis on the absoluteness of qualitative differences.

The idealistic philosophy of absolute wholeness serves Trotskyism as a basis for its "Left" talk of "permanent revolution," to be accomplished at one stroke on a planetary stale. It is not mere chance that Trotsky echoes the Hegelian, Lassalle. The theory of the

absolute isolation of the proletariat, which all other classes, including the peasantry, confront as a "united reactionary mass," the theory of revolution which arrives suddenly at the end of an epoch and
signifies the victory of the working class – these theories of Lassalle
were based on the idealistic doctrine of absolute breaks between
qualities. It is easy to recognize in the permanent revolution of Trotsky these same Lasallian features.

At the first stage of N.E.P., when socialist planning had not as
yet got its hands upon all the levers of the popular economy, Trotsky came out with a grand, all-embracing, all-accomplishing economic plan. In his abstract idealistic approach the whole was seen to
be separated from its parts; it was therefore quite unreal. But when
faced with practical difficulties Trotsky drew up a defeatist mechanistic programme of reducing the whole plan to the level of the
weakest sections of the national economy. Because of the backwardness of metallurgy (upon which the work of the machine building factories depended) Trotsky, in his speech at the Twelfth Party
Congress, proposed the closing of a number of our largest industrial
plants, including the famous Putilov works.

A clear example of his philosophy of absolute breaks is seen in
his attitude to the collectivization of the rural economy. Waxing
ironical on the question of our collective farm construction he wrote
that it was as impossible to construct a collective-farm out of the
sum of peasant farms as it was to build a steamer out of a collection
of little boats. Both Trotsky's comparison and his irony miss their
mark. In spite of his metaphysics our rural economy is developing
dialectically, quantitative change is leading to change of quality,
and the new quality is creating a new quantity, a new tempo of
growth.

Furthermore, in actuality the new never emerges ready-made
and finished. Breaks are never absolute. We have entered into the
period of socialism although a developed socialist society has not
yet been created and we have not yet emerged from the transition
period. It is this contradiction of living development that has never
been grasped by Trotsky, and is responsible for his errors.

And so both mechanistic "levelling down" and the idealism of
absolute wholeness are in their class-roots and their metaphysical
approach quite close to each other, and though they proceed from
different directions are all the time moving to the same conclusions.
It is clear from our enquiry that it is impossible to separate the

whole and the parts. They mutually penetrate each other. But in order to understand their real unity we must examine them not externally, not metaphysically, but in living contradictionary development. Independent qualities do not exist; all things are connected by a unity of development. The complex emerges out of the simple – *but unity of development does not denote the identity of all things.*

A living organism is something that arose out of inorganic matter. In it there is no "vital force." If we subject it to a purely external analysis into its elements we shall find nothing except physico-chemical processes. But this by no means denotes that life amounts to a simple aggregate of these physico-chemical elements. The particular physico-chemical processes are connected in the organism by a *new form of movement,* and it is in this that the quality of the living thing lies. The new in a living organism, not being attributable to physics or chemistry, arises as a result of the new *synthesis,* of the new *connection* of physical and chemical movements. This synthetic process whereby out of the old we proceed to the emergence of the new is understood neither by the mechanists nor by the vitalists.

The task of each particular science is to study the unique forms of movement of a particular degree of the development of matter. Social science studies the emergence and development of social formation, studies the development of productive forces and the relations of production, the class struggle and the changing of social forms. The production of tools and machines comprises the qualitative distinction of social man from animals and because of this qualitative distinction the development of society is accomplished not according to the laws of natural selection but according to laws that belong only to society.

Just as specific is the subject of biology. Biological sciences investigate the connection of different processes in the life of an organism, the laws of heredity and variation, the adaptability of the organism to the environment, development on the basis of natural selection, etc. All these processes are qualitatively unique, and attempts to reduce them to more simple laws can lead only to the distortion of the actual problems of knowledge.

How so? the mechanists will object; the complex is made up of the simple; life is wholly analysable into physico-chemical processes. Our mechanists do not understand that by subjecting the organic whole to external mechanical analysis this whole is destroyed.

By analysing an organism we get instead of the living, a nonliving thing, i.e. we destroy the very thing we set out to study.

Of course a more complex quality includes in itself elements of the simpler. Social man cannot exist without the physiological process of the exchange of substances, just as also there is no organic life without determined physico-chemical processes. But here is the point, the elements of the old, by being subordinated to the new system, by entering into the new synthesis, themselves become something new. Physico-chemical processes within an organism undergo a radical change; they cease in essence to be directly "dependent on" physics and chemistry.

The unique conditions of every chemical process within an organism are such that this process reaches results that under inorganic conditions are impossible.

"Albumen is the most unstable carbon compound that we know. It decomposes as soon as it loses the ability to fulfil its proper functions which we call life."[1]

Outside an organism albumen decomposes, within an organism it possesses a certain stability. However, this stability depends upon the constant renewal and the ceaseless change of various substances. "Life is the form of existence of albuminous bodies, whose essential moment is the *constant exchange of substances with the physical environment;* when this exchange ceases, the form too ceases and the decomposition of albumen ensues."[2] As we see, albumen within the conditions of an organism becomes qualitatively other.

But, some mechanist may object, exchange of substances is by no means proper only to organisms; we also meet with exchange in chemical reactions. No doubt, but the exchange of substances in an organism is qualitatively different from the exchange of the substances of inorganic nature and leads to directly opposite results. "The difference is this; in the case of inorganic bodies exchange of substances destroys them, in the case of organic bodies it is the *necessary* condition of their existence."[3]

---

[1] Engels, *Dialectic of Nature.*

[2] Loc. cit.

[3] Loc. cit.

Burning, i.e. the combination of carbon with oxygen, destroys bodies of non-organic structure, but the same process, in the form of the breathing going on within an organism, is the necessary condition of its preservation and development. It is the same process and yet at the same time quite another.

Quality, as the special system of a given whole, as the unique form of movement, lays its imprint on those elements from which it emerged itself.

As we see, in the reality of organic wholes, in their qualitative uniqueness, there is nothing mysterious and unknowable as vitalists and others declare. Wholeness is a qualitatively unique form of movement which, since it proceeds from previous stages of the development of matter, includes in itself elements of the old and re-fashions them in a new system which contains new contradictions.

The task of knowledge does not lie in reducing a whole to the parts, nor in studying a whole as such, but in the disclosure of the relations peculiar to each quality in its emergence and development.

Mechanists simply rejected the synthetic task of knowledge and reduced it to external mechanical analysis. The vitalists rejected analysis by converting synthesis into a previously given teleological force external to the particular parts. Neither these nor others understood development as the contradictory self-movement of matter. Actual scientific analysis has very little in common with mechanistic reduction. Of course in the study of an organism it is very important to know that the albumen of which the living tissue is made is a special type of carbon compound, that in the breathing process carbon dioxide is formed, that the hand acts on the principle of a lever, etc., etc. But the main problem for the physiologist in his analytic work is by no means *what* physico-chemical processes proceed in the organism, but what aspects, properties, features of each separate physical-chemical process make its specific role in the life of the organism possible. As we showed above, every physico-chemical process acquires in biological conditions a special significance and leads to results other than those found outside the organism. This specific thing in the chemical elements of life must also be sought for by the physiologist when he subjects the living being to analysis. Otherwise he will be not a physiologist but a chemist, he will have changed the subject matter of his investigation, and instead of studying the elements of the organism will be studying chemical processes as such. The mistake of certain physiologists who have constructed physical models of living cells is due to just such a change of their subject matter. In the movement of an amoeba a certain role is played by surface tension, but a drop of oil with its surface tension is only an external, remote analogy to the amoeba. In their acceptance of physical and chemical processes as removed from their organic connection as elements of life, physical mechanists have blundered badly.

Engels, disclosing the connection of different sciences with each other, wrote:

> "By calling physics the mechanics of molecules, chemistry the physics of atoms, biology the chemistry of albumens, I wish to express the transition of each one of these sciences into the other and therefore the connection, the continuity and also the distinction, the break between the two fields. Biology does not in this way amount to chemistry yet at the same time is not something absolutely separated from it. In our analysis of life we find definite chemical processes. But these latter are now not chemical in the proper sense of the word; to understand them there must be a transition from ordinary chemical action to the chemistry of albumens, which we call, life."[1]

Even in greater measure is it necessary to mark the qualitative uniqueness of the particular elements of human society. Society consists of people. It is true that people possess certain physiological needs and properties – they need food, they must secure shelter from cold, they multiply, etc. Without procreation there can be no social development. But only Parson Malthus and his followers (they include Karl Kautsky) have the effrontery to declare that unemployment under capitalism depends on the immoderate multiplication of the workers, has in fact a biological basis, whereas in actuality multiplication of social man is not his biological property, it is wholly subordinate to the specific law-system of the social whole. The growth of population is subordinate to social law-governance; the law of population, as Marx shows, is historical, it changes along with each form of society, is specific for each class, for each concrete situation.

---

[1] Engels, second note to *Anti-Dühring.*

And so the analysis of a qualitatively definite whole is not by any means its external mechanical dissection, is not by any means its reduction to such parts as have another, simpler qualitative definiteness. The particular parts always express in themselves the nature of the whole, and their separation from the whole is necessary only to Malthus, Kautsky, and other "priests" of the capitalist system, who use them as arbitrary logical figments and not as guides to an actual knowledge of capitalism. Thus in the contradictory unity of quality and its final limits, of qualitative and quantitative changes, of continuity and discontinuity, of the new and the old, is accomplished the eternal development of matter.

CHAPTER XI

THE NODAL LINE OF MEASUREMENTS

Pure quantity exists only in abstraction. In objective actuality every quantitative definiteness appertains to a certain quality. Three, four, five, etc. as generalities do not exist, but there are three or four trees, stones, tons of iron, metres of cloth, etc. Conversely quality also does not exist independently of quantity. Every quality belongs to a thing that has this or that magnitude, every qualitative definiteness has at every given moment a definite intensity and degree of its development, has this or that quantitative characteristic. A piece of iron that has no definite magnitude, weight and temperature does not exist. Nor does a tree exist without a definite diameter to its trunk, number of branches and leaves, etc. Every light-ray has this or that wave-length, every electric Current this or that voltage. The determined means of production in every country is characterized by this or that degree of development.

The establishment of such quantitative definitions, specific for each particular thing at each given moment of its development, has great practical and theoretical importance. However, the connection of quality and quantity in the examples just given has a more or less external character, each given magnitude is independent of the general characteristic of the quality. The fact that this piece of iron weighs three tons, and that four, is quite fortuitous for iron as a definite chemical element. The fact that in this country there are three trusts, in that ten, says in itself very little about the quality of capitalism as a special system of production.

In this way in every particular case the quantitative definiteness of a thing emerges as its external definiteness, "indifferent" to its quality. But as soon as we begin to scrutinize a thing in the whole course of its development we discover the profound internal connection of its quantitative and qualitative definitenesses.

Quality is developed on the basis of the internal contradictions of a thing. Development proceeds as determined by the form of movement characteristic of that quality and continues until the limiting stage within that type is reached. The contradiction of nascent capitalism pushes it inevitably to the development of machine technique, to the seizing of markets, to the annihilation of small-scale property, to domination in all fields of production. Socialism that has come into existence and has conquered but has still not yet fully developed proceeds inevitably to the full development of the possibilities of planned economy and goes on to the creation of productive forces adequate to socialism as a type of society.

In this case it is clear that quantitative development is by no means indifferent to the quality of the developing process, its connection with that quality is not external and fortuitous. Each particular quality has a corresponding quantitative measure so that the quantitative changes within a developing whole are determined by that quality. There are fixed limits in quantitative changes within which alone the quality can remain indifferent to the quantity. The point at which magnitude ceases to be indifferent is dependent upon the internal connection of quantitative and qualitative changes. Therefore change does not depend merely on quantitative development but on the special relation of quality to quantity in each particular case.

Conversely, we know that every quality is finite, that every qualitative definiteness has an internal final limit that belongs to it and that the fullest development of quality is at the same time the revelation of its limit.

Imperialism, the highest stage of capitalist development, is at the same time the last stage of its development.

> "But capitalism became capitalist imperialism only at a definite, very high stage of its development, when certain of its fundamental properties had begun to change into their opposites, when the features of a period of transition from capitalism to a higher socio-economic system had begun to take shape and reveal themselves all along the line."[1]

The concentration of powerful productive forces in the hands of a few capitalists is the highest stage of private property in the means of production. And at the same time the concentration reveals the final limit of private property, it makes possible and necessary the transition to socialism.

For a full knowledge of the quality of a thing it is necessary to determine its final limit, that highest stage of its development at which it goes over into another quality – into its opposite. To know the quality of a metal we need to determine the temperature at

---

[1] Lenin, *Imperialism*, chap. vii.

which it melts. To know the quality of a building material we must find out its resistance to strain, its conditions of fracture, its heat conductivity. Thus for the knowledge of a quality we must disclose the highest stage of its development, the point of demarcation for its changes, the quantitative final limit of its existence as the given quality.

That is to say, both quantity and quality are disclosed more fully in their unity. The disclosure of this unity is measurement in the widest sense.

The transition of quantity into quality and the reverse is nothing else than the revelation of the internal contradictions of measurement. And that nodal point of change, at which the transition of quantity into quality takes place, expresses very fully the measurement of the given thing.

Quantitative and qualitative changes, taken as themselves, seem to be something indeterminate, fortuitous, and external. In measurement we disclose their necessary connection, we reveal their importance in the unity of the process. Thus measurement is nothing else than the *law of the connection of quantitative and qualitative changes* – a law that belongs to everything.

"It is a great service to know the empirical numbers of nature, for example, the mutual distances of planets, but an immeasurably greater service is to make such empirically determined quantities vanish, by raising them to the *general form* of quantitative definitions, so that they become moments of law or measurement" (Lenin).

It was in this manner that Hegel determined the significance of the transition from external quantitative definiteness to measurement; he regarded measurement as the law-governed unity of a thing in its development, and development as that which gives the necessary basis to quantitative definiteness itself.

Knowledge of measurement plays an important role in science and practice. Every kind of physical energy, every chemical element has measure, which is reflected in a whole order of unalterable magnitudes – constants as they are called. Specific gravity, melting point, boiling point, atomic weight, valency, etc. – are such specific magnitudes as express the measurement of a chemical element. The constant of world gravitation, the magnitude of the quantum of energy, the mechanical equivalent of different aspects of energy,

Avogadro's constant – these are examples of magnitudes that reflect the measurement of physical processes. We measure the quality of a bridge by that load which the bridge can carry. Each machine has in given conditions the rate of output specific for it. A zoologist, in studying this or that animal, tries to establish its limit of growth, its age, its temperature, its blood constituents, etc. The differences in the qualification of workers of one and the same speciality finds its reflection, under equal conditions, in the different productivity of their labour.

In many cases serious political conflict centres round this question of measurement, as for instance when it is applied to the question of socialist advance or retreat, of finding the nodal point of a decisive turn. As an example we will consider the transition from the period of merely restricting the kulak to the period of the liquidation of kulaks as a class. Stalin in his speech at the Agrarian Conference gave convincing arguments for believing this transition to be opportune. He contrasted the quantity of wheat produced in kulak farms and in the socialist sector for the years 1927 and 1929, regarding these quantitative relationships as the index of the qualitative difference in the relation of two classes at the cited periods. In 1927 the relation of forces was such that a decisive advance on kulakism was impossible. The Zinoviev-Trotskyist party, which was at this time declaiming against the kulak, did not understand our unpreparedness for advance. Essentially the measures proposed by the opposition would have led to the policy of "scratching at kulakism," and not to its liquidation. "To advance on kulakism means so to prepare ourselves that when we do smite it it can no more rise to its feet."[1] This preparation was expressed in the Party line on collective farm and soviet-farm construction. And at last that moment came when the quantity of socialist wheat exceeded the quantity of kulak wheat; that was the nodal point of the related measurements, that was the moment when it was possible to introduce a qualitative change of tactics. In order to introduce this at the right time it was necessary to determine rightly the measurement of the relations of class forces. The Central Committee of our Party rightly determined this measurement and in 1929 initiated successfully the transition to the liquidation of kulaks as a class on the basis of all-round collectivization.

---

[1] Stalin, *Question of Leninism.*

In speaking of measurement in all the examples we have given we were at the same time speaking of the transition of one quality into another. Nor was it by chance. *Measurement, expressing the contradictions between quantity and quality, is the law of the transition of quantitative changes into qualitative changes and of the reverse process, and is therefore the law of transition from one process to a qualitatively different process.*

Measurement marks the final limit of a given quality. It is only possible to discover that limit by investigating the changes of a thing in a thoroughly practical and experimental way. To determine the measurement of the policy of *restricting* the kulak means to indicate that moment in which it passes over into the policy of *liquidating* the kulak. Measurement is found only in the process of change, in the process of turning one measurement into another.

Every measurement "exists only in that connection, which leads to the general" and expresses that connection by being the law of transition from one process to another. Every measurement is of internal necessity linked up with a number of others. In this internal connection they form a single line of development, a number of nodal points of qualitative changes – they form a *nodal line of measurements.*

An order of determined and logical changes in the length of a violin string gives a single order of musical tones and overtones. The solid, liquid and gaseous states of a substance are a single chain of quantitative and qualitative changes, a single nodal line of measurements of the aggregate states of the substance.

Knowledge finds in nature many different and, from their appearance, mutually unconnected, things and phenomena. The discovery of the nodal line of measurements leads to the disclosure of their internal connection, of the unity in the diversity, to the reflection in a concrete whole of the uniqueness of this or that field of nature. Engels, touching on the importance of the law of conversion of energy, wrote: "In science we have succeeded in ridding ourselves from the fortuitousness of the occurrence of this or that quantity of physical forces, because their mutual connection and their transition into each other have been revealed."[1]

Measurement is the law of the connection of quality and quantity. The nodal line of measurements is a yet wider and more gen-

[1] Engels, *Dialectic of Nature.*

eral law of a whole number of quantitative and qualitative changes. Where in appearance there is a simple, joint existence of separate things, a more profound knowledge will disclose their law-governed connection as links of a nodal line of the measurements of nature, a line complete in itself yet with infinite ramifications.

The nodal line of measurements expresses the internal connection of the development of material forms. However, it may happen the discovery of the nodal line of measurements will precede the discovery of the actual course of development. Even before the transmutation of chemical elements was verified in experiment chemists were occupied with the question of their classification. The great scientist, Mendeleyev, revealed what is called the periodic law of elements. He based this classification upon their atomic weights, a specific quantity belonging to each element, and by arranging the elements in the order of increasing atomic weights showed that the qualities of elements form a law-governed system – or, speaking in the language of dialectic, a nodal line of measurement.

Mendeleyev was led to his discovery by realizing the connection of particular elements with the quantity that is specific for them. He himself believed the conversion of elements into each other to be impossible and denied them any common origin. But when the general law was found it had great influence on the study of the properties of particular elements. Furthermore, on the basis of the periodic law Mendeleyev was able to foretell the properties of elements still undiscovered, whose places were then empty in the table of the periodic law. The investigations that followed brilliantly justified Mendeleyev's predictions. "Mendeleyev, by unconsciously applying the Hegelian law of transition of quantity into quality, accomplished a scientific exploit worthy to be set alongside with the discovery of Leverrier, who calculated the orbit of the unknown planet Neptune."[1] After Mendeleyev the periodic law underwent a number of essential changes and amplifications but its basic idea receives ever greater confirmation. The periodic law plays an important role in the study of that internal form of movement which lies at the basis of qualitatively different elements.

One of the greatest of the services of Marx in creating the theory of historic materialism was the discovery of the logical connec-

---

[1] Engels, *Dialectic of Nature.*

tion of a number of social formations. "In general features, the Asiatic, the antique, the feudal and modern bourgeois means of production can be established as progressive epochs of the economic history of society."[1] Social history as a whole, consisting as it does of the successive replacements of one social system by another each of which is characterized by the determined level of productive forces and of the productivity of social work, forms a single nodal line of measurements.

In politics the nodal line of measurements plays also an important role. As Lenin pointed out, the basic trait of opportunism is "the changing of principles, lack of principle... jumping over gaps." In contrast to opportunist lack of principle the Leninist policy is the conducting of a single line through all stages of revolutionary conflict. Lenin, in reckoning up the qualitative differences between stages, always indicated the internal connection of the particular stages with each other. Stalin on this basis has worked out the practical strategy and tactics of Bolshevism. Bolshevik strategy is built on the evaluation of the peculiarities of each stage, determines the measurement of the decisive turn from stage to stage, and realizes through a number of stages the one final aim of the proletariat. Trotsky opposes to the Leninist doctrine on the stages of revolution his own conception of the strategy of class struggle. In *The Lessons of October* he defined strategy very generally and abstractly, as "the art of conquering, i.e. of winning power." For Trotsky strategy is a plan "in general" that does not allow variation, nor takes account of the uniqueness of the stages in all the relations of class forces under all sorts of conditions. The dialectical unity of the nodal line of measurements in the Leninist doctrine of strategy is replaced by Trotsky by the abstract metaphysic of the single blow. It is quite clear that this conception of strategy is for Trotsky the foundation on which he justifies the armed Bolshevik rising of 1917. But this revolutionary strategy, which became necessary at the transition from bourgeois-democratic revolution to socialist revolution, was for Lenin the realization of a single line that had been thought out and expounded long before, the logical growing of one stage of revolution into another. Trotsky, however, declares this change of strategy to be a change of principles and is subsequently compelled

---

[1] Marx, Foreword to *Critique of Political Economy*.

to set in opposition to the Bolshevist dialectic the metaphysic of his own "permanent revolution."

Profoundly dialectical also is the Leninist plan of New Economic Policy. In his speech at the Eleventh Congress of the Party Lenin showed in the stages they had passed through and those that still awaited them that single line of development which included and justified N.E.P. The transition to a developed socialist offensive which the Party subsequently carried forward under Stalin's leadership was nothing else than the realization of one of the nodes of the Leninist fine.

And so, the nodal fine of measurements opens the road to the knowledge of the whole connection of development in all fields of nature and society. But no nodal line exists independent of the others. In essence everything in the world is the nodal line of its own internal differences and at the same time one of the measurements in some wider nodal line. The stages of capitalism form the nodal line of capitalist development, but capitalism in its turn is one of the measures in the general chain of the history of society, just as society is only one link in the eternal development of the universe of matter.

> "All nature, to the knowledge of which we can attain, forms some system, some accumulated connection of bodies, and under the word 'body' we understand all material realities, beginning with the stars and ending with the atom and even with a particle of ether, in so far as we admit the reality of the latter."[1]

Every partial measurement can be understood only as an expression of the general line of development. If the metaphysical fallacy lay in taking particular things in isolation, the dialectical conception of nature requires the finding of the place of a given process in the general connection of development. Through this connection of emergence and annihilation we can ever more completely and more deeply disclose all the uniqueness of a given thing.

---

[1] Engels, *Dialectic of Nature.*

SECTION IV

THE LAW OF THE NEGATION OF THE NEGATION

The dialectical process of the development of actuality and our knowledge is not exhausted by the law of the transition of quantity into quality and its converse nor by the law of the unity of opposites. We find in Marx and Engels the basis of a third fundamental law of dialectic – the negation of the negation.

What is the essence of this law? What connection has it with the kernel of dialectic – the law of the unity of opposites? In the exposition that follows we will show that the law of the negation of the negation emerges as one of the concrete forms of manifestation of the law of the unity of opposites, disclosing the connection of the qualitatively different stages in the dialectical development of processes, their relationship and the form of the change in each particular case.

As the starting-point of our exposition we will take the classic example of the law of the negation of the negation given by Marx, and we will establish on general lines those basic problems which make up the essence of this law.

In the first volume of *Capital,* in the section on "Historical Tendency of Capitalist Accumulation," Marx shows the course of development of private ownership in the means of work from its initial moments right down to its historically inevitable annihilation, to its transition into its opposite – into social ownership.

"Private property, as contrasted with social or collective property, exists only where the means of labour and the external conditions of labour belong to private individuals. But the character of private property differs according as the private individuals are workers or non-workers. The innumerable shades which, at the first glance, seem to be exhibited by private property are merely reflections of the intermediate conditions that he between these two extremes.

"The worker's private ownership of the means of production is the basis of petty industry; and petty industry is an indispensable condition for the development of social production and of the free individuality of the worker.

"This method of production presupposes a parcelling-out of the soil, a scattered ownership of the instruments of production. Just as it excludes concentration of these means into a few hands, so does it exclude co-operation, the division of labour within the process of production, the social mastery and regulation of the forces of nature, the free development of the social energies of production. It is only compatible with narrow limits for production and society. At a certain level of development, this method of production brings into the world material means which will effect its own destruction. Thenceforward there stir within the womb of society forces and passions which feel this method of production to be a fetter. It must be destroyed, it is destroyed. Its destruction, the transformation of the individual and scattered means of production, the transformation of the pygmy property of the many into the titan property of the few, the expropriation of the great masses of the people from the land, from the means of subsistence, and from the instruments of labour – this terrible and grievous expropriation of the populace – comprises the prelude to the history of capital.... Self-earned private property, the private property that may be looked upon as grounded on a coalescence of the isolated, individual, and independent worker, with his working conditions, is supplanted by capitalist private property, which is maintained by the exploitation of others' labour, but of labour which, in a formal sense, is free."[1]

Marx has shown how capitalist private, ownership, which *negates* small-scale private ownership, emerges; now he discloses the tendencies of its development:

"As soon as the capitalistic mode of production can stand upon its own feet – then the further socialization of labour and the further transformation of the land and of the other means of production into socially utilized (that is to say, communal) means of production, which implies the further expropriation of private owners, takes on a new form. What has now to be expropriated is no longer the la-

---

[1] Marx, *Capital,* vol. i, pp. 844-5.

bourer working on his own account, but the capitalist who exploits many labourers.

"This expropriation is brought about by the operation of the immanent laws of capitalist production, by the centralization of capital. One capitalist lays a number of his fellow capitalists low. Hand-in-hand with such centralization, concomitantly with the expropriation of many capitalists by a few, the co-operative form of the labour process develops to an ever increasing degree; therewith we find a growing tendency towards the purposive application of science to the improvement of technique; the land is more methodically cultivated; the instruments of labour tend to assume forms which are only utilizable by combined effort; the means of production are economized through being turned to account only by joint, by social labour. All the peoples and therefore the capitalist regime tend more and more to assume an international character. While there is thus a progressive diminution in the number of the capitalist magnates (who usurp and monopolise all the advantages of this transformative process), there occurs a corresponding increase in the mass of poverty, oppression, enslavement, degeneration, and exploitation; but at the same time there is a steady intensification of the wrath of the working class – a class which grows ever more numerous, and is disciplined, unified, and organized by the very mechanism of the capitalist method of production. Capitalist monopoly becomes a fetter upon the method of production which has flourished with it and under it. The centralization of the means of production and the socialization of labour reach a point where they prove incompatible with their capitalist husk. This bursts asunder. The expropriators are expropriated."[1]

Marx, having shown the whole historical course of private ownership now draws the following conclusions, among which we find the formulation of the law of the negation of the negation:

"The capitalist method of appropriation proceeding out of the capitalist method of production, and consequently

---

[1] Marx, *Capital,* vol. i, pp. 845-6.

capitalist private property, is the first negation of individual private property based upon individual labour. But, with the inexorability of a law of nature, capitalist production begets its own negation. It is a negation of a negation. This second negation does not re-establish private property, but it does re-establish individual property upon the basis of the acquisitions of the capitalist era; i.e. on co-operation and the common ownership of the land and of the means of production (which the labour itself produces)."[1]

What is the significance of Marx's exposition? Marx unfolds a dialectic of contradictory development of the forms of private ownership in which each successive stage, growing out of its predecessor and appearing as its negation, negates itself in turn by the force of the development of its contradictions. Both the conversion of small-scale private ownership into large-scale capitalist ownership and also the conversion of the latter into social ownership proceed on the basis of the development of the essential contradiction in the mode of production itself. Each phase in the development of the forms of private ownership resolves the determined form of the contradiction that belongs to the previous stage of development. Thus the individual forms of private ownership that preceded the capitalist grew out of the decomposition of feudal ownership. In it was given the solution of the contradiction between the development of productive forces and the forms of feudal ownership that had been keeping back the development of crafts and trade. "Private ownership by the worker of the means of production" (Marx) was the basis of small-scale production, which at that period was the necessary phase in the development of social productive forces to a new stage. But in the course of the development of this form of small-scale private ownership by the "many," a contradiction between the possession of the means of production of the small-scale producer and the further development of the forces in production emerged and proceeded to develop. Capitalism resolved this form of contradiction by the alienation of the means of production from the small-scale producer and their concentration into the hands of a few magnates of capital. But capitalism called into life another form of the same contradiction between the productive forces and private own-

---

[1] Ibid., p. 846.

ership – the antagonistic contradiction between the social organization of work and the private forms of appropriation.

Together with this it creates by its considerable expansion of productive forces the material premises for the resolution of this contradiction. Socialism, by developing productive forces to an unheard of degree and by finally abolishing private ownership of the means of production, completely fills in the gap between labour and the ownership of the means of production. The new "individual ownership" of the member of socialist society – ownership of consumption goods – only resembles in its external aspects that individual ownership from which capitalism grew, and is a wholly subordinate moment of the new socialist ownership of the means of production.

"Social property is spread over land and the other means of production, but individual property embraces the products, that is to say, consumption goods."[1]

And so the essence of the law of negation of the negation, as exemplified by Marx in application to the emergence and development of capitalism, amounts to the following basic propositions:

(1) Between the different phases of the contradictory development of private ownership, there exists a profound internal connection.

(2) Every phase, by overcoming the specific form of the contradiction of its predecessor, by negating it, brings forth the form of contradiction that belongs to it and by this means prepares its own negation.

(3) These phases, by negating each other, resolve the general contradiction that belongs to them and therefore the latter negation of the negation denotes a transition to a new law-system, to a new essential contradiction.

(4) The double contradiction unites in itself, in certain features, the preceding phases and from the external aspect represents a return to some features of the original form of the basic contradiction. The "synthesis" negates and overcomes both the "thesis" and also the "antithesis," but the

---

[1] Engels, *Anti-Dühring*.

external form of the "synthesis" reproduces certain features of the external form of the thesis.

Proceeding from these basic propositions we will try to estimate the concrete content of the law of the negation of the negation. The central movement in all the propositions we have indicated is development through contradiction, through the negation brought forth by the latter, and the negation of that negation. We will first attempt to make clear what we mean by dialectical negation. We already know from the foregoing exposition that the development of any process originates in its internal contradictions. Emerging as aspects of a contradiction, opposites mutually condition and mutually amplify each other. But the mutual conditioning of opposites rests basically on the fact that each of them is a negation of the other and an affirmation of itself.

Each aspect emerges therefore both as assuming and negating the other. Besides this they form a unity of opposites in which their mutual conflict leads to the negation of the given unity. Therefore, the moving contradiction of a process contains in itself "negation" as its moment.

"Dialectical materialism" – wrote Lenin – "requires the indication of difference, of connection, of transition. Without this a simple affirmation is not complete, is lifeless, is dead." This connection, this difference, is also given by the development of the contradiction in which also negation emerges as the initial impulse. The analysis of the development of any process demands above all the disclosure of its essential contradiction, the discerning of its "negativeness," which indeed is the actual source of its self-movement.

The capitalist mode of production grew out of the ruin of the mass of small-scale owners, peasants and craftsmen. This historic process of the expropriation of the small-scale producer, who had been at the same time owner of the means of production, led to the formation of a small class of large-scale owners, on the one hand, and of a large class of proletarians deprived of all property, on the other. Both opposites – capital and hired labour – mutually condition each other, and the abolition of one of these is at the same time the abolition of the other. Capital is above all a social relationship, the essential moment of which is the *relation of capital to hired labour*. Hired labour is a social relation and as such is impossible without capital, which is its essential moment. Besides this, both aspects make up a unity – the capitalist mode of production – a unity in which the class struggle between the proletariat and bourgeoisie develops.

Materialistic dialectic explains the emergence of negation as a result of the development of the internal contradictions of a process. And so negation emerges as a moment in the conflict of opposites and, together with this, serves as a true connection between the transitions from one set of stages to the others. Characteristic of merely "formal" logic is another conception of negation; negation is said to come from outside, to be an external and antagonistic force in relation to the given process. Metaphysical logic does not see development of contradictions as inside a process, as a self-negation of the process. For metaphysics negativeness does not emerge as an initial impulse inside the developing contradiction, but only as an external force. Such an external conception of negation is also fundamental to the mechanistic views. Thus Kautsky, in *The Materialistic Understanding of History*, comes to grief on the question of dialectical negation, which depends upon the self-movement of matter. There is, he says, no self-movement of matter. Self-movement is a superstition borrowed from Hegel, who spoke of self-movement of the spirit. Self-movement explains nothing. The actual source of movement, according to Kautsky, is the mutual action of two external forces. In such mutual action one of these forces negates the other. The environment negates the organism – that is, antithesis (first negation). The organism overcomes the negation of the environment – that is synthesis (negation of negation). Here both negation and negation of negation are purely external to each other. Kautsky thus completely fails to understand negation dialectically, fails to see that every unit contains a contradiction, and that each stage in the development of a process – both negation and negation of negation – emerges as a determined phase in the development of the unity of opposites. He does not understand that this very unity of opposites is also the impulse which initiates and carries through the development of the process.

"Movement," he writes, "flows out of the opposition or collision of opposing elements."

And so, for Kautsky, as also for every mechanist, the following moments in the understanding of negation are characteristic:

(1) Negation as an external moment in relation to the development of a process, which is understood to be a ceaselessly developing process, possessing in itself neither qualitative transitions nor stages that negate each other.

(2) Negation as absolute negation, as annihilation. The understanding of negation as absolute negation leads to the failure to understand that negation emerges as a moment of connection in the contradictory development of a process, that negation also emerges simultaneously as a positive moment in the development of a process and as an affirmation of new tendencies in contradictory unity.

"Dialectical 'moment'" – wrote Lenin – "requires an indication of 'unity'; i.e. of the connection of the negative with the positive, requires the finding of this positive in the negative. From affirmation to negation – from negation to a 'unity' with the affirmation; without this, dialectic becomes a barren negation, a word-play or a scepsis."[1]

Mechanistic methodology, denying the internal self-movement of a process, does not see this "unity" of negation with affirmation, but on the contrary, sunders them, opposes them to each other. The profound distinction between the dialectical conception of negation and the mechanistic was expressed by Lenin as follows:

"Neither barren negation, nor purposeless negation, nor sceptical negation, nor vacillation, nor doubt are characteristic and essential in dialectic, which undoubtedly does contain in itself the element of negation and moreover contains it as the most important element – No, this element of negation is a moment of connection, is a moment of development with a retention of the positive; i.e. without any vacillations, without any eclecticism."[2]

It follows that dialectical negation must be a determined negation, in order to express the connection of the phenomena in the development of a particular process.

---

[1] Lenin, vol. ix, p. 287. Russian edition.

[2] Ibid., p. 285. Russian edition.

"In dialectic to negate does not mean simply to say 'no,' or to declare a thing to be non-existent or to destroy it at will.... The mode of negation is determined here, in the first place, by the general, in the second place, by the special nature of the given process. Therefore, I must produce the first negation in such a way that there should be or should become possible a second negation. But how do I attain this? According to the special nature of each particular case. If I ground up a grain of barley, or crushed an insect, then, though I should have accomplished the first act of negation, I should have made the second impossible. For every category of objects there is thus a special mode of negation peculiar to it, and only from this is development to be obtained."[1]

The appearance of a plant from a seed that has been thrown into the ground is not the barren negation of the seed, but its further development. The emergence of a capitalist economy out of the small-scale-trading economy is the further development of the latter. But the simple destruction of a seed, the killing of an insect by a bird, do not express in themselves the internal law-governed connection of the stages of a process. On the contrary, the destruction of a seed, as such, by the appearance from it of a *plant* is at the same time also its preservation in the plant, which at a determined stage of development will produce other seeds. Negation is also affirmation, "destruction" is also preservation. Dialectical negation appearing as a stage in the development of a process, emerges on the one hand as the overcoming of the old, and on the other as the preservation of particular aspects of it as a subordinated moment. Such dialectical denial was called by Hegel "sublation." But according to Hegel, the idealist, it is not real things but ideas that "sublate" each other. Marx criticizing the idealistic character of this Hegelian conception, in which all actuality was shown as sublated in absolute knowledge, indicated its unreal character. "This sublation is assumed actually to overcome its subject, but in reality, leaves it untouched," wrote Marx, stressing the necessity of studying actual development. Marx also indicated the positive moments in Hegel's exposition of this problem of sublation. He showed that this process is really a mate-

---

[1] Engels, *Anti-Dühring.*

rial movement that recovers whatever disintegration has taken place, so that it emerges not only as an overcoming, but also as a preservation, a subordination to itself of the particular sides of the preceding stage in the development of the process. In a number of his works, Marx showed that in the ownership of the capitalist mode of production, small-scale private ownership was overcome as an independent law-system, but was preserved as a collateral sublated form of the capitalist law-system.

The problem of sublation plays an important role in the analysis of the tendencies of social development. One of the great contributions of Lenin was that he clearly and strongly urged the importance of using the old under the conditions of the new. In opposition to all "leftist" deviations, he stressed the necessity of such action as would avoid flat negation of the old, and would ensure at the same time that the latter should not be merely preserved in the new, merely joined on to it, but having been annihilated as a *system* with its own set of laws, should emerge merely as a collateral *form* of the new law system. It is along such lines that the dialectical conception of negation appears in the Leninist tactic of N.E.P. N.E.P. emerged as a form of contradictory development of socialism, in which occurred a special kind of negation of capitalism. This negation was allied with a partial sufferance of capitalism. Socialism and capitalism were in rivalry, but the conditions of the contest guaranteed the victory of the former. The development of N.E.P. denoted the resolution of this unstable situation, the victory of socialism and the abolition of capitalism within the frame of N.E.P. N.E.P., being a determined form of socialist development and at the same time the destroyer of capitalism, was preparing its own future negation by resolving its present contradictions, and thus paved the way for the final victory over the elements of capitalism.

The Trotskyists and the new opposition did not understand the dialectic of N.E.P. They identified it with capitalism. "N.E.P. is a capitalism that holds the proletarian state on a chain," Krupskaya[1] used to say. The Trotskyists declared the forms and methods of N.E.P. to be capitalist forms and methods, not seeing that the nature of trade, of money, of keeping accounts within the conditions of socialist construction was essentially altered, that the utilization of the old forms and methods does not denote their simple transfer into

---

[1] Krupskaya, Lenin's wife. Author of *Memories of Lenin.*

the frame of the soviet economy, but their critical adoption and ultimate overcoming. The Trotskyists did not see that in the setting up of the new law-governance the old forms and methods already occupy a subordinate position and are not a simple repetition of capitalist methods. Naturally, the Trotskyists, by not seeing the paths to the dialectical negation of capitalism within N.E.P., proposed to the Party a policy that aimed at the disruption of N.E.P. and consequently of socialist construction itself.

The "Right" also did not understand the dialectical negation in N.E.P., because their policy was to use capitalism with its forms and methods, to allow development of commerce, in such a way as could lead to nothing else than a strengthening of capitalist elements; i.e. they too threatened the disruption of socialist construction. The "Rights" meant by the "negation" of the kulaks a policy which merely encouraged their growth within socialism. The Trotskyists meant by their kind of "negation" a policy which would have caused the kulak groups to reappear. We have just quoted the analysis by Marx of the historic tendencies of the development of capitalism, where this very aspect of the law of negation of negation is stressed.

Engels, in *Anti-Dühring,* provides an illustration from a grain of barley. The grain is sown and under suitable conditions sprouts. "The seed, as such, vanishes, is negated and in its place there appears a plant – the negation of the seed. But what is the normal cycle of the life of this plant? It grows, flowers, is fertilized and finally produces barley seeds again; when these are ripe, the stalk withers, for now its turn has come to be negated. The result of this negation is that we have our barley seed again, not one, however, but more than a hundred."

Mikhailovsky interprets Engels's illustration in his own way. He says that in the development of a plant it is possible to count up more negations. For example, the stalk negates the seed, the flower negates the stalk, the fruit negates the flower. So where is the triad? Here there are *three* negations, not *two.* Further, Mikhailovsky interprets Engels as if the only difference that he sees between the original seed and the fruit is in the number of the seeds. Mikhailovsky's misinterpretation is twofold; in the first place, he has confused *any* succession of phenomena with development by negation; and secondly, he has substituted for the problem of qualitative development in the changing of stages a merely quantitative change.

The first is the more serious error. Mikhailovsky does not understand that the role of a negation or of a negation of a negation is not filled by *any* phenomenon that arises during the development of a process, but only by that stage which emerges as the complete "breaking down" of the previous stage.

"A flower," writes Plekhanov, "is an organ of a plant, and as such just as little negates the plant as the head of Mr. Mikhailovsky negates Mr. Mikhailovsky. But the 'fruit,' i.e. more exactly, the fertilized ovum, is actually a negation of the given organism because of its capacity to be the originating point in the development of a new life. Engels indeed considers the cycle of life of a plant from its beginning as a fertilized seed to its production of a fertilized seed."

Engels himself was prepared for such objections as those of Mikhailovsky. In *Anti-Dühring* he wrote:

"We have cited barley seed, but the same process takes place among the majority of insects, for example, among butterflies. They appear out of the egg by way of negating it, they pass through different phases of change till maturity, they copulate and then negate themselves (i.e. they die) as soon as the process of prolonging the species has been accomplished and the females have laid their many eggs.... *The fact that among the plants and animals the process is not so simply resolved, that they not once but many times produce seeds, eggs or young ones, before they die – is not our concern, our purpose here was to show that negation of negation actually proceeds in both realms of the organic world.*"

And so the matter is not in the quantity of negations but in the fact that the whole cycle of development includes in itself its own negation and negation of negation. Nay, more, Engels by looking at the whole process of development, for example, seed – plant – seed, shows further that here also the matter does not amount to a quantitative aspect of development.

"Cereals," he writes, "change very slowly so that modern barley is almost exactly the same as the barley of the last century. But let us take some plastic decorative plant, for example, the dahlia or the orchid; if we act artificially on the seed and on the plant that grows from it, then as the result of this negation of negation we shall obtain not only a *greater quantity* of seeds but also a *qualitatively* improved seed which is able to produce more beautiful flowers, and every repetition of that process, every new negation of negation will further enhance the quality."[1]

And so in the law of negation of negation Marx and Engels stress the internal connection and relationship of the successive stages of objective development, from the emergence of the contradiction in any process to its relative resolution in external forms of development. And in the illustration from seeds the cycle of life of a plant was taken by Engels from its embryonic state of seed, which are the result of another vegetative cycle, to the formation of new fruits, which at the same time appear as the initial stage of a new plant. Negation of negation thus emerges as:

(1) The result of the development of contradictions of a process.

(2) A moment in a contradictory unity of opposites.

(3) The *special stage* in the development of the process that breaks down in itself the foregoing phase, a stage that denotes the resolution of the basic contradictions, *the completion of the cycle of development and transition to a new unity of opposites.*

The thesis, antithesis and synthesis in the cycle of development of a seed (seed – plant – seed) express the different stages of development. Besides this, in the process of development antithesis is given in thesis, because the development of a seed takes place just in so far as it is negated as a seed and developed as a plant. This is also true as regards synthesis – it also is included as a moment in the development of a plant, since it takes place only in so far as the plant completes its cycle in fruit-bearing. Furthermore, synthesis as a moment includes itself in the new thesis because, as the completion of one cycle, it becomes the point of departure (thesis) of another cycle, or new process of development.

---

[1] Engels, Anti-Dühring.

Materialist dialectic, therefore, regards thesis, antithesis and synthesis as forms and stages of the development and resolution of the contradictions in the processes of actuality:

(1) As the one essential contradiction which appears at the same time as the point of departure of a new contradiction, that in turn negates it.

(2) As the development of this new contradiction.

(3) As the breaking of it down and the consequent relative resolution both of it and of the originating contradiction in the new process which has arisen as the outcome of all the preceding development.

Materialist dialectic besides this stresses the relativity of the stages in the development of processes; every stage be it thesis, antithesis or synthesis, by being a special form of the impulsive contradiction takes on the forms of thesis and antithesis and completes its development in synthesis. *Therefore the whole point of the problem of negation of negation lies just in this very problem of the emergence of the new law-system through development of the contradictions of the foregoing processes of actuality.*

Now we can show that the difference of the two opposite conceptions of the law of negation of negation – the dialectical and the metaphysical – consists in their different treatment of the problem of the emergence of the new.

Hegel, by the way in which he stated the question of the sublation of thesis and antithesis in synthesis disclosed the dialectical path of development that leads to the appearance of new law-systems. The problem of historical synthesis is the same as the problem of the emergence of the new. We will try to explain it and it will be seen that the essence of the law of negation of negation is very deeply involved in it.

The point is, can metaphysical negation explain the emergence of the new? We have already seen in the chapters devoted to criticism of the mechanists for their failure to understand the law of unity of opposites and the law of transition of quantity into quality and its converse, that mechanists cannot resolve the problem of development. By attributing all qualitative uniqueness to quantitative relations, they attribute all development to mechanical movement, i.e. to motion. The new is regarded by them as a new combination of elements that already existed earlier. The new can always be identified with the old by analysing it into its constituent elements. The new, the synthesis, therefore, is not distinguished by its quality, its law-governance, from the old. By treating continuity as something absolute, by not seeing the leap-like transition in the forming of new qualities, such a methodology naturally cannot explain the emergence of the new, the problem of development.

By being unable either to state or to resolve the problem of historical synthesis, mechanistic methodology finds it impossible to disclose the essence of the law of negation of negation; this law is reduced to a "triad." This is characteristic of all those who do not find themselves in sympathy with dialectic.

It is quite natural that Kautsky, who mechanistically opposes "thesis" to "antithesis" and the two of them to "synthesis," cannot arrive at a correct statement of the problem of the new. By Kautsky the new is declared to be the totally unexpected, to be "quite new." A cleavage between "thesis" and "antithesis" leads to a break of the connections in the development of actuality.

In the development of a plant the appearance of its fruits, its seeds, emerges as a negation of it, i.e. as a negation of the negation of the original seed. But seeds are brought forth by the development of the plant; they make up a moment of the plant, but such a moment as denotes the end of the development of the plant. The plant withers, the seed remains. The cycle of development is finished.

Kautsky is perplexed: what is this negation of negation when we have *simultaneously* both the plant (the negation of the seed) and the new seeds (the negation of the negation)? As a mechanist he would like to separate these two stages by an absolute interval in time, not understanding that in actual development the destruction of the old is also the emergence of the new.

Bukharin, with the schematism characteristic of his approach, forces all development into narrow categories. In his *Theory of Historic Materialism* he seeks to show how development originates. By attributing conflict of opposites to a conflict of opposite forces, Bukharin develops a theory of equilibrium instead of a theory of the unity of opposites on the basis of their conflict. He even goes on to declare that Hegel himself reduced all dialectic to a theory of equilibrium. Bukharin writes on this issue:

> "Hegel thus regarded the character of movement and expressed it in the following form: the primary state of

equilibrium he called thesis, the destruction of equilibrium – antithesis – the re-establishment of equilibrium on a new basis – synthesis (i.e. the unifying position in which contradictions are reconciled). This character of the movement of every existing thing comprised in the trinomial formula ('triad') he also named dialectic."[1]

Sarabyanov, too, takes the same mechanistic position; he demonstrates the existence of two triads in Hegel's philosophy. A triad is expressed in the following way:

(1) proposition,
(2) negation of proposition,
(3) negation of the negation of the proposition.

With this triad, Sarabyanov is fully in accord, after giving it a mechanistic trim. "You know quite well," he writes, "that from the seed to the ear there is an infinite number of stages. Now by these three stages, which we call the triad, we mean the past, the present and the future." But there is also a second triad – thesis, antithesis and synthesis. The first two stages are evident to Sarabyanov. But with regard to synthesis, he puts the question: "*Is* there a third stage – a 'synthesis,' that is to say, a combination of the first and second, a bond of thesis and antithesis?" Later, Sarabyanov explains that "synthesis is therefore formed as follows: one set of properties is connected with the thesis, the other set with the antithesis." By mechanistically interpreting the final synthesis as the combination of old (partly changed) properties, Sarabyanov shows that the second triad does not always explain the processes of development, although for the most part it can help towards their understanding.

And so all development amounts to a triad; a triad amounts to a sequence of equilibrium, the destruction of that equilibrium and its re-establishment; synthesis according to Bukharin is a reconciliation of opposites, according to Sarabyanov a combination of properties. It is clear that the problem of the new is resolved neither by Bukharin nor by Sarabyanov. We know already, to what *political* conclusion this theory of equilibrium and of reconciliation of opposites led. At the first successes of socialist construction, which evoked the furious opposition of the class enemy, the Right began to raise a

---

[1] Bukharin, *Theory of Historic Materialism*, p. 77.

clamour about the destruction of equilibrium and the need to re-establish it. "Synthesis" had to proceed on a "new basis." This "new basis" was in the opinion of the Right a return to the N.E.P. of 1923. In reality such a "synthesis" was reactionary; it was a useful argument for those who wished to stay within the frame-work of the old, who wanted merely to patch, not to renovate.

Both the Rights and the Lefts failed to understand the dialectic of contradictory development in the transition period and of the growth of socialism in it. In the contradiction between socialism and the small-scale trading economy from which capitalism is born anew, there is also included the basic contradiction of the transition period, namely the form of contradiction between socialism and capitalism specific for that period. War communism, N.E.P., the period of socialism – such are the basic stages which are passed through by the development of socialist construction, by the resolution of the contradictions of the transition period. War communism was that form of frontal attack against capitalism which was evoked by the conditions of the civil war and by the intervention of international capitalism against the country of proletarian dictatorship. War communism although it had resolved the contradiction between socialism and capitalism in its initial form and had laid the basis of socialist economy – the expropriation of the expropriators – yet could not resolve the basic contradiction of the transitional economy of the U.S.S.R., could not guarantee the construction of the second storey of socialist economy on that basis. N.E.P., which was the negation of war communism and the general economic policy of the transition period, emerged in addition (basing itself on the positive achievements of war communism) as that form of socialist construction which guaranteed the preparation of the resolution of the contradictions between the proletariat and the peasantry and consequently the resolution of the problem of which section was to prevail. In N.E.P. the contradictions of the transitional period are fully developed, because a fierce class struggle still goes on for the final eradication of the class enemy, for the consolidation and completion of the foundations of socialist economy, for the transference of the poorest and middle strata of the peasantry on to the path of socialist economy. As the energizing negative of the contradictions of N.E.P., socialist construction emerges, negating in its very movement the given form of its development, i.e. N.E.P. The entry into the period of socialism is the entry into the period of final resolution of the basic contradictions of N.E.P. Whereas the "negation" of war communism proceeded on the basis of the law-systems of N.E.P., the "negation of the negation" denotes the transition to the new law-system of socialism, on the basis of which the movement of the whole system of social relationships in the U.S.S.R. is proceeding, the capitalist classes are being liquidated and the edifice of socialist society is being raised.

The new emerges through leaps. Negation and negation of negation express themselves as this interruption of continuity, as manifestations of that new law-system which breaks down the old form of contradiction, but in the synthesis the old contradiction is itself broken down together with that contradiction which had served it as a premise and starting-point. Only concrete analysis can show how far opposites are overcome in the synthesis and to what extent they are "preserved." Concrete analysis shows that the resolution of the problem of who is to survive does not yet denote the abolition of N.E.P. as a whole; it shows that we have entered into a period of socialism and together with it into the last stage of N.E.P., that N.E.P. will be finally overcome in a developed socialist society. But the entry into the period of socialism also denotes that the development of the U.S.S.R. proceeds not on the basis of law-systems that are characteristic of the *first* stages of N.E.P., but on the basis of the law-systems *of socialism* that subjugate to themselves the law-systems of N.E.P.

The Right, taking its stand on positions of mechanistic methodology, could not understand the dialectic of a socialism that was interwoven with the last stage of N.E.P. They saw the presence of N.E.P. and denied that the U.S.S.R. had entered the period of socialism. They did not even notice the "negation of the negation" in relation to war communism, and the historic synthesis involved. Counter-revolutionary Trotskyism, like international capitalism and social reformism, also denies the entry of the U.S.S.R. into the period of socialism.

Neither the Right nor the Left understand the dialectic of social development as a succession of stages proceeding through a number of dialectical negations. And so, essentially, both these and others see nothing but a dilemma – either N.E.P. or socialism, and propose its solution in different ways.

The vulgar theory of evolution, based on mechanistic methodology, and that equally vulgar theory of absolute leaps which is based on the same foundation, cannot, therefore, explain the emergence of the new, nor disclose the essence of the problem of historic synthesis, i.e. the essence of the law of negation of negation.

Not only mechanists but also the Menshevist idealists have failed to interpret the problem of synthesis as the problem of emergence of the new and so have lapsed into an eclectic understanding of synthesis.

The negation of the negation – the synthesis, the new – does not emerge as they suppose by way of a simple uniting, concord, reconciliation, or external combination of opposites. Such a mechanistic interpretation of synthesis is mere eclecticism. When Lenin discusses the debate on trade unions during which conflicting viewpoints emerged he criticizes the eclecticism of Bukharin, who voiced a proposal to unite both the policy of the Central Committee and the policy of Trotsky. Lenin showed that the essence of the question was not to unite two opposite viewpoints. Every object or phenomenon has many opposite aspects and alternative ways of being described. However, in a concrete situation it is important to find that "new thing" which emerges as the progressive step in the mutual action of these aspects, it is important to disclose the new as the law of the movement of the whole. The eclectic cannot disclose this new progressive beginning.

The group of Menshevist idealists has on this question of synthesis lapsed into mechanism. It is sufficient to point to Deborin who understood under synthesis a fusion of opposite aspects. In his *Introduction to the Philosophy of Dialectical Materialism* Deborin depicts the philosophy of Marx as a synthesis of empiricism and rationalism, of French materialism and Hegelian idealistic dialectic. This is sufficient to show that the emergence of the new, which it is the whole achievement of Marx-Leninism to explain, is not disclosed by stating the question in this eclectic fashion. Dialectical materialism is not a mere synthesis of empiricism and rationalism; it *overcomes* their one-sidedness, their separation of sense experience and rational construction. It does not deny them, for they are equally essential moments in knowledge, nor does it preserve them as a permanent element in a final philosophy.

In the law of the negation of the negation the law of unity and conflict of opposites is made concrete as the law of the resolution of old contradictions and of the emergence of new ones. Engels sees in this the essence of the law of the negation of the negation. He writes:

> "A true, natural, historic and dialectical negation is (formally) the initial impulse of every development – the division into opposites, their conflict and resolution, in which (in history partly, in thought fully), on the basis of actual experience, the starting-point is reached anew, but at a higher stage."[1]

Engels in the passage quoted indicates one more aspect of the law of negation of the negation – the return to the beginning. This problem also is treated in different ways by the two opposite conceptions of development.

In his notes to Hegel's logic, Lenin enumerates and characterizes the elements of dialectic; he writes on the issue of development that in the higher stage there is "a repetition... of certain features and properties of the lower" and "a return as it were to the old" (a negation of negation).

Here is stressed the internal connection of the different stages of development, the problem of the "sublation" of the lowest stage of development within the higher. We discussed this above when we disclosed the dialectical character of negation. But along with it Lenin now sets the problem of the return "as it were to the old," to the beginning of the process, the problem of the fact that synthesis and thesis are analogous to each other.

In the *Dialectic of Nature,* Engels sketches a general picture of the development of our knowledge, enumerating its basic stages. At first the elemental dialectic of the Greek philosophers; then the period of its negation – the long domination of metaphysics; and at last the negation of the negation – the dialectical method as the overcomer of metaphysics, evoked by the growth of the internal contradictions of metaphysics, by its impotence, its inability to cope systematically with the accumulated material of the natural and social sciences. This contradiction requires "a return in some or other form from metaphysical thought to dialectical."

> "And here we are back again," writes Engels, "at the conceptions of the great founders of Greek philosophy,

---

[1] *Anti-Dühring.*

namely that all nature, from its smallest particular to its greatest bodies, from a grain of sand to the sun, is in eternal emergence and annihilation, in ceaseless flow, in incessant movement and change."

But is there a difference between the view of the Greek dialecticians on development and modern dialectic? There is an essential difference. "What with the Greeks was an inspired guess, is with us the result of strictly scientific experimental investigation and therefore has a much more clear and definite form." The dialectic of the Greeks was not developed or based on the development of all the sciences. The return to dialectic proceeds on a new basis, on the basis of the very rich development of experimental knowledge, of natural science and of social science.

What exactly is the relation of synthesis to the previous stages? On the subject of the relation of thesis and antithesis as seen in the relation of Greek philosophy to metaphysics, Engels argues that the metaphysical denial of the Greek doctrine of flux was true in relation to details, but the notion of flux is finally seen to be true as regards the metaphysical philosophy as a whole. The synthesis indeed consists in the return to the whole, which is now enriched and differentiated by the development of all science.

But how is a return to the beginning possible? It is possible only in virtue of the fact that the final point is the completion of the processes within the given law-system and becomes the point of departure of a new law-system, or of a new cycle. Thus proceeds the development of a plant (seed – plant – seeds). Thus proceeds the development of the forms of property (communal – private – social). Thus proceeds the development of knowledge of actuality (primitive dialectic – metaphysic – dialectical materialism). Each particular stage in the processes indicated itself disintegrates (because of the development of internal contradictions) into the more partial thesis and antithesis and finds a new completion in a synthesis that raises the whole system to a higher stage. Thus the contradictions of private ownership found their logical partial solution in the slave-owning, feudal, capitalist form of property. Because of the fact that each phenomenon in the course of its development brings forth its own opposite, and this latter is in turn converted into *its* opposite, there is a regression to a number of the features of the external form of the initial stage, now enriched by all the succeeding development.

> "Processes," wrote Engels, in *Anti-Dühring*, "which are antagonistic in their nature, contain in themselves a contradiction, a conversion of a known extreme into its opposite and finally as the basis of all – a negation of negation."

In other words, in any process, in virtue of its division into mutually-exclusive opposites and of the further resolution of this contradiction, there proceeds a double contradiction. All contradictory processes in nature and in society, by appearing as an expression of a negation, negate themselves by the further development of their contradictions. The double contradiction is the general form of movement of all actuality. It denotes the resolution of the contradiction, the completion of the process of development of the given essential unity of opposites, the return (as regards its external form) to the point of departure of the development. As regards its external form negation of negation denotes a breaking down of the negation, and consequently a return to the original position; as regards its content, negation of negation contains in itself all the positive material of the foregoing development.

And so synthesis breaks down within itself the previous stage and returns as it were to the thesis, but to a thesis enriched by the development of the antithesis. In such a conception, of returning to the beginning the difference between the dialectical doctrine of development and the metaphysical theory of cycles can be seen. The mechanistic theory of cycles in the eighteenth century affirmed that in nature and in society there is continuously proceeding a return to the starting-point, a simple repetition of the beginning. Thus all societies, when they raise themselves from primitive savagery to modern culture, reach the highest points of their development and pass again into decline. The next cycle begins again from the lowest degree, from savagery. Thus proceeds so-called development in the animal world. Animal species multiply, develop and perish. The next generations repeat the same cycle. The mechanistic theory of cycles does not notice that development is not a simple repetition, that a "cycle" expresses only the external form of development. Cycles do not exclude a movement to a higher level. The cycle of life, of living organisms, did not exclude the development of the world of animals. On the basis of the ruin and decline of many ancient cultures, society has proceeded to its higher stages, to more progressive forms. This of course does not exclude the possibility of a retrogressive movement in particular historic periods, of particular peoples, or of society as a whole. The mechanistic theory of cycles shows a lack of understanding of what the doctrine of synthesis makes so clear, that while we return as it were to the point of departure, we emerge at the same time as the product of enriched development, and at a higher level.

Hegel, speaking of the synthesis of ideas, wrote, that in it "the whole mass of its previous content is raised, and through its dialectical course forwards so far from losing anything, from leaving anything behind, it brings with itself all it has acquired and enriches and expounds its own being."[1] What was represented by Hegel as the self-development of idea appears in reality only as the enrichment of our knowledge at each new stage of development of social polity, as the reflection of that new aspect of actuality. The dialectical theory of cycles shows how processes in their development are raised from step to step. In place of the mechanistic theory of a cycle, dialectic bases the theory of development upon the motion of a spiral. Development is accomplished in circles, but the final point of the circle does not coincide with the beginning, but stands above the point of departure of the cyclic process. Synthesis emerges as the point of departure of further development, consequently as thesis in the new process of the cycle.

Development proceeds by spirals. The return to the point of departure is a return in external form, but is distinct because of its enriched content, its internal structure.

Lenin in *One Step Forward, Two Steps Back,* vividly discloses the dialectical character of the Party conflict at the Second Congress of the Party, between the revolutionary and opportunist wings of the Party. Lenin analyses the basic groups at the Congress – they are "Iskra"[2] – supporters of the majority, of the minority and of the cen-

---

[1] *Science of Logic*, part ii.

[2] *Iskra* (lit. "The Spark"), the famous newspaper which was to be "a red-hot spark flung into the tinder pile of the Russian Empire." This paper came under the control of Lenin and his group before the split in the Russian Social Democratic Party. At the Party Congress which concluded its sittings at the Brotherhood Church, Southgate Road, London,

tre, and the anti-"Iskra" group. He shows how according to the measure of the intensification and growth of disagreements on principle the composition of the majority and minority at the Congress was changed. The original majority at the Congress united all the "Iskra" supporters and a large part of the centre against the anti-"Iskra" group in the vote on questions not dealing with fundamental principles. On questions of organization all the "Iskra" supporters voted against the centre and the anti-" Iskra" group. Later, on quite a number of questions there began a movement of part of the "Iskra" supporters, both of the majority and minority, to the side of the anti-"Iskra" group and the centre; so the majority became a minority. The voting on the first paragraph of the programme sharply stressed the division into revolutionary and opportunist wings. Against the revolutionary wing voted the anti-"Iskra" group, an important part of the centre, almost all the minority supporters of "Iskra" and the vacillating members of the pro-"Iskra" majority. *The majority became the minority, and the minority the majority.* At last with the departure of the anti-"Iskra" group from the Congress the vote on the election of the Central Committee gave the victory to the majority group of the "Iskra" supporters against the minority groups and the centre and this denoted the final division of the Congress into its majority and minority.

Summing up the Congress, Lenin wrote:

> "The development actually went by the dialectical path, by the path of contradictions, the minority became the majority, the majority became the minority, each side went over from defence to attack and from attack to defence; the point of departure of the conflict of pure ideas (Clause 1 of the Programme) 'negated itself' and yielded place to a dis-

---

in 1903, a fierce struggle took place between Lenin's "Bolshevik" policy as set forth in *Iskra* and the "Menshevik" policy of Martov and Trotsky. Plekhanov and Lenin insisted on a highly disciplined Party entirely distinct from the liberals. This is the famous Clause 1 which Lenin speaks of in *One Step Forward, Two Steps Back.* The elections to the Central Committee also gave a majority to Lenin's group, but the minority refused to submit, won over Plekhanov and seceded. The result was that the Mensheviks seized the party machine and became the larger of the two parties. Lenin and the Bolsheviks were few and isolated for some time.

pute that involved the whole Congress, but thereupon the 'negation of negations' began and we returned to the point of departure of the conflict of pure idea; but now this 'thesis' was enriched by all the results of the 'antithesis' and was transformed into a higher synthesis, in which the isolated, fortuitous error on Clause 1 had grown into a system of opportunist views on the organization problem, so that the connection between this phenomenon and the basic division of our party into revolutionary and opportunist wings became more and more apparent to all. In a word, not only does the seed grow according to Hegel, but the Russian Social Democrats fight each other according to Hegel."[1]

The law of negation emerges as the further concretization of the law of the unity of opposites. It appears as the general law of development of processes in nature, in society and in our thought. Along with the other basic laws of dialectic it discloses the forms of the development of the contradictory processes of actuality and is a methodological implement of our knowledge that helps us to see the perspectives of historical and scientific changes and consciously to influence their transition from one stage to another, from one phase of the contradiction to its higher forms.

---

[1] Lenin, *One Step Forward, Two Steps Back.*

INDEX OF PROPER NAMES
and
DETAIL INDEX TO ENGELS, HEGEL, LENIN, MARX, PLEKHANOV, STALIN

DETAIL INDEX TO ENGELS, HEGEL, LENIN, MARX, PLEKHANOV, STALIN

ENGELS

LENIN

MARX

PLEKHANOV

STALIN